Charles Edward in 1745

The Chevalier de Johnstone

A MEMOIR
OF THE
'FORTY-FIVE

Edited with an Introduction
by Brian Rawson

Folio Society, London, 1958

The design for the binding of this volume is reproduced, with permission, from an Edinburgh binding of the period in the possession of the National Library of Scotland. The maps for this edition were drawn by K. C. Jordan F.R.G.S.

Second edition (revised) 1970

PRINTED IN GREAT BRITAIN
by Alden & Mowbray Ltd at the Alden Press, Oxford
Set in 12 point Fournier leaded 1 point
Illustrations printed by D. H. Greaves Ltd, Scarborough
Bound by W. & J. Mackay & Co Ltd, Chatham

CONTENTS

ILLUSTRATIONS

———◇———

Reproduction of 'The Engagement between the Lyon *and the* Elizabeth' *is by courtesy of Lord Hinchingbrooke and 'The Duke of Cumberland with his army crossing the Spey' by kind permission of Hulton Picture Library.*

INTRODUCTION

————— ◇ —————

THE history of the Jacobite movement, which was born in the revolution of 1688 and died in the dismal failure of the Elibank plot in 1750, is largely one of mishandled opportunity. Even in the earliest stages (when those who were later to become Jacobite revolutionaries were still the supporters of the ruling dynasty), had James II been capable of leading a determined opposition against the invading William as he landed at Torbay, he would almost certainly have retained his throne. Instead he vacillated and the first chance was lost. Even so, there was such an immediate upsurge of popular feeling directed against a foreign king, that if James had returned immediately from France, he would have received sufficient support to enable him rapidly to overthrow the recently and surprisingly victorious William.

The next real opportunity came twenty years later, when to every patriotic Scot the Act of Union was anathema. If James III, the Old Pretender, had had sufficient imagination fully to appreciate the situation, he would, in 1708, have landed in Scotland, even had he done so alone. There he would have been welcomed, in England there would have been too little antagonism for effective opposition, and he would, provided he remained north of the border, have been able to bide his time. When Anne died, he could have seized his opportunity and have assumed his rightful crown in peace before the importers of the House of Hanover could crystallize their wishes into action. Even if James had been still in France when Anne died, he could have crossed the Channel sooner than George and, by virtue of being first in the field, might well have won the day. But like his father he too vacillated and again the opportunity was lost; the Elector of Hanover ascended the English

7

throne and the support of interest ranged itself in his train. On each of these occasions all that was really necessary was that the Jacobite claimant should have been in the right place at the right time and should have shown an unshakeable belief in both the justice of his cause and the certainty of success. From then on, however, the governing factors became more complex; thenceforth it became a question of armed rebellion and of conquering by force of arms. From then on also, pro-Jacobite sympathies in England and even in Scotland tended to become more passive than active. Many were the toasts that were still drunk to 'the King over the Water', but increasingly fewer people were willing to run any risk in order to set a Stuart on his throne. In moments of optimism, or full of grievances against the existing regime, they would pledge their support, but when the time came for them to implement their pledge, many were found wanting.

It had been to a large extent on religious grounds that James II had been overthrown, and it is in many ways surprising that this same question of religion does not seem, during the subsequent rebellions, to have been of any very great significance. It is admittedly true that the Old Pretender, although he remained a staunch Catholic, showed none of his father's desire to proselytize his subjects, but this was something that the people would have to take on trust; they could have no direct knowledge that it was true. When, thirty years later, his son landed in Scotland he too, at least theoretically, was still a Catholic but, though the cry of 'Papist' may be found in the occasional individual letter, anti-catholicism never assumed the proportions of a rallying cry. Had this question of religion really been of any vital importance, it seems unlikely that Charles Edward, who wore his religion lightly, would have failed to realize the fact; he could easily have turned Protestant before landing in Scotland, instead of some years later when it was no longer of material importance. It was not, then, fear of a resurgence of religious intolerance that deprived both Pretenders of active support. Had such a fear existed it would have resulted in active opposition. The truth lay in a pervasive feeling of apathy where people could see good and bad in both sides and were quite prepared to sit on an uncommitted fence.

This diminution of pro-Jacobite feeling was a gradual process and, for some years, it remained a force to be reckoned with. When, in 1715, the Earl of Mar raised the standard of rebellion at Braemar, he had with him fifteen of the leading Scottish peers and chieftains, supported by the large majority of the Macdonalds, the Camerons and the Stewarts. The one notable exception was the ever changeable and far too canny Simon Fraser, Lord Lovat. In all, the Jacobite forces at the outset numbered not less than eight thousand, whereas the government forces, under Argyll, numbered only two thousand. But Argyll was a general of considerable ability and the Earl of Mar was not; the former's two thousand were more than a match for the latter's eight, while James himself, who should have been present at the beginning to be an inspiration to his troops, only arrived in time to witness defeat and failure. And when he did arrive, his pensive melancholy acted only as a depressive; he had neither the character nor the magnetism of personality necessary to fire the beacon of revolt and arouse that feeling of devotion which can overcome all obstacles. In his memoirs of the rebellion the Master of Sinclair left a picture of James that was only too apt:

> ... and yet I must not conceal that when we saw the Person who they called our King, we found ourselves not at all animated by his Presence, and if he was disappointed in us, we were tenfold more so in him; we saw nothing in him that look'd like Spirit; he never appear'd with Cheerfulness and Vigour to animate us; his Countenance look'd extremely heavy.

Had Charles Edward stood in his father's place, events might well have taken a different course. Had Lord George Murray been in command of the rebel forces, the despairing cry of 'O for one hour of Dundee'* might never have been heard. But, in the event, the rebellion of 1715, which had stood so excellent a chance of success, fizzled out in failure, and the Old Pretender, whose many virtues might have made him an excellent if uninspiring king, retired with his melancholy and his uncomplaining goodness first to France and later to Rome.

It was the elements, rather than any human weaknesses, that were responsible for the failure of the next two attempts to restore the Stuarts to the throne. The first of these, in 1719, was, in many respects, the best organized of all. A Spanish fleet, carrying five thousand Spanish soldiers under the command of the Duke of Ormonde, was to sail from Cadiz and, having been joined by James at some northern Spanish port, was to embark on an invasion of England. At the same time, the Earl Marischal was to proceed to Scotland and, at his instigation, the standard of revolt was to be raised by the Marquis of Tullibardine. But the fleet was dispersed by storms shortly after leaving Cadiz, and Tullibardine's rebel forces, numbering little more than a thousand, were soon defeated by General Wightman.

After this attempt—the last in which James himself was directly involved—the strength of the Jacobite movement suffered a marked decline. The birth of a son to James in the following year was the only sign of hope; now that the father was so obviously disinclined to make any further effort to reclaim his birthright, it was in that son that the supporters of the House of Stuart placed all their aspirations. As he grew up, his charm, his courage and his evident determination to win for his father a crown he would not seek for himself, initiated yet another era of plot and counter-plot.

By 1740 it was obvious that not only would any further

*Attributed to John Gordon of Glenbucket.

attempt to restore James have to be backed by foreign aid, but
also that such aid would have to come from France, whose
general attitude towards the exiled Jacobites was one which
wished them well. But to transmute good wishes into active
support was a very different matter. None the less when, in
1743, Cardinal Fleury died and French policy lay (in so far as
Louis XV would allow it to lie) in the hands of Cardinal de
Tencin, the propitious moment seemed to have arrived. Yet,
even so, it was not until January 1744, after innumerable discus-
sions and representations, that Charles Edward was invited to
come from Rome to Paris. Almost unwillingly, for he had little
hope of success, James let him go. After further negotiations, a
French expedition was finally agreed on, but, just as the prince
was about to join it at Gravelines, it was, as in 1719, dispersed
by a storm. The French, reading the omens, showed little
inclination to help further. Had the Young Pretender's attitude
been less uncompromising and had he been willing to accept
the crown of Scotland only, the French might have proved
more co-operative. But they can hardly be blamed for refusing
to support a prince who, on his side, steadfastly refused to
modify his own aims to accord with those of his would-be allies.

Unlike his father, Charles Edward was incapable of patient
resignation; if no one could be found to go with him along the
road he was determined to follow, then he would go alone.
After considerable difficulties, he managed to secure a frigate, a
man-of-war and a certain quantity of arms and ammunition.
With these, with the 'seven men of Moidart', and against the
advice of anyone who had been in touch with local feeling in
Scotland, he set out. The future looked bleak enough, but
worse was to follow. His expedition in miniature was sighted
by an English man-of-war and, in the ensuing engagement, his
own escort was so disabled that it was with only the frigate that
he finally reached the Isle of Eriskay.

His welcome was anything but heart-warming; no one had

expected him and no one wanted him to come. Everywhere the advice he was given was the same: 'Go home'. The prince's refusal and his 'I am come home, Sir, and I am persuaded that my faithful Highlanders will stand by me', showed, in itself, the world of difference between him and his father. Never would he accept reversal as a fate decreed; he was a man of action against whom no obstacle, however great, could stand. Until dissension and defeat sapped his optimism, he emanated confidence to those around him. With these positive assets—worth far more than any token following of foreign troops—coupled to the charm which no one denied him, it is small wonder that he so soon succeeded in winning over many of those who had at first held back in doubt. Admittedly McLeod of McLeod went over to the government and Lord Lovat continued to flirt with both sides, but these two apart, the majority of the remaining chieftains rallied to his cause.

Charles Edward's virtues seemed to make possible the otherwise impossible, but it was in many respects his own failings that betrayed him. From his birth he had been surrounded by intrigue and plot, by suspicion and jealousy and, amid such a welter of continual conspiracy, it was only to be expected that his sense of judgment and his ability to distinguish who were his friends and who his enemies should have become blunted. Also, since he and his father were complete opposites in character, he naturally mistrusted the latter's counsellors and placed more faith in the free and easy Irish who surrounded him. He believed in Murray of Broughton, the one man who was to betray him, and he believed in the promises of the French government, which came to nothing. The setbacks he was continually faced with would have been enough for many men, but because of his invincible faith in himself, Charles Edward was able to overcome them all. All except one. His reliance on Murray of Broughton led him to distrust Lord George Murray. Working together and in harmony, these two could have conquered England, but they were continually at variance. It is revealing to note that, in their memoirs, both O'Sullivan and Sir John MacDonald, two of the men of Moidart who accompanied the prince from France, show the same marked bias against Lord George. They imply that if the conduct of the campaign had been left entirely in the hands of the prince all would have been well. Johnstone, who did not join the expedition until several days after it had arrived in Scotland, takes the opposite view. 'Had Prince Charles slept during the whole of the expedition, and allowed Lord George to act for him, according to his own judgement, there is every reason for supposing he would have found the crown of Great Britain on his head when he awoke.' The mass of evidence is on Johnstone's side, though not with such exaggeration. Lord George had served throughout the 'fifteen and had very considerable campaign experience. Throughout the 'forty-five he was hampered and hindered in every possible way by those nearest to the prince, and was only suspiciously tolerated by the latter himself.

The opening of the campaign was more successful than even the most sanguine of Jacobite supporters could have hoped for. Due partly to the incompetence of General Cope and partly to the fact that he had insufficient troops at his disposal, the rebels were able to reach Edinburgh without meeting any opposition. The victory of Prestonpans was followed by the invasion of England with an army now between seven and eight thousand strong. The majority of the prince's council had been against this, but Charles overruled them. He had, he said, had innumerable offers of aid and reinforcement, and he convinced them that only a spectacular advance, not a passive consolidation, would bring the waverers openly out in support. Rapidly the army advanced to Preston, to Manchester and finally to Derby, but the prince's forecasts were equally rapidly proved false. The numbers who rallied to his standard were negligible and the councils of war were becoming increasingly dissentient and doubtful.

That Charles had, in fact, received offers of assistance is incontestable; why that assistance failed to materialize is far more open to conjecture, though a number of potential adherents undoubtedly continued to sit on the fence, unwilling to commit themselves. The government forces under the Duke of Cumberland had still to be overcome; they would wait to see the outcome of the inevitable battle. Then, if all went well, they would join the rebels. The only forces still to be overcome would be a few regiments of guards and the militia stationed in London—large in numbers possibly but of very doubtful quality and reliability. The tide would be overwhelming. This apathy, this waiting until the issue was all but certain, was in part due to the success achieved by an omnipresent and highly efficient government spy service in inducing a feeling almost of paralysis in the would-be Jacobites. But another, more serious reason, is quoted by Lawrence Woulfe, the apologist for the failure of the English Jacobites.

> I have hear'd from very good authority that several leading men . . . were very forward to rise, but they expected . . . to hear of a Body of Troops landed in England, which for a long time was dayly thought would have been effected. . . . The principal reason for which the well affected People dared not rise in any other form and join the Prince's Army, is the want of Officers to lead their undisciplined men which the Prince would not spare them.

From Rome, James himself seems to confirm this explanation:

> I don't see how it is possible for our friends in England . . . without arms, without regular troops, without, enfin, any support, [to] pretend to rise in arms. . . . I have often blamed the indolence and timidity of our friends in England;

but, in the present moment, I own I think they would act imprudently and even rashly not to ly quiet still.

But even though the prince's army remained unaugmented, the position was by no means desperate. During the advance from Macclesfield, Lord George, with half the army, had moved by way of Congleton,* thus giving the impression that he was heading for Wales. Cumberland fell into the trap, sent a large part of his force to meet what he thought was the whole rebel army, and so enabled Lord George to double back and join up with Charles and the other half of the army at Derby. By this manoeuvre Cumberland was outflanked and only a comparatively small portion of his forces lay directly in the rebels' way. The success of the advance on London would depend only on the rebels' ability to advance rapidly enough to prevent Cumberland's outflanked force from catching up with them. Of even greater importance was the fact that Sir Watkin Williams-Wynn was on the point of marching to join the prince with a considerable force of Welsh supporters.

To their undoing, however, the rebel forces remained in ignorance of how strong their position was. Also, the most famous of the government spies, the notorious Captain Bradstreet, had managed to infiltrate into the prince's camp at Derby and had there succeeded in gaining the ear of the Council. Representing himself as a volunteer to the prince's cause, he announced that he had just come from Lichfield and that the Duke of Cumberland was on the point of entering that town with an army eight thousand strong. That his intelligence should have been believed is little short of amazing, but some of the prince's followers had come so far to fear the worst that they automatically accepted as true any statement that tended to confirm those fears. Then, also, the prince had heard no definite news from Williams-Wynn, and those about him tended to

*See map p. 57.

regard this promised support as being no more reliable than all the others. Time fought on the side of the government, for the messenger from Wales arrived two days too late.

In the Council at Derby there seemed, therefore, in the light of the available information, little to be said in favour of continuing the advance. On the other hand, information had been received which favoured retreat. A report had arrived from Lord John Drummond in the north in which he not only said that he himself had succeeded in levying a considerable force, but also that three thousand troops were on the point of arriving from France. A junction between the two armies seemed eminently desirable. That this report was as false as the information given by Captain Bradstreet in no way detracted from its effect; nor did the consideration that here might be sufficient troops to keep the government forces in the north more than fully occupied.

The prince was overruled and the retreat that marked the beginning of the end was under way. That Charles Edward himself now rode despondently at the rear of the army rather than eagerly in the van was indication enough of the temper of his troops. They, who had been so full of enthusiasm and who had asked for nothing better than to be allowed to come to grips with the enemy as soon as possible, now lost all stomach for the fight and wanted nothing so much as to be able to return to their homes. Even the victories of Clifton Hall and Falkirk failed to rekindle the spark and the *débâcle* of Culloden was only a question of time. This loss of morale was the really vital consequence of the decision at Derby, and the prince's defeatism was reflected in those about him. Had it been otherwise, the purely tactical decision would have been of slight importance. Even after Culloden, the rebel forces were stronger than they had ever been. But the psychological effect was irrevocable.

Except for minor outbreaks whose chances of success were

Lord George Murray

negligible, the course of the Jacobite movement had now run full circle; the last opportunity had, like the first, been mishandled.

Born on 25 July 1719, James Johnstone was the only son of an Edinburgh merchant and was closely connected with some of the best Scottish families—a fact of which he is continually reminding us. With an automatic entrée into Society, his youth was spent in the pursuit of pleasure, and his dissipation was such that his father was hard put to it to find a remedy. Finally it was resolved to send him on a visit to two of his uncles then living in Russia, in the hope that a temporary absence might serve to bring him to his senses. By agreeing to go Johnstone may, temporarily at least, have ingratiated himself with his parent, but from his own account of his private life after his return, his voyage can hardly be held to have effected a reformation.

Underlying his dissolute amiability, however, there were still the firm Episcopalian and Jacobite principles in which he had been educated, and when news arrived in Edinburgh that the Young Pretender had landed, he was one of the first to join the cause. Through relations, he gained an introduction to Lord George Murray and was appointed his aide-de-camp. Also, for a short period, he was assistant aide-de-camp to the prince himself. This composite duty he not unnaturally found increasingly wearing, and when, after Prestonpans, he was given a captain's commission, he raised his own company and with it joined the Duke of Perth's regiment.

His own account tells how he fought through the whole campaign and of his wanderings following Culloden. After a number of narrow escapes, some feats of considerable endurance, and not a few interludes of amorous dallying, he finally escaped to Holland. Once there, his first thoughts were to go again to Russia where his uncles could have exerted some influence on his behalf. Instead, however, he was persuaded to go

B

to Paris where, finding his portion of the government fund set
aside for Scots exiles insufficient for his needs, he joined the
French service. For a while he served with the French forces
in Canada, part of the time as aide-de-camp to Montcalm, and
there is some evidence to suggest that his talents were warmly
appreciated. After the English had completed their conquest of
Canada, he returned to France. There, however, although he
was created Chevalier de Saint-Louis in 1762, the deaths of his
protectors and a variety of accidents cut him off from prefer-
ment and despite all he had done, he was finally condemned
to a life of penury and rather petulant petitioning. On one
occasion, recapitulating his service in Canada, he lamented
(referring to himself in the third person) that 'utterly exhausted
from doing so many different jobs, having had no other bed
but the ground throughout the whole campaign, having been
unable to sleep for more than two hours out of every twenty-
four, and having never taken off his clothes except to change
his linen nor his boots except to change his socks, he had
hoped to rise to the highest military rank ... But fate had
condemned him to a distasteful stagnation in the French service,
and to growing old in unrelieved misery.'* In 1792, in a letter
to his son James, he wrote: 'I only wish for bread which the
Eternal Almighty God has had the bounty to give me until
the age of 74 years', and talked of 'my present cruel, distressed
and desperate situation' and of 'my unhappy life through
which from my infancy I have never had the smallest enjoy-
ment which was not embittered with pain, trouble, crosses &
persecutions'.†

Mention of his son James highlights one of the uncertain-
ties in the Chevalier's life—when he was married and to whom.

*From an undated letter (in French) to M. de Sartine, Ministre de la
Marine.
†The extracts from this letter are quoted by kind permission of Mrs.
Malcolm Morley, whose husband was a direct descendant of the
Chevalier.

According to a pedigree produced in 1852, he married a daughter of Ballard Beckford, of New York, probably between 1762 and 1764. The truth of this, however, is highly suspect, and it is far more likely both that he was married and that his son James was born sometime between his return from Russia and his joining Charles Edward. Evidence to support this can be found in *Waverley* where Sir Walter Scott wrote: 'It would not, for instance, be supposed that at the time he was favouring us with the highly wrought account of his amour with the adorable Peggie, the Chevalier de Johnstone was a married man whose grandchild is now alive'. This would also explain why Peggie did not accompany him to France.

The date of Johnstone's death is again uncertain, but it was probably about 1800.

The memoirs themselves seem to have been written shortly after his return from Canada, and they were first published in 1820. Inevitably the lapse of time resulted in a number of inaccuracies. Particularly is this so where distances are concerned, for added to lapses of memory there was also the confusion between French leagues and English leagues, and between Scottish miles and English miles. In the present edition these have all been amended where possible to read the distance by road in English miles. In other cases, where what the author says gives a totally inaccurate picture of relative strengths, or where he implies that the impossible was possible, footnotes have been added to rectify the position. In the main, however, every effort has been made to avoid unnecessary editorial apparatus and, where misconceptions are (as frequently happens) the misconceptions of bias, they have been left unaltered. Such bias is almost the hallmark of all personal accounts of the Rebellion and is one of the reasons why so many points remain open to conjecture. No one source can be taken as completely reliable and any conclusions, especially as to the relative merits of the main protagonists, can only be based (possibly wrongly) on majority opinion.

On the whole Johnstone gives a fairer picture than many of his contemporaries. Although Lord George was obviously his hero he is never blind to his faults, and though he does occasionally allow himself a gratuitous remark when writing of Charles Edward's failings, he still remains aware of all the qualities he had to commend him.

Apart from ending with Johnstone's arrival in Holland and not following the uninteresting itinerary of his journey to Paris, the only cuts that have been made in this part of the original text are of minor passages which are either repetitious or irrelevant. The original manuscript of Johnstone's memoirs, including the journal of his time in Canada, is now in the Clan Macpherson Museum in Newtonmore.

BRIAN RAWSON

THE FORTY-FIVE

I

PRINCE CHARLES EDWARD STUART, grandson of James the Second, unable to support any longer the endless delays in the embarkation of the troops destined by the court of France for an invasion of Scotland, at length formed the resolution of repairing secretly to that country, and throwing himself into the arms of the Scotch. Their fidelity and attachment to his family had been amply proved in the different attempts made by them since the Revolution to replace the Stuarts on the throne,* and he entertained a hope of succeeding in his enterprise by the efforts of his subjects alone, without the assistance of foreign powers.

He embarked at Belle Isle, on the 12th of July 1745, on board a small frigate, escorted by the *Elizabeth*, a ship of sixty guns. These two vessels were armed and fitted out at the expense of Mr Welsh,† a merchant of Nantes, for the conveyance of the Prince to Scotland; but the court of France afterwards reimbursed that individual for all the expenses of the expedition.

The Prince was only accompanied by seven individuals: the Duke of Athol, attainted and an exile since the year 1715; Macdonel, an Irishman; Kelly, an Irishman, formerly secretary to the Bishop of Rochester; Sullivan, an Irishman; Sheridan, an Irishman, who had been governor to the Prince; Macdonald, a Scotsman; Strickland, an Irishman;‡ and Michel, his valet-de-chambre, an Italian: a most extraordinary band of followers, no doubt, when we consider the daring enterprise on which they were entering, which was no less than that of attempting to wrest the crown of Great Britain from the house of Hanover.

*The attachment to the house of Stuart was general only in the Highlands.
†Anthony Walsh, descended from an Irish family.
‡An Englishman of an old Westmorland family.

Mr Sullivan, who had been aide-de-camp to Marshal de Maille-
bois, in Italy, was the only individual of the suite who possessed
any knowledge of military affairs. The other Irishmen, drawn
into Scotland by the allurement which the enterprise held out
to them of making their fortune, were extremely injurious to
the interests of the Prince, from the bad advice they gave him;
and unfortunately they enjoyed his full confidence.

The Prince, having lost all hopes of landing in Scotland with
an army of regular troops, ought, at least, to have been accompanied by officers distinguished for their talents in the art of
war, well qualified to combine with judgment, and conduct
with prudence, the operations of the field; possessing minds
fertile in resources, enlightened by experience, and capable of
discerning and of turning to advantage every momentary
success which fortune might present. Officers of this description, at the head of his army and in his councils, would have
rendered the disembarkation of regular troops less necessary,
and would have enabled him to avoid those faults which even-
tually produced the ruin of his cause in Scotland; for this
Prince, though he gained battles, was never able to derive
from them any of the advantages to which they ought to have
led. It is certain that no general officer in France would have
refused to embark with the Prince on an enterprise so well
calculated to procure him instant celebrity throughout all
Europe, the attention of which was fixed on this expedition. It
was a rare opportunity for developing talents, for the display
of which an opportunity might never occur in a more numerous
army.

The *Elizabeth* was attacked, in the latitude of 47° 57′ about
thirty-nine leagues to the westward of the Lizard point, by the
Lion, an English man-of-war of sixty guns. The two vessels
were of the same force, and the fight was maintained with the
utmost fury and obstinacy for the space of six hours, until they
were both so greatly disabled that they could hardly be kept

afloat. When the combat ceased, each vessel was obliged to consult its safety by endeavouring to gain some port without delay. The Prince, who in his little frigate beheld this obstinate conflict, was extremely uneasy as to the result and, as the *Elizabeth* had on board a considerable quantity of arms and military stores, he ordered his vessel to advance under her stern, for the purpose of ascertaining her real situation. He was informed that she had lost a great number of men; that the captain and several other officers had been killed, besides many soldiers of the regiment of Maurepas, who had volunteered their service in the expedition; that the vessel was so pierced with balls that she could with difficulty be kept from sinking; and that they would be obliged to put into the first port of France which they could reach, being totally incapable of continuing the voyage. Thus the *Lion* and the *Elizabeth*, equally shattered by the combat, were obliged to regain their respective coasts. The Prince, in his frigate, continued his course for Scotland, where he landed at Loch Sunart, on the 24th of July, and took up his quarters in the house of Mr Macdonald of Kinloch Moidart. There he was soon joined by Cameron of Lochiel, with his clan of Camerons; by Macdonald of Clanranald, with his clan of Macdonalds; by the clan of the Stuarts of Appin; and by the clans of the Macdonalds of Keppoch, Glengarry, and Glencoe. The Macdonalds of Keppoch commenced hostilities in their march to join him by attacking two companies of the Royal Scots, whom they made prisoners, and presented to the Prince as a happy omen of his future success.

No positive information of the descent of the Prince reached Edinburgh till the 8th of August, when a courier was received from Campbell of Lochnell, with a letter to the magistrates of that city, containing a circumstantial account of his progress from his first landing. As King George was then abroad in Hanover, the Regency, which he had appointed to govern the kingdom in his absence, issued orders to Sir John Cope, the commander-in-chief for Scotland, to assemble all the regular troops in Scotland with the utmost diligence, and to march against the Prince without loss of time, in order to crush this enterprise in its birth; and it is highly probable that he would have succeeded had he conducted himself as he ought to have done. But he lost his advantage over the enemy, by delaying like Fabius (not indeed with the wisdom of Fabius*) to come to an engagement, although his army was far superior in number to that which he had to encounter. Perhaps he hoped that, by allowing the Highland army to be joined by all the partisans of the Prince, he would gain more honour by their defeat, and render himself of more importance to the court of London.†

General Cope assembled his army at Stirling. It was composed of the infantry regiments of Lee, Lascelles, and Murray; five companies of a Highland regiment, two companies of Guise's regiment, and Gardiner's and Hamilton's regiments of dragoons: he had six field-pieces, and two mortars. With this army he set out from Stirling, in obedience to the orders received by him from the Regency, in order to make head against the Prince. But, as there are several roads to the north of Scotland, he chose that which goes along the eastern coast;‡

*Quintus Fabius, the Roman dictator, who continually harassed Hannibal's army but would never allow himself to be drawn into a pitched battle, so giving his own forces time to rally their strength.

†Evidence adduced at General Cope's trial proved this opinion of him to be utterly unfounded.

‡Cope left Stirling on the 20th and proceeded not along the route suggested by Johnstone, but by way of Crieff, Amulree, Aberfeldy, Trinafour and Dalnacardoch. Only when he reached Dalwhinnie did he become aware that the Pretender's forces were both stronger and further advanced than he had previously been led to understand. To continue his own advance might well be to court disaster, and Cope was therefore left with the choice of either returning to Stirling or of heading for Inverness. In the delusory hope that reinforcements would rally to him and that the mere presence of a government army at Inverness would deter the prince from leaving Scotland, he chose wrong—and so left the route to the south open.

whilst the Prince, having certain information of the route taken
by General Cope, made choice of the road across the mountains
by Blair Athol, by which he reached the low country, adroitly
contriving to leave the English army behind him. Thus General

.... Route followed by
Charles Edward
– – – Route followed by
General Cope

INVERNESS

Fort Augustus

Glenfinnan

Fort William

Moidart

Corryarrack

Ruthven

Dalwhinnie

Dalnacardoch

Trinafour

Blair Atholl

Aberfeldy

Amulree

Dunkeld

PERTH

Crieff

STIRLING

EDINBURGH

ABERDEEN

THE OPENING OF
THE CAMPAIGN

Cope constantly directing his march to the north, and the
Prince to the south, by two different roads, it was impossible
they could ever meet.

The conduct of Sir John Cope was the more inconceivable,
as he was generally looked upon in England as an experienced
general, and he had distinguished himself very much in
Flanders. There is an arm of the sea at Leith, the port of

Edinburgh, about six miles in breadth, which becomes gradually narrower till we reach the town of Alloa, twenty-eight miles west of Edinburgh, where it terminates in the mouth of the river Forth. The magistrates of Edinburgh had taken the precaution to withdraw all the ships and boats of every description to Leith, thereby depriving the Prince of all means of crossing this arm of the sea. Consequently General Cope, in order to prevent him from penetrating to the south, had only to throw up entrenchments at the fords, near the town of Stirling where all the great roads from the Highlands meet, to enable him to oppose successfully the passage of the river. Stirling is situated at a distance of thirty-seven miles from Edinburgh, eight miles from Alloa, and two miles from the chain of mountains that stretch to the north and north-west of Scotland. There is a stone bridge across the river, but it is commanded by the guns of the castle, and General Cope might have shut up the Prince in the mountains by merely remaining with his army at Stirling. The position was central and very advantageous for covering Edinburgh, an object of which he never ought to have lost sight, because it was obvious that the Prince would endeavour to become master of the capital of Scotland so that, by inspiring his friends with confidence, he might induce them to declare themselves openly in his favour. It is an incontrovertible axiom, and one which ought to serve as a rule of conduct in military operations, that whatever is to our advantage is contrary to that of our enemy, and whatever is to the advantage of the enemy is contrary to ours. Hence we may often form a just conclusion as to the designs of the enemy by supposing ourselves in his position and by carefully examining what we should do in a similar situation, provided the enemy acts according to the principles of the art of war; for if the general opposed to us is ignorant of his profession, even a Marshal Turenne would be as much puzzled to divine his intentions as the most inexperienced soldier.

By shutting up the Prince in the mountains, General Cope would have prevented him from performing any of those brilliant achievements which were so essential, in the beginning of his enterprise, to insure its success; and the Prince would never have attempted to pass the river by force, had entrenchments lined with field-artillery been thrown up at all the fords.* To pass the river secretly, by ascending towards its source, was hardly possible, as he would then have been obliged to go through the country of the Campbells, a clan of Highlanders extremely numerous, of whom the Duke of Argyle was the chief, and who were the implacable enemies of the house of Stuart. Supposing even that the Prince had effected his passage, General Cope could still have advanced and given him battle, with every possible advantage and without losing his position between him and Edinburgh. If the Prince's army had advanced by the roads leading to the fords, as it certainly would, all that General Cope had to do was, when the Prince was so near that he could not possibly escape, to pass Stirling bridge with his army, and fall suddenly on the Highlanders whilst they were employed in examining the fords. The result of the combat could not have been doubtful, General Cope having from three to four thousand regular troops,† against twelve or fifteen hundred undisciplined mountaineers. But now, either from ignorance in the art of war (notwithstanding the reputation he had acquired), from policy, or from bad intentions towards the government, General Cope, instead of crushing the Prince at the outset, permitted an enterprise whose rapid and astonishing progress surprised and fixed the attention of all the powers of Europe. Thus the Prince, with a small and contemptible number of Highlanders, shook the throne of Great Britain and

---

*But Cope was unable to do this. In a letter to Lord Tweedale, of the 3rd of August, he said: 'If I come to want to make use of a field-train, or any artillery at all, we have not any gunners for that purpose.'
†He had in fact less than 2,000.

was on the point of being crowned in London. He kept his ground against the whole force of England strengthened by the addition of the Hessian and Dutch troops, and gained several battles against disciplined armies much superior in number to his own.*

On the 5th of September, the Prince arrived at Perth, where the Highlands begin to extend to the west and north-west, a town about forty miles from Edinburgh. There he immediately proclaimed his father, James the Third, King of Great Britain, published a manifesto and, at the same time, the commission appointing him Regent of the kingdom, both of them dated from Rome. On his arrival at Perth he had not above a thousand followers;† but the day after, he was joined by the Duke of Perth with a part of his vassals, Lord George Murray with a part of the vassals of his brother the Duke of Athol, and likewise by Lord Nairn, and several other persons of distinction, who attached themselves to his fortunes. On the 7th he sent a detachment to Dundee, a town situated twenty-two miles from Perth, to proclaim his father as king.

As soon as the news of the Prince's landing was confirmed at Edinburgh, I immediately repaired to the house of Lord Rollo, a Scots peer, the father-in-law of my sister, to wait the arrival of the Prince at Perth, which is about four miles from his mansion; and on the sixth of September I left it to join the Prince, accompanied by the two Misses Rollo who presented me to their relations, the Duke of Perth and Lord George Murray. On my arrival at Perth, I was greatly surprised to find so few followers with the Prince, as public report at Edinburgh had increased them to a prodigious number. The Prince having

---

*The armies were never *much* superior, nor were the rebel forces without discipline.
†When the Pretender erected his standard on the 19th, at Glenfinnan, he had about 1,000 men; by this time he had nearer 1,850.

appointed Lord George and the Duke of Perth his lieutenant-generals, Lord George proposed that I should be his aide-de-camp, which proposal I accepted and began immediately to enter on the exercise of the duties attached to the situation. And as the Prince had then only one aide-de-camp, Mr Maclaughlan, he employed me as much as Lord George himself did; so that, night and day, my occupations were incessant, and I could scarcely find time to sleep two hours in the four-and-twenty.

II

THE Prince set out from Perth on the 11th of September, and on the 13th crossed the Forth at the ford of the Frew, about four miles from Stirling. On the evening of the 14th, our army reached the neighbourhood of Corstorphin, a village about three miles from Edinburgh, and passed the night in a field at Gray's Mill, where the Prince lodged in the miller's cottage. While remaining there, deputies arrived from the city to treat about a capitulation, to whom the Prince replied, that he could not treat with his subjects. However, matters were soon arranged, and next morning the Prince was conducted to Holyrood House, the palace of his ancestors, amidst the acclamations of an immense crowd, whom curiosity had brought to meet him a quarter of a league from the city. The next day King James was proclaimed at Edinburgh, and the Prince declared Regent to govern the kingdom in the absence of his father at Rome.

General Cope arrived, on the 11th of September, at Aberdeen, a city one hundred and fifteen miles north of Edinburgh: and having embarked his army, sailed with a fair wind, and landed at Dunbar, a town twenty-eight miles east of Edinburgh, on the 17th. Here he was immediately joined by Brigadier General Fowke, newly arrived from England, as also by the dragoon regiments of Hamilton and Gardiner, whom he had left behind him at Stirling on setting out for the North.

Lord George Murray, who had the charge of all the details of our army and the sole direction of it, possessed a natural genius for military operations, and was indeed a man of surprising talents, which, had they been cultivated by the study of military tactics, would unquestionably have rendered him one of the greatest generals of the age. He was tall and robust, and brave in the highest degree, conducting the Highlanders in the most heroic manner, being always the first to rush sword in

The Engagement between the *Lyon* and the *Elizabeth*

hand into the midst of the enemy. He used to say when he advanced to the charge, 'I do not ask you, my lads, to go before, but merely to follow me'—a very energetic harangue, admirably calculated to excite the ardour of the Highlanders, but which would sometimes have had a better effect in the mouth of the Prince. He slept little, was continually occupied with all manner of details, and was altogether most indefatigable, for he alone had the planning and directing of all our operations: in a word, he was the only person capable of conducting our army. His colleague, the Duke of Perth, though brave even to excess, every way honourable, and possessed of a mild and gentle disposition, was of very limited abilities and interfered with nothing. Lord George was vigilant, active, and diligent; his plans were always judiciously formed, and he carried them promptly and vigorously into execution. However, with an infinity of good qualities, he was not without his defects: proud, haughty, blunt and imperious, he wished to have the exclusive disposal of everything and, feeling his superiority, would listen to no advice. There were, it is true, few persons in our army sufficiently versed in military affairs to be capable of advising him as to the conducting of his operations. The Highland chiefs, like their vassals, possessed the most heroic courage; but they knew no other manoeuvre than that of rushing upon the enemy sword in hand, as soon as they saw them, without order and without discipline. Lord George could receive still less assistance from the subaltern Irish officers, who, with the exception of Mr Sullivan, possessed no other knowledge than that which usually forms the whole stock of subalterns, namely, how to mount and quit guard. We can hardly, therefore, be astonished that Lord George, possessing so many of the qualities requisite to form a great general, should have gained the hearts of the Highlanders; and a general who has the confidence of his soldiers may do wonders. Hence, possessing the art of employing men to

C

advantage, without having had time to discipline them, but taking them merely as they came from the plough, he made them perform prodigies of valour against various English armies, always greatly superior in number to that of the Prince, though the English troops are allowed to be the best in Europe. Nature had formed him for a great warrior; he did not require the accidental advantage of birth.

The Prince ordered a body of Highlanders to enter the city of Edinburgh, who immediately formed the blockade of the Castle, where there was a garrison of five or six hundred men, to prevent their sallies and deprive them of the means of disturbing us in the city. At the same time he ordered the rest of his army to remain encamped at Duddingston, a village about a quarter of a league from his palace of Holyrood House.

On the 19th of September, General Cope encamped his army at Haddington, about seventeen miles to the east of Edinburgh, and on the 20th he approached to within six miles of our camp. As it was absolutely indispensable, in our situation, to give battle as soon as possible (because a great number of the Prince's friends only waited the event to declare themselves in his favour), he assembled his army on the morning of the 20th of September and immediately set out to meet the enemy. His army was composed of about eighteen hundred men, badly armed, a part of them having only bludgeons in their hands. They had found very few arms at Edinburgh, as the inhabitants, before the capitulation, had deposited them in the Castle, which is situated on the summit of a steep rock, impregnable from its elevation and only to be taken by famine or bombardment. The army of General Cope was composed of four thousand regular troops, besides several volunteers, whom a fanatic zeal had induced to join his standard, but who had not sufficient courage to do us any injury.*

*General Cope's army was by now 2,300 strong, the prince's 2,400.

We arrived, about two o'clock in the afternoon, within musket-shot of the enemy, where we halted behind an eminence, having a full view of the camp of General Cope, the position of which was chosen with a great deal of skill. The more we examined it, the more we were convinced of the impossibility of attacking it; and we were all thrown into consternation, and quite at a loss what course to take. On even ground, the courage and bravery of the Highlanders might supply the place of numbers, but what could eighteen hundred men do against four thousand in a position inaccessible on every point? The camp of the enemy was fortified by nature, and in the happiest position for so small an army. The General had on his right two enclosures, surrounded by stone walls from six to seven feet high, between which there was a road of about twenty feet broad, leading to the village of Prestonpans. Before him was another enclosure, surrounded by a deep ditch filled with water and from ten to twelve feet broad, which served as a drain to the marshy ground. On his left was a marsh which terminated in a deep pond, and behind him was the sea, so that he was enclosed as in a fortification, which could be attacked in no other manner than by a regular siege. We spent the afternoon in reconnoitring his position: the more we examined it, the more our uneasiness and chagrin increased, as we saw no possibility of attacking it without exposing ourselves to be cut to pieces in a disgraceful manner. At sunset our army traversed the village of Tranent, which was on our right, and took a new position opposite to the marsh. General Cope, at the same time, ordered his army to take a new front, supporting his right by the ditch of the enclosure, his left by the sea, and having his front towards the lake.

Mr Anderson, proprietor of the marsh, came to the Prince in the evening, very *à-propos*, to relieve us from our embarrassment. He assured him that there was a place in the marsh where we could pass it with safety, and that he himself had frequently

crossed it when hunting. The Prince, having instantly caused
the place to be examined, ascertained that this account was correct, and that General Cope, not deeming it passable, had
neglected to station a guard there. He caused the army to pass
through the place in question during the night, the Highlanders
moving along in files without meeting with any opposition
from the enemy. As soon as they came out of the marsh they
took up their formation, their line extending towards the sea.

At break of day, General Cope took our first line of twelve
hundred men, formed in order of battle at the distance of two
hundred paces from his army, for bushes. Our second line, of
six hundred men, was composed of those who were badly
armed, many of them, as we have already observed, having only
staves or bludgeons in their hands. Captain Macgregor of the
Duke of Perth's regiment, for want of other arms, procured
scythes, which he sharpened and fixed to poles of from seven to
eight feet long. With these he armed his company, and they
proved very destructive weapons.

When our first line had passed the marsh, Lord George dispatched me to the second line, which the Prince conducted in
person, to see that it passed without noise or confusion. Having
examined the line and seen that everything was as it should be,
in returning to Lord George, I found the Prince at the head of
the column, accompanied by Lord Nairn, just as he was beginning to enter the marsh, and I passed it the second time along
with him. We were not yet out of the marsh when the enemy,
seeing our first line in order of battle, fired an alarm-gun. At the
very end of the marsh there was a deep ditch, three or four feet
broad, which it was necessary to leap over, and the Prince, in
making this leap, fell upon his knees on the other side. I laid
hold of his arm and immediately raised him up. On examining
his countenance, it seemed to me, from the alarm expressed in
it, that he considered this accident as a bad omen.

Lord George, at the head of the first line, did not give the

English time to recover from their surprise. He advanced with such rapidity that General Cope had hardly time to form his troops in order of battle, before the Highlanders rushed upon them sword in hand. They had been frequently enjoined to aim at the noses of the horses with their swords, without minding the riders, as the natural movement of a horse, wounded in the face, is to wheel round, and a few horses wounded in that manner are sufficient to throw a whole squadron into such disorder that it is impossible afterwards to rally it. They followed this advice most implicitly, and the English cavalry were instantly thrown into confusion.

Macgregor's company did great execution with their scythes. They cut the legs of the horses in two, and their riders through the middle of their bodies. Macgregor was brave and intrepid, but, at the same time, altogether whimsical and singular. When advancing to the charge with his company, he received five wounds, two of them from balls that pierced his body through and through. Stretched on the ground, with his head resting on his hand, he called out to the Highlanders of his company, 'My lads, I am not dead! By G—, I shall see if any of you does not do his duty!'

The Highlanders instantly fell on the flanks of the infantry which, being uncovered and exposed from the flight of the cavalry, immediately gave way. Thus, in less than five minutes, we obtained a complete victory, with terrible carnage on the part of the enemy. It was gained with such rapidity that, in the second line, where, not having been able to find Lord George, I was still by the side of the Prince, we saw no other enemy on the field of battle than those who were lying on the ground killed and wounded, though we were not more than fifty paces behind our first line, running always as fast as we could to overtake them, and near enough never to lose sight of them. The Highlanders made a terrible slaughter of the enemy, particularly at the spot where the road begins to run between the two

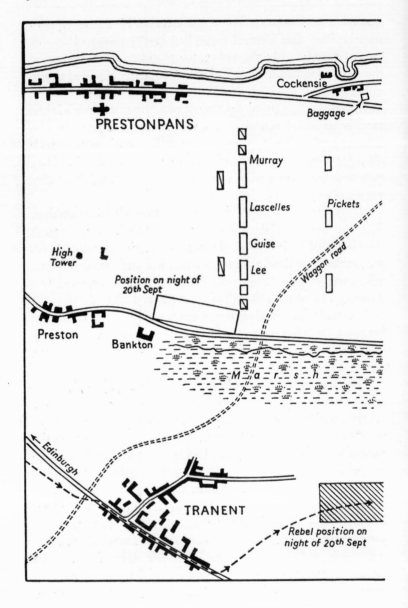

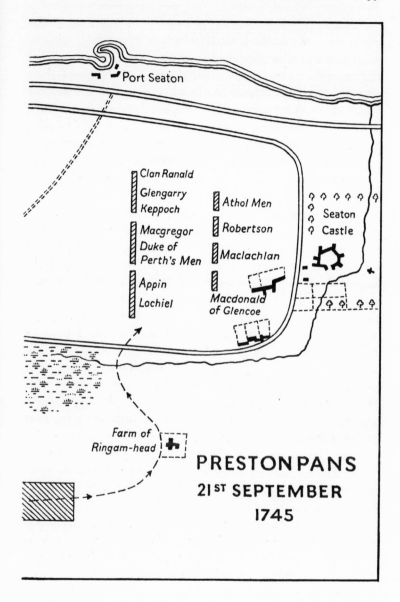

Port Seaton

Clan Ranald
Glengarry
Keppoch

Athol Men

Macgregor
Duke of
Perth's Men

Robertson

Maclachlan

Appin

Lochiel

Macdonald
of Glencoe

Seaton
Castle

Farm of
Ringam-head

PRESTONPANS
21ST SEPTEMBER
1745

enclosures, as it was soon stopped up by the fugitives; as also along the walls of the enclosures, where they killed, without trouble, those who attempted to climb them. The strength of the enemy's camp became their destruction. Some of them attempted to rally in the enclosure, where there was an eminence which commanded the field of battle, and from which they fired some shot; but they were soon put to flight by the Highlanders, who immediately entered the enclosure in pursuit of them.

The panic-terror of the English surpassed all imagination. They threw down their arms that they might run with more speed, thus depriving themselves by their fears of the only means of arresting the vengeance of the Highlanders. Of so many men in a condition, from their numbers, to preserve order in their retreat, not one thought of defending himself. Terror had taken entire possession of their minds. I saw a young Highlander, about fourteen years of age, scarcely formed, who was presented to the Prince as a prodigy, having killed, it was said, fourteen of the enemy. The Prince asked him if this was true? 'I do not know,' replied he, 'if I killed them; but I brought fourteen soldiers to the ground with my sword.' Another Highlander brought ten soldiers to the Prince, whom he had made prisoners, driving them before him like a flock of sheep. This Highlander, from a rashness without example, having pursued a party to some distance from the field of battle along the road between the two enclosures, struck down the hindermost with a blow of his sword, calling, at the same time, 'Down with your arms.' The soldiers, terror-struck, threw down their arms without looking behind them, and the Highlander, with a pistol in one hand and a sword in the other, made them do exactly as he pleased. The rage and despair of these men, on seeing themselves made prisoners by a single individual, may easily be imagined. These were, however, the same English soldiers who had distinguished themselves at Dettingen and Fontenoy, and who might justly be ranked amongst the bravest troops of Europe.

However, when we come to consider the matter attentively, we can hardly be astonished that Highlanders, who take arms voluntarily from attachment to their legitimate Prince and their chiefs, should defeat thrice their number of regular troops, who enlist from seduction or a love of idleness and dissipation. Such men are strangers to the love of glory, affection for their Prince, the enthusiasm of patriotism, the intense feeling of the justice of their cause, the hope of rich spoil or honourable promotion.

It is the general who can inspire his army with confidence in his capacity, talents and experience, who is the best leader, for soldiers who are prepossessed in his favour will conduct themselves like heroes, in the belief that they are marching to a certain victory. With troops as animated as the Highlanders were in this extraordinary battle, a general ought not to think of the number of his army, however inferior to that of the enemy, but merely of the frame of mind in which his soldiers are.

The field of battle presented a spectacle of horror, being covered with heads, legs, arms and mutilated bodies; for the killed all fell by the sword. The enemy had thirteen hundred killed, while we made fifteen hundred prisoners, and took six field-pieces, two mortars, all the tents, baggage and the military-chest. General Cope, by means of a white cockade, which he put in his hat, similar to what we wore, passed through the midst of the Highlanders without being known and escaped to England, where he carried the first news of his defeat. This victory cost us forty killed, and as many wounded.* The greatest advantage we derived from it was the reputation that the Prince's army acquired in the outset, which determined many of his partisans, who were yet wavering, to declare themselves openly in his favour. The arms of the vanquished, of which we stood in need, were also of great service to us. The

*The author's estimate of the Highlanders' losses is reasonably accurate, but that of Cope's obviously exaggerated. At most the number of killed was not above 400 or 500.

Prince slept next night at Pinky-house, about a quarter of a league from the field of battle. He committed to my care one hundred and ten English officers, who were our prisoners, with orders that they should want for nothing.

Having been several times in armies which have been put to rout since this action, I have always remarked, that much fewer men were lost on the field of battle than in the subsequent flight. Seized by a panic-terror, and frequently borne away by their companions without knowing why, even when they have lost fewer men than the enemy who remains victorious, they disperse like sheep, and, unable to defend themselves, come voluntarily forward like so many victims to be sacrificed. Thus it required no extraordinary courage in this young Highlander to bring down fourteen soldiers, but merely an arm sufficiently strong to give fourteen blows with his sword on the heads of so many fugitives, and legs sufficiently swift to pursue and overtake them. The other Highlander, who took ten prisoners, would have paid dearly for his rashness, if they had had sufficient presence of mind to look behind them, when he ordered them to lay down their arms.

The rallying of troops has ever appeared to me one of the most essential requisites in military science. To impress on the minds of soldiers the necessity of this, and of retiring slowly before the enemy with their arms always in readiness to defend themselves, it is only necessary to show them that on this depends their safety and their lives; and that if they fly in confusion and disorder, without being able to defend themselves, they will infallibly meet with their destruction. The soldier who betakes himself to a disorderly flight does not do so with the idea of losing his life, but with the hope of preserving it and of being sooner out of danger. But he deceives himself as to his means, and rushes on death instead of avoiding it. Soldiers are mere machines, and we must direct and guide them to prevent them from being tyrannised over by their imagination. In an attack I have seen the same men advance like lions, who, when repulsed, became in an instant as cowardly and timorous as hares. However, it is not the diminution of their numbers in the fight that can occasion such a sudden change, for they cannot know what is passing throughout the army; but they turn their backs mechanically, without any other reason for doing so, than that they follow the example of those who happen to be near them. The contagion spreads through the army like wild-fire: an unexpected resistance on the part of the enemy, instantly deranges the order of the whole machine and destroys, in an instant, the faculty of discernment and reflection, and the whole becomes one scene of confusion.

III

NEXT day, being the 22nd of September, the Prince returned to Edinburgh, where he was received with the loudest acclamations by the populace, always equally inconstant in every country in the world. He there published several edicts, one of which prohibited all public rejoicings on account of the victory obtained over General Cope, as it was purchased at the expense of the blood of his subjects. In another, he granted a general amnesty for all treasons, rebellions, or offences whatever, committed against him or his predecessors since the Revolution of 1688; provided the aggressors repaired to the palace of Holyrood-house within the space of four days, and made a declaration in presence of his secretary, that they would live in future under his government as quiet and peaceable subjects. He also sent circular letters to the magistrates of all the towns in Scotland, commanding them to repair immediately to Edinburgh to pay their proportion of the contributions which he imposed on every town, and he dispatched other letters to all the collectors and controllers of the land-tax and customs, ordering them to bring to his palace their books and the public money in their hands, on pain of high treason.

The victory of Prestonpans, however unimportant it at first seemed, made the Prince the entire master of Scotland, where the only English troops which remained were the garrisons of the castles of Edinburgh and Stirling. As the whole of the towns of Scotland had been obliged to recognize the Prince as regent of the kingdom in the absence of his father King James, all that he had to do now was to retain possession of it. His chief object ought to have been to endeavour, by every possible means, to secure himself in the government of his ancient kingdom, and to defend himself against the English armies (which would not fail to be sent against him) without attempting, for the present, to extend his views to England. This was the advice which every one gave the Prince and, if he had followed it, he might still perhaps have been in possession of that kingdom. He was strongly advised to dissolve and annul the union between Scotland and England, made during the usurpation of Queen Anne by a cabal of a few Scots peers, whom the English court had gained over to its interests by force of gold, contrary to the general wish of the Scottish nation, all ranks of which, down to the lowest peasant, have ever held this act in abhorrence. Such a step would have given infinite pleasure to all Scotland, and the sole consideration of being freed from the English yoke would have induced the Scots to declare themselves generally in his favour.

By thus fomenting the natural hatred and animosity which the Scots have in all times manifested against the English, the war would have become national, and this would have been a most fortunate circumstance for the Prince. The Scots, though much inferior to the English in numbers, had withstood them during a long and almost uninterrupted war of a thousand years, and had preserved their liberty and independence down to the union of the two kingdoms in 1707. Besides, if the Prince could have kept his ground in Scotland, the court of France would have found it their interest to maintain him on the throne and would have exerted themselves to the utmost to prevent an union with England. It was further observed, by those who gave this advice to the Prince, that as the Union, from its being an act passed during the usurpation and injurious to the house of Stuart, was necessarily void, it was proper to issue writs for the immediate meeting of the Scottish parliament at Edinburgh, to impose taxes in a legal manner and obtain supplies for the support of his army.

As this parliament could only at first be composed of the partisans of the Prince, it would not certainly have been considered as a free parliament; but the taxes imposed in this

manner on the nation would have appeared less arbitrary, and
borne a greater appearance of justice and lawfulness than the
military contributions which were then levied.

The Scots who were most distinguished for their talents,
experience and good sense, proposed this wise and salutary
plan of operations to the Prince, which, however, he did not
seem to relish.* He had inherited the sentiments of his ancestors,
who always entertained an extravagant attachment to the
English people, and who were always the victims of the ill-
judged mildness with which they governed them, instead of
ruling them with a rod of iron, like their former sovereigns,
Henry VIII and Queen Elizabeth. The Prince constantly
rejected every proposition which he thought calculated to
displease them or even to give rise to the slightest umbrage.
The unfortunate house of Stuart have been always abhorred
and detested by the English nation since their accession to the
throne, and have never received any other return for their
tender regard than incessant persecution, the English shedding
their blood even on the scaffold, and at last driving the whole
family from the country, after stripping them of their crown.
The mind of the Prince, however, was occupied only with
England, and he seemed little flattered with the idea of possessing a kingdom to which the family of Stuart owes its origin and
its royalty.

The army of the Prince, after this victory, increased in
numbers every day, and soon amounted to from four to five
thousand men. He then became impatient to enter England, and
for that purpose assembled a council of all the chiefs of clans,
where his opinion was approved of by no one. King George
had returned to London on the 11th of September, and, alarmed

---

*When, earlier, the Cardinal de Tencin had offered assistance to recover
England and Scotland on condition that Ireland was ceded to France,
Charles Edward's only reply, even then, was 'All or nothing.' He would
never consider any form of compromise.

at the defeat of General Cope, had recalled the whole of the English troops in the army of the allies in Flanders. The chiefs represented to the Prince that nothing could be more ridiculous than to attempt an invasion of England with such a handful of men, when it was defended by fifty thousand regular troops and a numerous militia. Some of the chiefs even told him, that they had taken arms, and risked their fortunes and their lives, to seat him on the throne of Scotland, but that they wished to have nothing to do with England. However, the Prince indicating that he had received letters from several English lords, assuring him that he should find them in arms on the borders ready to join him with a considerable English force, the chiefs of the clans suffered themselves at length to yield and, after many debates, gave their assent to his proposition.*

Thus the Prince, instead of remaining in Scotland on the defensive, set out with his army on the 1st of November from Edinburgh, where he had scarcely stayed long enough to perceive that he was entirely master of the kingdom, and that it was only necessary to adopt proper measures and follow judicious counsels, to preserve his conquest. The enterprise was bold, nay rash, and unexampled. What man in his senses could think of encountering the English armies and attempting the conquest of England with four thousand five hundred Highlanders? It is true they were brave, resolute, and determined to fight to the very last, selling their lives as dearly as possible, having no alternative but victory or death. Nonetheless the disproportion between this handful of men and the whole force of England was so great as to preclude the slightest hope of success.

Our army remained in the town of Dalkeith, seven miles from Edinburgh, till the 3rd of November, when we set out for England. But before our departure, two vessels, the one French

*These letters were no invention; that there were a number of offers of support is amply borne out by an examination of the Stuart archives.

and the other Spanish, laden with money, arms, military stores, and six Swedish field-pieces with a detachment of French artillery-men, having reached Montrose in safety on the 11th of October, their cargoes were forwarded to Dalkeith. These vessels also brought several Irish officers in the service of France, who joined us at the same place. Mr Grant, an able mathematician, who had been employed for many years with Monsieur Cassini in the observatory at Paris, was of the number, as also Monsieur d'Aiguille, brother to the Marquis d'Argens, who took the title of ambassador of the king of France.

Our march was very judiciously planned and equally well executed, resembling, on a small scale, that of Marshal Saxe some years before, when he advanced to lay siege to Maestricht. There are three great roads from Edinburgh to London: one of them runs along the eastern coast of Scotland, enters England at Berwick-upon-Tweed and passes through Newcastle-upon-Tyne. This is the road generally taken. Another goes along the western coast of Scotland* and enters England at Carlisle, a city formerly the frontier-defence of the English against the incursions of the Scotch on the west, as Berwick was on the east. The third road lies between the other two.

Our army was formed into three columns, each of which took a separate road on setting out from Dalkeith, with the view of keeping the enemy, by this stratagem, ignorant of the place where the Prince intended to enter England. This plan succeeded so well that Marshal Wade, who was at Newcastle with eleven thousand men whom he had lately brought from Flanders, including a corps of Swiss troops in British pay, continued to cover and protect that city, which is one of the most important in England. Secrecy in this case, was so well observed that hardly any person in our army had the least idea of the

*It ran, in fact, through the centre of the country, and only approached the Solway Firth at the English border.

The Battle of Prestonpans

place where the junction of the three columns would take place, and we were very much surprised on finding ourselves all arrive, on the 9th of November, almost at the same instant, on a heath in England, about a mile from the town of Carlisle. This march was arranged and executed with such precision that there was not an interval of two hours between the arrival of the different columns at the place of rendezvous.

Carlisle, a considerable town and capital of the county of Cumberland, is only about ten miles from the borders of Scotland. The river Esk, which is fordable and about half the breadth of the Seine at Paris, here separates the two kingdoms as the river Tweed does on the side of Berwick. The fortifications are in the old style and have been entirely neglected for several centuries, in consequence of the cessation of the long wars between the two countries, and the final union of the crowns, on the death of Queen Elizabeth. It is surrounded by walls flanked with towers, and a fosse, and contains a castle well furnished with artillery, and defended by a garrison of invalids. This castle was formerly a place of considerable strength, but at present its walls, like those of the town, are falling from age into decay. We opened our trenches before this place, under the orders of the Duke of Perth, on the night of the 10th of November, at a distance of eighty yards from the walls. Mr Grant, an Irish officer of Lally's regiment, our principal engineer, ably availed himself of the ditches of enclosures, by which we were enabled to approach close to the town sheltered from the fire of the enemy. Our artillery consisted of the six Swedish field-pieces received from France with Mr Grant, and the six other field-pieces of a smaller calibre, which we had taken at the battle of Prestonpans.

Having learned that Marshal Wade was on the march to force us to raise the siege of Carlisle, and that he had already advanced with his army to the town of Hexham, the Prince left the Duke of Perth, with a small body of troops, to conduct

D

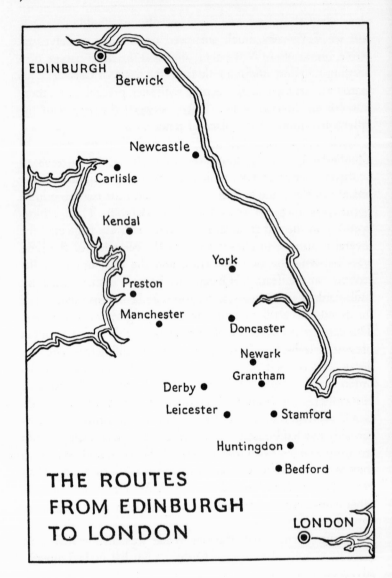

EDINBURGH

Berwick

Newcastle

Carlisle

Kendal

York

Preston

Manchester

Doncaster

Newark

Grantham

Derby

Leicester

Stamford

Huntingdon

Bedford

**THE ROUTES
FROM EDINBURGH
TO LONDON**

LONDON

the siege, and immediately marched against him, as it was of the highest importance to us to give battle before we advanced into England, in order to preserve a free communication with Scotland. The Prince, after waiting for the Marshal some days at Brampton, a small town nine miles from Carlisle, received positive information that he had abandoned Hexham and fallen back upon Newcastle, on which we returned to Carlisle. The Prince, on his return, had the satisfaction to receive the keys of the city from a deputation sent to him to propose terms of capitulation. It surrendered the third day after the opening of the trenches, rather from our threatening to fire red-hot balls upon the town and reduce it to ashes, than from the force of our artillery, for we did not discharge a single shot, lest the garrison should become acquainted with the smallness of their calibre, which might have encouraged them to defend themselves.

The town first proposed to surrender without the castle, but as the Prince refused to receive the one without the other, the inhabitants became alarmed, and obliged the garrison to join in the capitulation. The military were made prisoners of war and dismissed, after taking an oath not to bear arms against the house of Stuart for the space of one year.

It is impossible to conceive why Marshal Wade, generally allowed to be the best general officer in the service of England, did not advance to Brampton and endeavour to stop the progress of the Prince by giving him battle, having an army of regular troops more than double the number of that of the Prince. He may have been afraid of exposing himself to the Highlanders, after the disgrace of his brother-officer, General Cope; he may have been unable to move because of disease in his army as his soldiers were not accustomed to the fatigues of winter-campaigns; or he may have had particular instructions from King George to risk nothing, and not to leave Newcastle, lest the colliers, who amount to more than twenty thousand, should seize this favourable opportunity for revolting, and join the Prince in order to liberate themselves and their posterity from perpetual slavery in the mines. It is impossible to say which, but whatever the truth of the matter, he remained always inactive under the walls of that town.

The Prince then held a council of all the Highland chiefs, in which he again held that he had received fresh letters from his friends in England, assuring him that he should find all of them in arms, on his arrival at Preston. The chiefs represented in strong terms the danger of attempting to penetrate farther into England with such a small army, and maintained that, as all the succours expected from the English who had promised to join him on the borders had vanished into smoke, his most prudent course was to return to Scotland, fix his residence at Edinburgh, and carry on a defensive war in that country, till such time as he was in a condition to change it into an offensive one. The Prince, however, insisted always on advancing into England, and the chiefs at length gave their consent.

Our cavalry left Carlisle on the 20th of November, and marched that day to Penrith, a distance of eighteen miles. It consisted of two companies of life-guards, composed of young gentlemen, with Lord Elcho, a nobleman equally distinguished for his illustrious birth and his singular merit, commanding the first company, and Lord Balmerino the second. Besides the life-guards, there was a body of one hundred and fifty gentlemen on horseback, commanded by Lord Pitsligo. On the 21st, the Prince followed with the infantry, and passed the night at Penrith. Lord Elcho, with the cavalry which he commanded as first captain of the life-guards, passed the night at Shap, a village ten miles south from Penrith. The Prince, on quitting Carlisle, left a garrison of two or three hundred men in the castle.

On the 22nd the cavalry advanced to Kendal, and the infantry, with the Prince, remained at Penrith; and on the 23rd the cavalry and infantry met at Kendal. On the 24th, the cavalry passed the night at Lancaster, whilst the infantry rested at

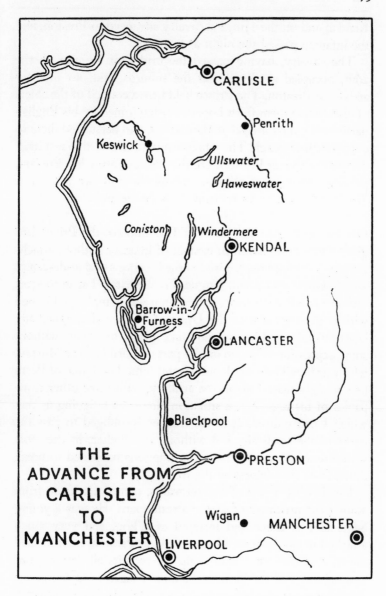

CARLISLE

Penrith

Keswick

Ullswater

Haweswater

Coniston

Windermere

KENDAL

Barrow-in-Furness

LANCASTER

Blackpool

THE
ADVANCE FROM
CARLISLE
TO
MANCHESTER

PRESTON

Wigan

MANCHESTER

LIVERPOOL

Kendal; and on the 25th, the cavalry advanced to Preston, and the infantry passed the night at Lancaster.

The cavalry, having passed the bridge of Preston on the 26th, occupied a village near the suburbs, and our infantry arrived at Preston. The Prince held here a council of the chiefs of clans, gave them fresh hopes of being joined by his English partisans on their arrival at Manchester, and persuaded them to continue their march. The whole army was allowed to rest itself during the 27th at Preston. On the 28th our army left Preston, passing the night at Wigan, and on the 29th we arrived at Manchester, where we remained during the 30th.

On the evening of the battle of Prestonpans, the Prince had given me a commission of captain of infantry without attaching me to any regiment. Tired of the functions of aide-de-camp, which wore me out with fatigue, I immediately began to exert myself to raise a company, and when it was completed, I joined with it the regiment of the Duke of Perth and resigned my laborious office. This did not take place, however, without some expression of pique on the part of Lord George Murray, who was unwilling that I should quit him. The Duke of Perth immediately placed me in the artillery, with three other companies of his regiment, a situation almost as fatiguing as that which I had quitted, as I was frequently obliged to pass the night in the open air, and without any shelter, in the most severe weather, when any of the waggons happened to break down from the badness of the roads.

I had enlisted one of my sergeants, named Dickson, from among the prisoners of war at Prestonpans. He was a young Scotsman, as brave and intrepid as a lion, and very much attached to my interest. On the 27th, at Preston, he informed me that he had been beating up for recruits all day without getting one, and that he was the more chagrined at this as the other sergeants had had better success. He therefore came to ask

my permission to get a day's march ahead of the army by setting out immediately for Manchester, a very considerable town
of England, containing forty thousand inhabitants, in order to
make sure of some recruits before their arrival. I reproved him
sharply for entertaining so wild and extravagant a project,
which exposed him to the danger of being taken and hanged,
and I ordered him back to his company. Having much confidence in him, I had given him a horse and entrusted him with
my portmanteau, that I might always have it with me. On
entering my quarters in the evening, my landlady informed me
that my servant had called and taken away my portmanteau and
blunderbuss. I immediately bethought myself of his extravagant project, and his situation gave me much uneasiness. But
on our arrival at Manchester, on the evening of the following
day, the 29th, Dickson brought me about one hundred and
eighty recruits, whom he had enlisted for my company.

He had quitted Preston, in the evening, with his mistress and
my drummer. Having marched all night, he arrived next morning at Manchester, which is about thirty miles distant from
Preston, and immediately began to beat up for recruits for
'the yellow-haired laddie'. The populace, at first, did not inter-
rupt him, conceiving our army to be near the town; but as soon
as they knew that it would not arrive till the evening, they surrounded him in a tumultuous manner, with the intention of
taking him prisoner, alive or dead. Dickson presented his
blunderbuss, which was charged with slugs, and threatened to
blow out the brains of those who first dared to lay hands on
himself or the two who accompanied him. By turning round
continually, facing in all directions and behaving like a lion, he
soon enlarged the circle which a crowd of people had formed
round them. Having continued for some time to manoeuvre in
this way, those of the inhabitants of Manchester who were
attached to the house of Stuart, took arms and flew to the assistance of Dickson, to rescue him from the fury of the mob, so

that he soon had five or six hundred men to aid him, who dispersed the crowd in a very short time. Dickson now triumphed in his turn, and putting himself at the head of his followers, he proudly paraded, undisturbed, the whole day, with his drummer, enlisting for my company all who offered themselves.

On presenting me with a list of one hundred and eighty recruits, I was agreeably surprised to find that the whole amount of his expenses did not exceed three guineas. This adventure of Dickson gave rise to many a joke at the expense of the town of Manchester, from the singular circumstance of its having been taken by a sergeant, a drummer, and a girl, a circumstance which serves to show the enthusiastic courage of our army, and the alarm and terror with which the English were seized.

I did not derive any advantage from these recruits, to the great regret of Dickson. Mr Townley, formerly an officer in the service of France, who had joined us some days before, obtained the rank of colonel with permission to raise a regiment entirely composed of English, and the Prince ordered me to deliver over to him all those whom Dickson had enlisted for me. It was called the Manchester regiment, and never exceeded three hundred men—of whom the recruits furnished by my sergeant formed more than the half. These were all the English who ever declared themselves openly in favour of the Prince, and the chiefs of the clans were not far wrong, therefore, in distrusting the pretended succours on which the Prince so implicitly relied.

Our army left Manchester on the 1st of December and passed the night at Macclesfield. On the 2nd, our cavalry reached Congleton, a town twelve miles from Newcastle-under-Lyme, where the Duke of Cumberland was posted with an army of ten thousand men, who retired to Lichfield on the approach of our troops. Lord Elcho having suddenly entered Newcastle-under-Lyme, to reconnoitre the enemy, took Mr Weir, the principal spy* of the Duke of Cumberland, prisoner. On the 3rd, our cavalry advanced to Ashbourne, having passed through Leek, where our infantry stopped for the night.

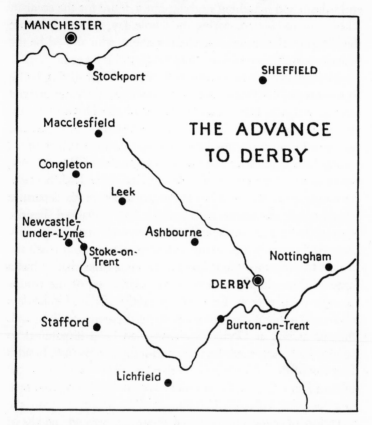

On the 4th, the whole of our army reached Derby, a considerable town, one hundred and twenty-five miles distant from London. The Duke of Cumberland being only a few miles from Derby,† our army employed the 5th in making preparations for giving battle to him next morning. There was a great

*John Vere, an Irishman.   † See Introduction p. 15.

disproportion between the numbers of the two armies, but the inequality was balanced by the heroic ardour of the Highlanders, animated, on that occasion, to the highest pitch of enthusiasm and breathing nothing but a desire for the combat. They were to be seen, during the whole day, in crowds before the shops of the cutlers, quarrelling about who should be the first to sharpen and give a proper edge to his sword.

Whilst every preparation was being made for giving battle to the Duke of Cumberland next morning, a courier arrived from Lord John Drummond, brother to the Duke of Perth, and the dispatches of which he was the bearer, totally changed the face of our affairs. His Lordship informed the Prince of his having landed at Montrose with his regiment of Royal Scots, newly raised in France, and some pickets of the Irish brigade. He added, in his letter to the Prince, that before his departure from France, the whole Irish brigade had embarked, besides several French regiments, and that there was every probability they would arrive in Scotland before his letter could reach the Prince. He informed the Prince, at the same time, that he had a force of three thousand men, partly composed of the troops brought by him from France, and partly of the Highlanders who could not join the Prince before his departure for England. On our arrival at Derby, a courier had been dispatched to London, who returned next day and informed us that, besides the army of the Duke of Cumberland, which was within a few miles of Derby, there was another army of thirty thousand men encamped on Finchley Common;* this, however, with the exception of some regiments of guards, consisted mostly of militia.

In the afternoon of the 5th, the Prince held a council on the accounts which the two couriers had brought. The council sat a

---

*Sir John Macdonald confirms this figure as being the number of people who were expected to join the army when the prince's army approached London. Their reliability was, however, open to doubt.

long time, and the debates were very keen. The question for deliberation was whether we should continue to advance on London, or return to Scotland and avail ourselves of the reinforcement of three thousand men with Lord John Drummond, and wait in that country for the succours from France, the speedy arrival of which was held out to us by Lord John. The Prince obstinately insisted on giving battle next morning (the 6th) to the Duke of Cumberland, and advancing to London; but he was the only one who was of that opinion.

Since the council held at Preston, the chiefs of the Highland clans had never opposed the Prince in anything, as they saw themselves too far advanced in England to be able to retreat. Having embarked in this extravagant enterprise, they felt that they had no alternative but continuing the adventure, and conquering or dying with arms in their hands. In case of a defeat in England, no one in our army could by any possibility escape destruction, as the English peasants were hostile towards us in the highest degree, and the army of Marshal Wade was in our rear, to cut us off from all communication with Scotland.

But this intelligence from Lord John Drummond totally changed our views and the state of our affairs, by announcing three thousand men and succours from France, which would in all probability have arrived in Scotland by that time, and would be ready to join us on the frontiers of England. The chiefs of clans, therefore, unanimously represented to the Prince that, with an army disposed as ours was, there could be no doubt but that we should easily beat the army of the Duke of Cumberland, though much superior to us in point of numbers; but that a victory could not be obtained without more or less loss, and that an army of four thousand five hundred men, opposed to the whole strength of England, could not admit of the smallest diminution. Especially was this so as a second battle must soon after be fought against another English army on Finchley Common, before we could enter London; and that, supposing that by some miracle we should arrive at this capital without losing a man, what sort of figure would four thousand men make amidst a population of a million of souls? They added, besides, that the Prince ought now to see clearly how the matter stood with regard to his English partisans, since, after traversing all the provinces which had the reputation of being the most attached to his family in order to enable them to join him, not a single person of distinction had yet declared himself.* The Duke of Perth alone took no part, at first, in these debates between the Prince and the chiefs of the clans, resting his head against the fireplace and listening to the dispute without uttering a single word; but at last he declared himself loudly of the opinion of the other chiefs.

The Prince always obstinately insisted on going to London. He maintained that we were in greater danger of being cut to pieces in retreating to Scotland than in advancing, because the Duke of Cumberland, the moment he knew of our retreat, would be sure to pursue us hotly, and to be constantly at our heels. Meanwhile Marshal Wade, who would certainly receive orders to interpose his army between us and Carlisle, would cut off our communication with Scotland; so that we should be placed between two fires and all caught, as it were, in a net.

The chiefs of the clans answered the Prince, that our army, being without the incumbrance of baggage, and the High-landers extremely agile and hardy (as they had often proved since they entered England by marching twenty miles a day without leaving any stragglers) would, by having merely the start for a few hours of the Duke of Cumberland, prevent him from ever overtaking us. With bad roads, his army could scarcely march twelve miles in a winter day without leaving the

*The prospect was not, in fact, as bleak as this implies. In Wales Sir Watkin Williams-Wynn, with pledges of support from many of the leading families, was already on the march, while, further south, the Duke of Beaufort was also standing ready.

half of the soldiers behind. We had, therefore, little to fear from this army. As for the army of Marshal Wade, we had no greater reason for fearing it now, than when we entered England: nay, nothing was more desirable than that we should fall in with it, because, by beating it, we should retire gloriously from England with arms in our hands, which would console the Highlanders, whose hopes would be disappointed by their retreat.

The retreat was, at length, fixed for next morning, the 6th of December, and the better to conceal it, we left Derby some hours before day-break. The Highlanders, conceiving at first that they were on the march to attack the army of the Duke of Cumberland, displayed the utmost joy and cheerfulness, but as soon as the day allowed them to see the objects around them and they found that we were retracing our steps, nothing was to be heard throughout the whole army but expressions of rage and lamentation. If we had been beaten, the grief could not have been greater.

IV

OUR arrival at Derby was known at London on the 5th of December, and the following Monday, called by the English *Black Monday*, the intelligence was known throughout the whole city, which was filled with terror and consternation. Many of the inhabitants fled to the country with their most precious effects, and all the shops were shut. People thronged to the Bank to obtain payment of its notes, and it only escaped bankruptcy by a stratagem. Payment was not indeed refused, but as those who came first were entitled to priority of payment, the Bank took care to be continually surrounded by agents with notes, who were paid in sixpences, in order to gain time. These agents went out at one door with the specie they had received, and brought it back by another, so that the *bona fide* holders of notes could never get near enough to present them. By this artifice the Bank preserved its credit and literally faced its creditors. It being known at London that our army was within a few miles of that of the Duke of Cumberland, the news of a battle—for the result of which they were in the greatest alarm—was expected every moment, and they dreaded to see our army enter London in triumph in two or three days. King George ordered his yachts, in which he had embarked all his most precious effects, to remain at the Tower quay, in readiness to sail at a moment's warning. I was assured on good authority, when I was in London some time after our unfortunate defeat, that the Duke of Newcastle, then secretary of state for the war-department, remained inaccessible in his own house the whole of the 6th of December, weighing in his mind the part which it would be most prudent for him to take, and even uncertain whether he should not instantly declare himself for the Pretender. It was even said in London, that fifty thousand men had actually left that city to meet the Prince and join his army. Everybody in the capital was of opinion that, if we had beaten the Duke of Cumberland, the army of Finchley Common would have dispersed of its own accord: and that by advancing rapidly to London, we might have taken possession of the city, without the least resistance from the inhabitants and without exchanging a single shot with the soldiers, as the King had formed the resolution of embarking immediately in one of his yachts and setting sail for Holland, in case the battle, which was expected at Derby, had proved unfavourable to his son. Thus a revolution would have been effected in England, so glorious for the few Scotsmen by whom it was attempted, and altogether so surprising that the world would not have comprehended it, and posterity would scarcely have credited it. It is true, the English were altogether ignorant of the number of our army, from the care we took in our marches to conceal it; and it was almost impossible for their spies ever to discover it, as we generally arrived in the towns at night-fall and left them before the break of day. In all the English newspapers our numbers were uniformly stated as high as twelve or fifteen thousand men.

I dare not attempt to decide whether we did right or wrong in returning to Scotland. The Supreme Being alone can penetrate into futurity and foresee those obscure and unexpected events which frequently counteract the best combined projects and most maturely digested plans of the greatest of men. The human mind is extremely limited in its foresight with regard to accident: it can only judge from probabilities, and decide as to the consequences that ought naturally to result from measures. If we had continued to advance to London and had encountered all the troops of England, with the Hessians and Swiss in its pay, there was every appearance of our being immediately exterminated without the chance of a single man escaping. Bravery, even when carried the length of ferocity, cannot effect impossibilities and must necessarily yield to numbers. It is in analysing projects that we must judge of their solidity and find out the truth; not in considering the event.

There was no reason for supposing that fifty thousand men would leave London to join our army, as in every place we passed through we found the English very ill-disposed towards us, except at Manchester, where there appeared some remains of attachment to the house of Stuart. But even if we had been certain of this reinforcement from London, it would still have been absolutely necessary for us to defeat both enemy armies before reaching it, for the English people make a great noise, but are not fond of blows, nor of quitting their fire-sides. Even supposing us to have completely beaten the army of the Duke of Cumberland, the wreck of his army would have fallen back on Finchley Common, and strengthened the army there.

Had Lord John Drummond, on his landing, advanced by forced marches, as he ought to have done,* and joined us on the borders of England with his three thousand men, instead of remaining inactive in Scotland, it is certain that no one in our army would ever have thought of a retreat, whatever assurances we might have received of succours from France. And it is equally certain that, if Lord John had not landed with his regiment in Scotland, we had now penetrated so far into England, that as we had no better prospect than to follow up the enterprise, we should all of us have fallen, like brave men, with arms in our hands, or made ourselves masters of London and driven King George from his throne. There was no alternative. Lord John was likewise inexcusable in having communicated to the Prince the false intelligence of a certain aid of ten thousand men from France,† which, from the positive assurances in his letter,

*The reports concerning Lord John Drummond's forces were considerably exaggerated and several of the units were heavily depleted. Also, some of his troops had to be detached to contain the government forces at Stirling and Glasgow who, otherwise, would have been able to overwhelm those of the prince's supporters who were still in Scotland.
†Three thousand.

was so implicitly believed that every individual in our army deemed this force already landed in Scotland. The first thing we did in the morning was to see whether the wind was favourable, and every moment we expected to receive an account of the disembarkation. This false report of Lord John Drummond had undoubtedly great influence in producing the resolution taken at Derby of retreating to Scotland.

On the 6th of December our army passed the night at Ashbourne; on the 7th, we reached Leek; the 8th, Macclesfield; the 9th, Manchester; the 10th, Wigan; and the 11th, Preston, where we remained during the 12th. We arrived at Lancaster on the 13th, where we recruited ourselves during the 14th; and on the 15th we reached Kendal, where we received certain information that we had left Marshal Wade behind us, and that we were no longer in any danger of having our retreat to Scotland cut off. Lord George Murray, who was always informed of whatever took place in the armies of the enemy, and often, by means of his emissaries, even knew all the movements they intended to make, had a great advantage over them, for they were totally ignorant of every thing that related to our army. In order to ascertain more particularly the position of the army of Marshal Wade, which was very near us at Kendal, Lord George took a detachment of life-guards, and went himself, as soon as it was dark, to reconnoitre. In about two hours he returned, with several English whom he had made prisoners, and who gave him all the information he desired.

The Prince having acquired a strong relish for battles, from the facility with which he had gained the victory at Prestonpans at so small an expense, was always for fighting, and sometimes even reproached Lord George for his unwillingness to incur the risk of an engagement, when no advantage could be derived from a victory, and for his having prevented him from fighting the Duke of Cumberland at Derby. Lord George said to him in the morning, when we were about to leave Kendal,

E

'As your Royal Highness is always for battles, be the circumstances what they may, I now offer you one, in three hours from
this time, with the army of Marshal Wade, which is only about
two miles distant from us.' The Prince made no reply, but
mounted into his carriage, and we immediately put ourselves in
motion to continue our retreat.

On the 16th, our army passed the night at Shap, but our
artillery remained at the distance of a league and a half from
Kendal, some ammunition-waggons having broken down, so
that we were obliged to pass the whole night on the high-road,
exposed to a dreadful storm of wind and rain. On the 17th, the
Prince, with the army, arrived at Penrith; but the artillery, with
Lord George, and the regiment of the Macdonalds of Glengarry,
consisting of five hundred men who remained with us to
strengthen our ordinary escort, could only reach Shap, and that
with great difficulty, at night-fall.

We set out from Shap by break of day on the 18th to join the
army, which waited for us at Penrith; but we had scarcely
begun our march when we saw a great number of the enemy's
light-horse continually hovering about us, without venturing,
however, to come within musket-shot. The appearance of these
light-horse appeared the more extraordinary as, hitherto, we
had seen none in the whole course of our expedition into
England. We arrived at mid-day at the foot of an eminence
about half-way between Penrith and Shap, which it was
necessary to cross in our march. The moment we began to
ascend, we instantly discovered cavalry, marching two and
two abreast on the top of the hill, who disappeared soon after
as if to form themselves in order of battle with the intention of
disputing the passage. We heard, at the same time, a prodigious
number of trumpets and kettle-drums. Mr Brown, colonel in
the train of Lally's regiment, was at the head of the column,
with two of the companies which the Duke of Perth had
attached to the artillery, of which mine was one. After them

followed the guns and ammunition-waggons, and then the two other companies attached to the artillery. Lord George was in the rear of the column, with the regiment of Macdonalds.

We stopped a moment at the foot of the hill, everybody believing it was the English army, from the great number of trumpets and kettle-drums. In this seemingly desperate conjuncture, we immediately adopted the opinion of Mr Brown, and resolved to rush upon the enemy sword in hand and open a passage to our army at Penrith, or perish in the attempt. Thus, without informing Lord George of our resolution, we darted forward with great swiftness, running up the hill as fast as our legs could carry us. Lord George, who was in the rear, seeing our manoeuvre at the head of the column, and being unable to pass the waggons in the deep roads confined by hedges in which we then were, immediately ordered the Highlanders to proceed across the enclosure, and ascend the hill from another quarter. They ran so fast that they reached the summit of the hill almost as soon as those who were at the head of the column. We were agreeably surprised when we reached the top to find, instead of the English army, only three hundred light-horse and chasseurs, who immediately fled in disorder. We were only able to come up with one man who had been thrown from his horse and whom we wished to make prisoner to obtain some intelligence from him. But it was impossible to save him from the fury of the Highlanders, who cut him to pieces in an instant. From the great number of trumpets and kettle-drums which the light-horse had with them, there is every reason for supposing that it was their design to endeavour to induce us to turn aside from the road to Penrith, by making us believe that the whole English army was on the hill before us. Had we fallen into the snare which was laid for us, in a few hours every man of our detachment would either have been killed or taken prisoner.

We immediately resumed our march, but in less than an

hour one of our ammunition-waggons broke down from the badness of the roads, and we were obliged to halt. The singular adventure of the light-horse had filled me with some uneasiness, as I was unable to account for their audacity, unless the army of Marshal Wade were much nearer us than we imagined.* I communicated my fears to Mr Grant and, in order that we might not lose time in repairing the broken waggon, I suggested to him that we should go to a farm, which we saw on our right, about a quarter of a league from us, and try to procure one. He consented, and we took seven or eight men with us, of whom my sergeant, Dickson, was one. Having found a waggon in the courtyard of the farmer, we immediately carried it off and our march was retarded no longer than the time necessary for transferring the ammunition from one waggon to another. In returning from the farm, Dickson called our attention to something which appeared blackish to us, on a hill about four miles to our left. He alone, contrary to the opinion of everyone else, maintained that he saw it moving, and that it was the English army advancing towards us. As we took what he saw for bushes, and as nobody excepting himself could distinguish anything, I treated him as a visionary. But he still persisted, till I ordered him to be silent, telling him that fear alone could have filled his imagination with the idea of an army. However his last word was, that we should see in an hour whether or not he was in the right.

When we had advanced about two miles, we were soon convinced that Dickson's eyes were much better than ours. The Duke of Cumberland, having followed us by forced marches with two thousand cavalry and as many foot-soldiers mounted behind them, fell suddenly on the Macdonalds, who were in the rear of the column, with all the fury and impetuosity

*With the exception of General Oglethorpe's dragoons, Marshal Wade's forces were always a considerable distance from the Highlanders throughout their retreat.

imaginable. Fortunately the road running between thorn-hedges and ditches, the cavalry could not act in such a manner as to surround us, nor present a larger front to us than the breadth of the road. The Highlanders received their charge with the most undaunted firmness. They repelled the assailants with their swords, and did not quit their ground till the artillery and waggons were a hundred paces from them and continuing their rout. Then the Highlanders wheeled to the right and ran with full speed till they joined the waggons, when they stopped again for the cavalry, and stood their charge as firm as a wall. The cavalry were repulsed in the same manner as before by their swords. We marched in this manner about a mile, the cavalry continually renewing the charge and the Highlanders always repulsing them, repeating the same manoeuvre and behaving like lions.

The Prince, at Penrith, having received an imperfect account of our adventure with the light-horse, immediately ordered the army to advance to our assistance. The English cavalry accompanied us in this manner till we arrived opposite the castle of Clifton-hall, which is three miles from Penrith, but halted as soon as they saw our army drawn up in order of battle. They then entered the enclosures of the castle, which were defended by thorn-hedges, and, having dismounted, formed themselves in battle order in front of our army, which was upon a heath. The hedges separated the two armies, which were within a musket-shot of each other.

Mr Cameron of Lochiel,* who was at the head of our army, having passed the bridge to wait for us and assist us, was the first to join Lord George with his regiment of Camerons, and rescue him and the Macdonalds of Glengarry from the English cavalry. The sun was setting when our detachments formed a junction with the army. The Highlanders immediately ran to the enclosures where the English were, fell down on their

*It was, in fact, Macpherson of Clunie.

knees, and began to cut down the thorn-hedges with their dirks; a necessary precaution as they wore no breeches, but only a sort of petticoat which reached to their knees. During this operation, they received the fire of the English with the most admirable firmness and constancy. As soon as the hedge was cut down, they jumped into the enclosures sword in hand, and, with an inconceivable intrepidity, broke the English battalions, who suffered so much the more as they did not turn their backs as at the battle of Prestonpans, but allowed themselves to be cut to pieces without quitting their ground. Platoons of forty and fifty men might be seen falling all at once under the swords of the Highlanders; yet they still remained firm and closed up their ranks as soon as an opening was made through them by the sword.

At length, however, the Highlanders forced them to give way, and pursued them across three enclosures, to a heath which lay behind them. The only prisoner they took was the Duke of Cumberland's footman, who declared that his master would have been killed, if the pistol, with which a Highlander took aim at his head, had not missed fire. The Prince had the politeness to send him back instantly to his master. We could not ascertain the loss of the English, in this affair, which some estimated as high as six hundred men. We only lost a dozen Highlanders who, after traversing the enclosures, continued the pursuit with too much ardour along the heath.

Our army did not withdraw from Clifton-hall till some hours after the night had set in, but our artillery was sent off in the beginning of the action, with orders to continue to advance to Carlisle without stopping at Penrith. We learned, from the footman, that the Duke of Cumberland, having given all his trumpeters and kettle-drummers to the light-horse, had hoped to retard the march of our detachment, with the artillery. If we had been in any manner the dupes of this artifice, we should have been all destroyed, for, in half an hour, the

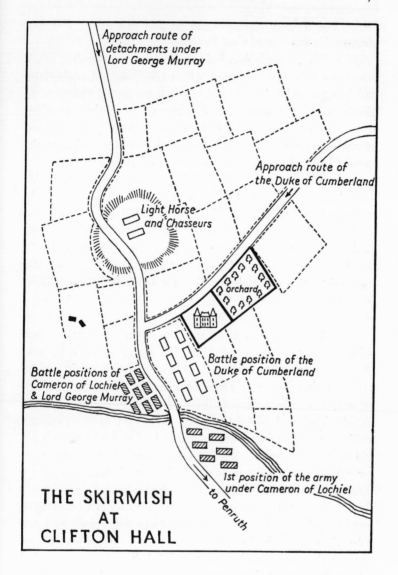

Approach route of
detachments under
Lord George Murray

Approach route of
the Duke of Cumberland

Light Horse
and Chasseurs

orchard

Battle position of the
Duke of Cumberland

Battle positions of
Cameron of Lochiel
& Lord George Murray

1st position of the army
under Cameron of Lochiel

to Penruth

THE SKIRMISH
AT
CLIFTON HALL

Duke would have got between us and our army, and our communication would thus have been cut off.

As we very much dreaded the junction of Marshal Wade with these four thousand men, whom the Duke of Cumberland had brought with him to Clifton-hall by forced marches, to harass us in our retreat, as well as the arrival of the rest of his army which he had left behind him, we marched all night and arrived at Carlisle about seven o'clock in the morning of the 19th of December. Next morning, before the break of day, we quitted Carlisle, where the Prince left the unfortunate Mr Townley, with the English regiment raised at Manchester, in command of the town, and Mr Hamilton, with some companies of the regiment of the Duke of Perth, in command of the castle. The Prince promised to return to their assistance in the course of a few days, though this appeared to be morally impossible, as we ourselves were obliged to make every effort to escape from the whole of the forces of England, which were on the point of forming a junction.

I could never comprehend the reason for voluntarily sacrificing these unfortunate victims, left by us at Carlisle. The Prince was not overburdened with men, and it could not be supposed that they would be able to defend themselves, in such an untenable place, against the united forces of the Duke of Cumberland and Marshal Wade, possessed of a numerous artillery. It was well known that we had taken it with the utmost facility on our entering England. It was not in a condition to resist a cannonade of four hours, being utterly untenable and a thousand times worse than an entrenched camp in open country. Besides, it could not be supposed that the Duke of Cumberland would neglect to lay siege to it without delay and, as Lord John Drummond had not marched to join us, we were obliged to retreat into the heart of Scotland to join him. Some pretended that policy dictated the abandonment of this unfortunate garrison as a bait to amuse the Duke of Cumberland and prevent him from pursuing us closely, that we might have time to retreat at our ease, without being disturbed by the English armies. Others were of opinion, that the measure originated in a spirit of vengeance* against the English nation, as no one of all the persons of distinction in England who invited the Prince to make a descent in Great Britain, had declared themselves openly in his favour, by attaching their fortunes to his as the Scots had done.

It would seem that our audacity and temerity had confounded those English generals who were most distinguished for their talents, capacity, and experience in military affairs, and completely deprived them of all presence of mind. The conduct of Marshal Wade is incomprehensible; he had only to perform a march of about sixty miles, the distance from Newcastle to Carlisle, to cut off our retreat to Scotland, whilst, when our return was decided on at Derby, we were more than one hundred and fifty miles from Carlisle. Yet, notwithstanding the repeated orders which he received from the Duke of Cumberland to that effect, and the vast disproportion between his march and that which we were necessarily obliged to perform, he was too late, by several hours, in reaching Kendal, to be able to throw himself between us and Scotland.† Every man in our army was of opinion, from the position of General Wade, that there was no possibility of our leaving England without giving him battle, a circumstance which would not have displeased the Highlanders in the excellent disposition for fighting in which they were. But even a victory would then have been of no great utility to us, and would have led to nothing, as in England it would not have augmented the number of our army, and this was our principal object.

*There is no evidence to support this statement and, in any case, there were twice as many Scots as English in the garrison force.
†Wade was, at the time, near Wakefield but, even though he set out immediately he heard news of the retreat, he was too late. All he could do was to send Oglethorpe's dragoons in pursuit.

We left Carlisle on the 20th of December at three o'clock in the morning, and arrived on the banks of the river Esk, which separates Scotland from England, about two o'clock in the afternoon. This river, which is usually shallow, had been swelled by an incessant rain of several days to a depth of four feet. However, we were obliged to cross it immediately, lest a continuation of the rain during the night should render the passage altogether impracticable. Our position had become extremely critical. We had not only to encounter all the English troops, but likewise the Hessians and Swiss, with six thousand Dutch, of the garrisons of Dendermonde and Tournai, who had been landed in England.

Nothing could be better arranged than the passage of the river. Our cavalry formed in the river, to break the force of the current, about twenty-five paces above that part of the ford where our infantry were to pass: the Highlanders formed themselves into ranks of ten or twelve abreast, with their arms locked in such a manner as to support one another against the rapidity of the river, leaving sufficient intervals between their ranks for the passage of the water. Cavalry were likewise stationed in the river, below the ford, to pick up and save those who might be carried away by the violence of the current. The interval between the cavalry appeared like a paved street through the river, the heads of the Highlanders being generally all that was seen above the water. By means of this contrivance, our army passed the Esk in an hour's time, without losing a single man, and a few girls, determined to share the fortune of their lovers, were the only persons who were carried away by the rapidity of the stream. Fires were kindled to dry our people as soon as they quitted the water, and the bagpipers having commenced playing, the Highlanders began all to dance, expressing the utmost joy on seeing their country again—forgetting the chagrin which had incessantly devoured them, and which they had continually nourished ever since their departure from Derby.

V

WE entered England on the 8th of November, and left it on the 20th of December, the birthday of the Prince, without losing more than forty men, either from sickness or marauding, including the twelve at the affair of Clifton-hall. Our stragglers seldom failed to be attacked by the English peasants, who were all implacable enemies of the Prince but too cowardly to dare to take up arms against us, though the different provinces through which we passed might have easily formed an army of a hundred thousand men to oppose us. They were deficient neither in hatred towards us, nor in the wish to injure us, but they wanted courage and resolution to expose themselves to the swords of the Highlanders.

The terror of the English was truly inconceivable, and in many cases they seemed quite bereft of their senses. One evening, as Mr Cameron of Lochiel entered the lodgings assigned to him, his landlady, an old woman, threw herself at his feet and, with uplifted hands and tears in her eyes, supplicated him to take her life but to spare her two little children. He asked her if she was in her senses, and told her to explain herself. She answered that everybody said the Highlanders ate children, and made them their common food. Mr Cameron having assured her that they would not injure either her or her little children, or any person whatever, she looked at him for some moments with an air of surprise, and then opened a press, calling out with a loud voice, 'Come out children, the gentleman will not eat you.' The children immediately left the press, where she had concealed them, and threw themselves at his feet.

They affirmed in the newspapers of London, that we had dogs in our army trained to fight, and that we were indebted for our victory at Prestonpans to these dogs, who darted with fury on the English army. They represented the Highlanders as monsters, with claws instead of hands. In a word, they never ceased to circulate, every day, the most extravagant and ridiculous stories with respect to the Highlanders. The English soldiers, indeed, had reason to look upon us as extraordinary men, from the manner in which we had beaten them with such inferior numbers, and they probably told these idle stories to the country people, by way of palliating their own disgrace. The men again, in repeating these stories to their wives, improved, no doubt, on the exaggerations of the soldiers, till, passing from mouth to mouth, the original falsehoods became at length so absurd, that none but English peasants, the most stupid and credulous of mortals, would listen to them. But, indeed, there is nothing so absurd that the English will not readily believe it. A better proof of this cannot be given than what took place when I was in London. A man advertised that he would, in the Haymarket Theatre, enter a pint bottle. The price of admission was half-a-crown; and the Duke of Cumberland, who was one of the crowd that flocked to see this miracle, lost his sword in the throng. But the actor, who had more sense than they, after appearing in the theatre to request an additional quarter of an hour before commencing his operations, contrived, in the mean time, to escape with a few hundred guineas which he had taken at the door, leaving them to cool their heels till his return to perform his promise, and treating them as such a set of fools ought to be treated. After this instance of credulity, their folly and extravagance ought not to surprise us.

As soon as we had passed the river, the Prince formed our army into two columns, one of which took the road by Ecclefechan, conducted by the Prince in person, and the other, under the orders of Lord George Murray, took the road that leads to Annan. Lord Elcho, with the cavalry, went straight to Dumfries, a considerable town, full of fanatical Calvinists who had seized some of our ammunition-waggons when we entered England. We punished the inhabitants by levying a considerable fine on them. As there is no town nearer than eight or ten miles from the ford of the Esk, we were obliged to march all night, though it had never ceased raining since the affair at Clifton-hall. Highlanders alone could have stood a march of two nights of continual rain in the midst of winter, and drenched as they were in crossing the river: they were inured to fatigue and of a strong and vigorous constitution, frequently marching six or seven leagues a-day, our ordinary marches in England, without leaving any stragglers behind. They might even have destroyed an army of a hundred thousand regular troops by marching alone, had they persisted in continually following us. The principal object in the disposi-tion of our marches, was to keep the English always in a state of uncertainty with regard to our movements, the towns to which we intended to go, and the roads we meant to take. Continually baffled by our manoeuvres, they were obliged to remain in-active till they could learn our real object, by the re-union of our columns. As a result they lost a great deal of time.

The column led by Lord George arrived next morning at Annan, where it reposed during the 22nd. On the 23rd, it reached Moffat. On the 24th, it abandoned the road it had hitherto followed, which goes directly to Edinburgh, and took a cross-road to the left for Glasgow, where it formed a junction with the column of the Prince on the 26th. The latter column slept at Ecclefechan on the 21st; on the 22nd, at Dumfries; and on the 23rd, advanced straight to Glasgow. Lord Elcho, with the cavalry, reached that city on the 25th, the day before the arrival of the two columns. The Duke of Cumberland, unable from our movements to conjecture what our intentions were, ceased to follow us, and the two English armies took up their quarters at Carlisle.

Messrs Brown and Gordon, two officers in the service of France, who had been left at Carlisle, joined us on our arrival at

Glasgow. They informed the Prince that the town and castle were taken by the Duke of Cumberland two days after our departure, being totally incapable of resisting, for twenty-four hours, the heavy artillery of the enemy. By the capitulation, the Duke of Cumberland had granted to the garrison their lives, with an assurance that they should not be tried for having borne arms.* They added, in their declaration, that they only escaped from Carlisle the moment the capitulation was signed.

The garrison of Carlisle was confined in the prisons of London, and the Duke of Cumberland, on his arrival there on the 5th of January, had so little regard for good faith as to maintain that they were not bound in honour to observe a capitulation with rebels. Thus twelve of the unfortunate officers of the English regiment, with Messrs Townley and Hamilton at their head, were afterwards hanged and quartered in London, and the head of Townley still remains exposed on Temple-bar, one of the gates of the city

The Prince at first seemed inclined to disbelieve the report of Messrs Gordon and Brown, and some even accused them of falsehood; but those who had any knowledge of fortification were disposed to believe them. Had the Prince foreseen the fate of these unfortunate victims, he would undoubtedly have prevented it by evacuating the place on our retreat—the only plan reconcileable, not merely with humanity towards those who had exposed their lives and fortunes in his cause, but with regard to his own particular interest, as he had not a superfluity of men in his army. We must draw a veil over this piece of cruelty, being altogether unable either to discover the motive for leaving these four hundred men at Carlisle, or to find an excuse for it.

Glasgow is the second city in Scotland, from the number of

*The actual wording ran: 'All the terms His Royal Highness will or can grant to the rebel garrison at Carlisle are, that they shall not be put to the sword, but be reserved for the King's pleasure.'

THE RETREAT
TO
GLASGOW

its inhabitants and the extent of its commerce. Our army was allowed to remain there, to recover from its fatigues, till the 2nd of January, when we quitted it in two columns, one of which took the route to Cumbernauld, where it passed the night, whilst the other went to Kilsyth. By this movement the Prince, according to every appearance, seemed to entertain the intention of proceeding to Edinburgh, especially as Lord Elcho with the cavalry had advanced as far as the town of Falkirk, which is only twenty-six miles' distance from it. But the column which had passed the night at Kilsyth quitted the Edinburgh road next morning, and, falling back upon its left, the two columns met in the evening, at the village of Bannockburn, three miles from Stirling.

The object of the Prince, in approaching Stirling, was to accelerate his junction with Lord John Drummond, whom he had ordered to repair to Alloa with the three thousand men under his command, and the artillery and military stores which he had brought from France. When the town of Stirling, protected by the castle, in which there was a strong garrison commanded by General Blakeney, the governor, refused to surrender, the Prince, on the 4th of January, ordered a part of his army to occupy the villages of St Dennis and St Ninians, which are within cannon-shot of the town, on the south. By this position it was blockaded and invested on every side, the stone bridge to the north of the town having been broken down when General Cope was there with his army.

On our reaching Bannockburn, Lord George Murray, who took the charge of everything, and attended to everything, repaired immediately to Alloa, where Lord John Drummond had already arrived, in order to take measures for the speedy advance to Stirling of the troops and artillery, brought by Lord John from France. After giving the necessary directions for the conveyance of the guns, he returned next day to Bannockburn. He then put himself at the head of eleven hundred men and

A Scottish and French Camp

stationed himself with them as a fixed post at Falkirk. Lord Elcho, with the cavalry, occupied the town of Linlithgow, which is eighteen miles from Edinburgh and eight from Falkirk. The rest of our army was quartered in the villages of St Dennis and St Ninians, and at Bannockburn where the Prince had his headquarters.

Lord John Drummond immediately repaired to Bannock-burn with his regiment of Royal Scots and five pickets of the Irish brigade, as also did Lord Lewis Gordon and six hundred vassals of his brother the Duke of Gordon, Mr Fraser the eldest son of Lord Lovat and six hundred of his father's vassals, the Earl of Cromarty, his eldest son Lord Macleod, and his vassals, the Mackenzies. The Prince was then joined by many other Highlanders of the clans of Mackintosh and Farquharson, so that our army was suddenly increased to eight thousand men, the double of what it was when we were in England.*

What a pity that the Prince had not these eight thousand men at Derby! They would have succeeded in crowning him at London. If he could only have restrained his impatience, and remained in Scotland till his partisans had had time to join him at Edinburgh, from the most remote provinces of Scotland, he might then, after his affairs had been firmly established in that country, have made an attempt on England. It would appear that the difficulty of transporting the six pieces of cannon sent from France, and the fear of their falling into the hands of the English, detained Lord John Drummond in Scotland.†

The importance commonly attached to artillery, their supposed utility, or rather the absolute necessity for them on all occasions, are greatly over-rated, and I do not doubt but that, in the course of time, an army will think itself lost, if it has not

---

*Reports as to the actual strength of the prince's army vary from 7,000 (quoted by O'Sullivan) to a maximum of 9,000.
†See note p. 64.

F

these enormous masses to drag after it, the cause of so much embarrassment, just in the same manner as infantry have been taught to tremble for their safety, unless they have cavalry to protect their flanks. The Highlanders, however, entertain a sovereign contempt for cavalry, from the facility with which they have always defeated them, throwing them into disorder in an instant by striking at the heads of the horses in the manner I have already mentioned.

In the present state of things, it is certainly necessary for an army of regular troops to have a numerous artillery. The sword has been laid aside for the musket and it would appear, from the victories obtained in the late war, almost entirely by a great superiority of artillery, that it is wished to lay aside the musket for cannon. I know not whether this new inclination be well or ill founded, but I am very certain that our artillery was very troublesome, and even very injurious to us.

On all occasions it is necessary to consult the genius of those whom we command, and to conform ourselves to their particular habits. If we had remained firing at a certain distance instead of rushing impetuously upon the enemy, two thousand regular troops, regularly trained to fire and unaccustomed to the sword, would have beaten four thousand Highlanders with ease. Their manner of fighting is adapted for brave but undisciplined men. They advance with rapidity, discharge their pieces when within musket-length of the enemy, and then, throwing them down, draw their swords, and holding a dirk in their left hand with their target, dart with fury on the enemy through the smoke of their fire. When within reach of the enemy's bayonets, bending their left knee, they cover their bodies with their targets, which receive the thrusts of the bayonets, while at the same time they raise their sword-arm and strike their adversary. Having once got within the bayonets and into the ranks of the enemy, the soldiers have no longer any means of defending themselves, the fate of the battle is decided in an instant, and the carnage follows—the Highlanders bringing down two men at a time, one with their dirk, in the left hand, and another with the sword.

The reason assigned by the Highlanders for their custom of throwing their muskets on the ground is not without its force. They say they embarrass them in their operations, even when slung behind them, and on gaining a battle, they can pick them up again along with the arms of their enemies; but, if they should be beaten, they have no occasion for muskets. They themselves proved that bravery may supply the place of discipline at times, as discipline supplies the place of bravery. Their attack is so terrible, that the best troops in Europe would with difficulty sustain the first shock of it, and if the swords of the Highlanders once come in contact with them, their defeat is inevitable.

On the 6th of January, we opened the trenches before the town of Stirling, under the direction of Mr Grant; but the mere threat of laying siege to the town induced the magistrates to repair to Bannockburn and propose a capitulation. The Prince having granted them the conditions which they required, we took possession of Stirling next day. The castle was not included in the surrender. To the summons of the Prince, General Blakeney answered very politely, 'That His Royal Highness would assuredly have a very bad opinion of him, were he capable of surrendering the castle in such a cowardly manner.'

An army of about thirteen thousand men, composed of the best troops of the armies of the Duke of Cumberland and Marshal Wade, entered Scotland under the command of Lieutenant-general Hawley. The first division, under General Husk, reached Edinburgh on the 4th of January, and General Hawley himself arrived there on the 6th. The whole of General Hawley's army having assembled in Edinburgh, General Husk was detached to Linlithgow on the 13th with the five old regiments of Monro, Cholmondeley, Price, Ligonier, and Battereau, and the remains of the two dragoon regiments of Hamilton and Gardiner which had escaped from the battle of Prestonpans, and entered that small town at one end, whilst Lord Elcho, with our cavalry, went out at the other, to fall back on Lord George Murray at Falkirk. On the 14th, the regiments of Howard, Pulteney, and Burrel, marched on Borrowstownness, which is half-way betweeen Edinburgh and Stirling; and they were followed, on the 15th, by the regiments of Fleming, and Blakeney, and a battalion of the regiment of Sinclair. On the 16th, General Hawley encamped with his army and a train of ten field-pieces at Falkirk, and Lord George Murray fell back, at his approach, on Bannockburn, with the detachment of which he had for some time the command at Falkirk.

Monsieur Mirabelle de Gordon, a French engineer and chevalier of the order of St Louis, was sent into Scotland with Lord John Drummond, and arrived at Stirling on the 6th. Great hopes were at first entertained of his being able to reduce the castle, which was the cause of much chagrin to the Highlanders by annoying them in their going to and returning from their own country. It was supposed that a French engineer, of a certain age and decorated with an order, must necessarily be a person of experience, talents, and capacity; but it was unfortunately discovered, when too late, that his knowledge as an engineer was extremely limited, and that he was totally destitute of judgment, discernment and common sense. His figure being as whimsical as his mind, the Highlanders, instead of Monsieur Mirabelle, called him always Mr Admirable.

Mr Grant had already communicated to the Prince a plan of attack on the castle, which was to open trenches and establish batteries in the burying-ground on that side of the town which is opposite to the castle-gate. He assured the Prince that this was the only place where they could find a parallel almost on a level with the batteries of the enemy, and that, if a breach were effected in the half-moon which defends the entry of the castle from a battery in the burying-ground, the rubbish of the work would fill the ditch and render an assault practicable. He added that it was entirely useless to think of making an attack in any other place, from the impossibility of succeeding, and that as the hills in the neighbourhood of the castle were forty or fifty feet lower than the castle itself, our batteries could produce little or no effect, whilst their batteries would command ours. Besides, supposing it even possible to effect a breach on that side, we could never mount to the assault, the rock on which the castle is built being everywhere very high and almost perpendicular, except towards that part of the town opposite to the burying-ground.

The inhabitants of Stirling having remonstrated with the Prince against this plan, as the fire from the castle would, they said, reduce their town to ashes, he consulted Monsieur Mirabelle, with a view to ascertain whether there were any other means of taking the castle. As it is always the distinctive mark of ignorance to find nothing difficult, not even the things that are impossible, Monsieur Mirabelle immediately undertook to open the trenches on a hill to the north of the castle, where there were not fifteen inches depth of earth above the solid rock, and it became necessary to supply the want of earth with bags of wool, and sacks filled with earth, brought from a distance. Thus the trenches were so bad that we lost a great many men, sometimes twenty-five in one day. The six pieces of artillery sent from France, two of which were eighteen, two twelve, and two six-pounders, arrived at Stirling on the 14th.

In the evening of the 16th, the Prince gave orders for collecting together the whole army to be reviewed next morning at break of day on a moor to the east of Bannockburn. Nobody supposed that there was any other object in this general review than to choose a field of battle and obtain the necessary information respecting the nature of the ground, which was the more essentially necessary as we every moment expected an attack from the English army, then encamped at Falkirk. When the review was over, about ten o'clock in the morning, he made the army face to the right to form a column, and immediately moved off without any person in the army being able to penetrate his design, particularly as he did not appear at first to take the roads leading towards the English army.

Our army marched across the fields, and by bye-roads, to Dunipace, leaving the highway from Stirling to Falkirk at a considerable distance on our left, and making a great circuit to conceal our movement from the enemy. Having passed through the village of Dunipace, which is about three and a half miles from Falkirk, at two o'clock in the afternoon, we suddenly found ourselves upon the heights near that town, in sight of the English army and within nine hundred yards of their camp, before General Hawley knew of our departure from Bannock-burn. Their surprise on seeing us may easily be conceived. They immediately flew to arms, and, with great precipitation, ascended to a part of the height between us and the town of Falkirk. There was a high wind, accompanied by a heavy rain, which the Highlanders, by their position, had in their back, whilst it was full in the face of the English who were blinded by it. They were, besides, incommoded with the smoke of our discharge, and the rain, getting into their pans, rendered the half of their muskets useless. The English fruitlessly attempted to gain the advantage of the wind, but the Prince, extending to the left, took care to preserve this advantage by corresponding movements on his part.

General Hawley drew up his army in order of battle in two lines, having three regiments of infantry in a hollow at the foot of the hill. His cavalry was placed before his infantry on the left wing of the first line. The English began the attack with a body of about eleven hundred cavalry, who advanced very slowly against the right of our army, and did not halt till they were within twenty paces of our first line, to induce us to fire. The Highlanders, who had been particularly enjoined not to fire till the army was within musket-length of them, discharged their muskets the moment the cavalry halted and killed about eighty men, each of them having aimed at a rider. The commander of this body of cavalry, who had advanced some paces before his men, was of the number. The cavalry closing their ranks, which were opened by our discharge, put spurs to their horses and rushed upon the Highlanders at a hard trot, breaking their ranks, throwing down everything before them and trampling the Highlanders under the feet of their horses. The most singular and extraordinary combat immediately followed. The Highlanders, stretched on the ground, thrust their dirks into the bellies of the horses. Some seized the riders by their clothes, dragged them down and stabbed them with their dirks, several again used their pistols, but few of them had sufficient space to handle their swords. Macdonald of Clanranald, chief of one of the clans of the Macdonalds, assured me that whilst he was lying upon the ground under a dead horse which had fallen upon him, without the power of extricating himself, he saw a dismounted horseman struggling with a Highlander. Fortunately for him, the Highlander, being the strongest, threw his antagonist, and having killed him with his dirk, he came to his assistance and drew him with difficulty from under his horse.

The resistance of the Highlanders was so incredibly obstinate that the English, after having been for some time engaged pell-mell with them in their ranks, were at length repulsed and forced to retire. The Highlanders did not neglect the advantage they had obtained, but pursued them keenly with their swords, running as fast as their horses, and not allowing them a moment's time to recover from their fright. Then the English cavalry, falling back on their own infantry drawn up in order of battle behind them, threw them immediately into disorder and carried the right wing of their army with them in their flight.

The clan of Camerons, which was on the left of our army, having attacked at the same time the right of the English army, where there were only infantry, put it also to flight; but the Highlanders, when descending the hill in pursuit of the enemy, received, on their left flank, a discharge from the three regiments placed in the hollow at the foot of the hill, which they did not perceive till the moment they received their fire, which greatly incommoded them. Mr John Roy Stuart, an officer in the service of France, afraid lest this might be an ambuscade laid for us by the English, called out to the Highlanders to stop their pursuit, and the cry of stop flew immediately from rank to rank and threw the whole army into disorder. However, the enemy continued their retreat, and the three regiments at the foot of the hill followed the rest, but with the difference that they retreated always in order, acting as a rear-guard of the English army, and continued a fire of platoons on us till their entrance into the town of Falkirk.

As night began to appear, the English army entered the town and fires were immediately seen in every part of their camp, from which we all supposed that they had retreated to it and that we had not obtained a complete and substantial victory. The honour of remaining masters of the field was of little avail to us. We had no reason for believing that we had lost the battle as the English army had retreated, but as we supposed them still in their camp, we considered it at most as undecided, and expected a renewal of the combat next morning.

Fortunately the enemy did not perceive the disorder which had crept into our army, and of which Colonel John Roy Stuart was the innocent cause by his excessive precaution and foresight. The Highlanders were in complete disorder, dispersed here and there with the different clans mingled pell-mell together, whilst the obscurity of the night added greatly to the confusion. Many of them had even retired from the field of battle, either thinking it lost or intending to seek a shelter from the dreadful weather. It is often more dangerous to stop the fire and impetuosity of soldiers, of whom the best are but machines, and still more of undisciplined men who do not listen to any orders, than to let them run all risks in order to carry everything before them.

I met, by accident, Colonel Brown, an Irishman, to whom I proposed that we should keep together, and share the same fate. He consented, but observed at the same time that the Prince having made him the bearer of an order, he wished to find him, with the view of communicating an answer. After having sought the Prince for a long time to no purpose, and without finding anyone who could give us the least information respecting him, we fell in with his life-guards, in order of battle near a cottage on the edge of the hill, with their commander Lord Elcho, who knew as little of what had become of Charles as we did ourselves. As the night was very dark and the rain incessant, we resolved to withdraw to the mansion of Mr Primrose, of Dunipace, about a quarter of a league from Falkirk.

On our arrival at the castle, we found Lord Lewis Gordon, brother of the Duke of Gordon, Mr Fraser, son of Lord Lovat, and six or seven other chiefs of clans; but none of them knew what had become of their regiments. Other officers arrived every instant, all equally ignorant of the fate of the battle and equally in doubt whether we had gained or lost it. About eight o'clock in the evening, Mr Macdonald of Lochgarry joined us, and revived our spirits by announcing for certain that we had gained a most complete victory, and that the English, instead of remaining in their camp, had fled in disorder to Edinburgh. He added, in confirmation of this news, that he had left the Prince in Falkirk, in the quarters which had been occupied by General Hawley, and that the Prince had sent him to Dunipace, for the express purpose of ordering all of us to repair to Falkirk next morning by break of day.

It is impossible, without having been in our situation, to

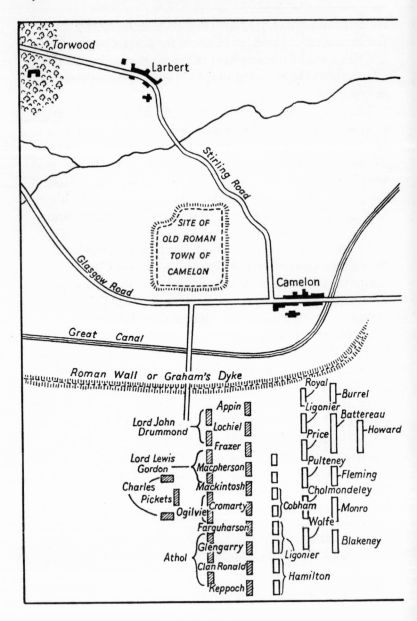

R. Carron

Great Canal between
Forth & Clyde

Falkirk

Bantaskin

Road to
Edinburgh

FALKIRK
17TH JANUARY
1745

form an idea of the extreme joy which we derived from this agreeable surprise. As the enemy, in their retreat, had abandoned all their tents and baggage, their camp was soon pillaged by the Highlanders, and the booty carried away, notwithstanding the obscurity of the night and the badness of the weather. The enemy lost about six hundred in killed, and we took seven hundred prisoners.

It was Lord Kilmarnock who first discovered the flight of the English. Being well acquainted with the nature of the ground, as a part of his estates lay in the neighbourhood, he was sent by the Prince to reconnoitre the enemy, and, having approached the great road to Edinburgh beyond the town of Falkirk, passing by bye-paths and across fields, he saw the English army panic-struck and flying in the greatest disorder as fast as their legs could carry them. With an account of this fortunate discovery, Lord Kilmarnock immediately returned to the Prince, who still remained on the field of battle, notwithstanding the dreadful wind and rain; but he then descended from the hill about half past seven o'clock in the evening, immediately entered the town of Falkirk, and detached as many troops as he could suddenly assemble to harass the English in their flight, who were yet at a short distance from us.

The enemy were unable to avail themselves of their artillery during the action or to carry it with them in their flight, and we found, next day, ten field-pieces, half-way up the hill, which they had not had time to draw up to the top. They lost a great many men in the hollow at the foot of the hill, where the cornfields were thickly strewed with dead bodies.* In their flight they took one prisoner in a very singular manner. Mr Macdonald, a major of one of the Macdonald regiments, having dismounted an English officer, took possession of his horse which

---

*Reports as to the losses suffered by the armies vary considerably but those of the government forces were probably in the region of 300 or 400 whereas the rebels lost only about 40.

was very beautiful, and immediately mounted it. When the English cavalry fled, the horse ran off with the unfortunate Mr Macdonald, notwithstanding all his efforts to restrain him; nor did it stop till it was at the head of the regiment, of which, apparently, its master was the commander. The melancholy, and at the same time ludicrous figure, which poor Macdonald would cut, when he thus saw himself the victim of his ambition to possess a fine horse, may be easily conceived. Ultimately it cost him his life upon the scaffold.

Had General Hawley possessed sufficient coolness and presence of mind, when he saw our army appear upon the height, to have dispassionately examined the advantages and disadvantages of attacking us immediately, and had he remained in his camp, prepared to defend himself if we attacked him, the Prince would have been dreadfully disconcerted, and I really know not what course we could have adopted. Our army could not pass the night in the open air, during such a terrible tempest; and it would have been a sort of victory for General Hawley, if the Prince had been obliged to return by a night-march in such dreadful weather, without effecting his object. But such is the nature of man, that everything unexpected and unforeseen produces an impression on the mind in proportion to its importance, or the consequences which may result from it. Hence there are few surprises judiciously planned and executed, which do not succeed.

VI

THE bad weather which had been so favourable to us during
the battle and contributed so much to our obtaining the victory,
proved very injurious to us afterwards, by preventing us from
pursuing the vanquished enemy and totally dispersing that
army without leaving a vestige of it in Scotland. This would
have obtained for us repose and tranquillity for a long time in
that country, as the army was composed of old regiments and
the best troops of the English.

The tempest raged with such violence, during the whole of
the next day, the 18th, and the rain poured down in such torrents, that none of us quitted our lodgings. Having repaired to
the Prince's quarters, at about seven o'clock in the evening, I
found no one in his anti-chamber, but when I was about to
withdraw, Mr Sullivan issued from the Prince's closet and informed me that, from the badness of the weather, the cannon
taken from the enemy had been left on the field of battle without any guard, and he requested me to go instantly with a
guard of a sergeant and twenty men and pass the night beside
them. He added that I should find the guard below, ready to
march. I set out with this detachment. The sergeant carried a
lantern, but the light was soon extinguished, and by that accident we immediately lost our way and wandered a long time at
the foot of the hill among heaps of dead bodies, which their
whiteness rendered visible notwithstanding the obscurity of a
very dark night. To add to the disagreeableness of our situation
from the horror of this scene, the wind and rain were full in our
faces. I even remarked a trembling and strong agitation in my
horse, which constantly shook when it was forced to put its feet
on the heaps of dead bodies and climb over them. However,
after we had wandered a long time amongst these bodies, we at
length found the cannon.

On my return to Falkirk, I felt myself relieved as from an oppressive burden, but the horrid spectacle I had witnessed was, for a long time, fresh in my mind. How inconsistent is man! During a battle, we frequently see our dearest friends fall by our side (as has repeatedly happened to myself) without being sensibly affected with sorrow and regret at the moment of their unfortunate death. Yet when we coolly proceed over a field of battle, we are seized with horror at the sight of dead bodies, a spectacle repugnant to human nature, though, when living, they may have been perfectly unknown to us. So much does man differ from himself, according to the situations in which he happens to be placed.

The Prince received news from Edinburgh every moment, with details of the consternation and panic-terror of the English in their flight. He was informed that for several days after their defeat they were still under the influence of their alarm, and that at the review by their commissary of war there were not four thousand present in Edinburgh, out of the thirteen or fourteen thousand of their army before the battle.* The friends of the Prince exhorted him to repair with all haste to the capital, to disperse this wreck of the English army and resume the possession of that city. This, in the opinion of every one, was the only sensible course which the Prince could adopt, but it was soon seen that it is much easier to gain a victory than to know how to profit by it. The gaining a battle is very often the effect of pure chance, but to reap all the advantages of which a victory is susceptible, requires genius, capacity, and superior talents, and it is in turning a victory to account that we particularly discover the great soldier. One thing is certain, and that is, that the vanquished will always have great resources in the negligence of the victorious party. We ought to have pursued the English with the rapidity of a torrent, in order to prevent them from recovering from their fright, and we should have

*The total of the government forces at Falkirk was about 8,000.

kept continually at their heels, and never relaxed, till they were no longer in a condition to rally, without thinking of reaping the fruits of our victory, till their complete defeat should enable us to do so with safety, leisure and tranquillity.

On the 19th, when the weather became favourable, it was natural to think we should take the route to Edinburgh. But—what fatal blindness!—instead of pursuing a vanquished and routed enemy, the Prince resolved to return to Bannockburn to continue the siege of Stirling Castle. This determination was the result of a consultation with Monsieur Mirabelle, the senseless individual already mentioned, who promised to reduce it in the course of forty-eight hours. The possession of this petty fort was of no essential importance to us; on the contrary, it was of more advantage to us that it should remain in the hands of the enemy, in order to restrain the Highlanders, and prevent them from returning, when they pleased, to their own country, for, whenever they got possession of any booty taken from the English, they were constantly going home in order to secure it. This fatal resolution of returning to Stirling induced Mr Peter Smith, the Freron* of our army, to observe, 'that our whole enterprise had been one continued series of blunders, but that, fortunately for us, the Almighty had hitherto turned all our blunders to our advantage.' However, this stupid and gross blunder of not pursuing the enemy with vigour, and not keeping continually at their heels to disperse them completely, without relaxing so long as one Englishman remained on the soil of Scotland, could never be of any advantage to us, and could not fail, sooner or later, to effect our ruin.

Effects, far from corresponding to their causes, frequently give rise to events altogether different from what appearances might lead us to anticipate. Who could have imagined that the six pieces of heavy artillery, sent by the court of France to our assistance, would become our ruin? And yet they certainly

*A contemporary French journalist.

The Duke of Cumberland

were our ruin, for without them we should never have dreamed
of laying siege to Stirling Castle, as no one could have thought
of a siege without artillery. After the victory of Falkirk, all of
us would have agreed as to the propriety of effecting the complete destruction of the English army, by following up the
victory by a hot pursuit and taking possession of Edinburgh.

Our trenches, traced on a hill to the north of the Castle by
Mirabelle, advanced very slowly because of the mere covering
of earth, and we lost a great many men, particularly of the Irish
pickets. What a pity that these brave men should have been
sacrificed to no purpose by the ignorance and folly of Mirabelle!
These pickets, who behaved with the most distinguished
bravery and intrepidity at the battle of Falkirk, preserving
always the best order when the whole of the rest of our army
was dispersed, and keeping the enemy in check by the bold
countenance which they displayed, ought to have been reserved
for a better occasion.

At length, on the 30th of January, Monsieur Mirabelle, with
a childish impatience to witness the effects of his battery, un-
masked it as soon as three embrasures of the six of which it was
to have been composed were finished, and immediately began a
very brisk fire with his three pieces of cannon. But it was of
short duration, and produced very little effect on the batteries
of the Castle, which being more elevated than ours, enabled
the enemy to see even the buckles of the shoes of our artillery-
men. As their fire commanded ours, our guns were immediately dismounted: in less than half an hour we were obliged to
abandon our battery altogether, as no one could approach it
without meeting with certain destruction, while our guns,
being pointed upwards, could do no execution whatever. Thus
a work of three weeks, which had prevented us from deriving
any advantage from our victory at Falkirk and which had cost
us the lives of a great number of brave men, was demolished in
an instant, like a castle of cards.

G

Justice ought to be done to the merit and good conduct of General Blakeney, who perceived our ignorance from the position of our battery and did not disturb us while constructing it. Convinced that we could do him no injury from that quarter, he remained quiet, like a skilful general, and allowed us to go on, that we might lose these precious moments which we ought to have employed in pursuing the enemy. Well he knew that he could destroy our battery whenever he pleased, and level it in an instant with the ground.

This error of amusing ourselves before the Castle instead of pursuing the enemy, the punishment of which followed so soon afterwards, was the beginning of our calamities. Up to this time fortune seemed to have blindly favoured us. The English soldiers, in their flight, had dispersed so much up and down the fields that five days after the battle four thousand men could scarcely be assembled at Edinburgh, which, by our mismanagement, became a rallying point for them and the source whence all our disasters flowed. The fugitives, finding they were not pursued, began to recover by degrees from their fright, took courage from our inactivity and lethargy, and at length joined their colours in the capital. By the reinforcement of two regiments of infantry, Sempell's and the Scots fusiliers, the dragoon regiments of Bland and St George, with Kingston's light-horse, detached from the army of Marshal Wade, the army of the enemy in eight or ten days was stronger than it had been before the battle of Falkirk.

General Cope is said to have enjoyed with evident satisfaction the news of the defeat of General Hawley. He had, according to the English custom, offered bets to the amount of ten thousand guineas, in the different coffee-houses in London, that the first general sent to command an army against us in Scotland would be beaten, as he himself had been at Prestonpans, and by the defeat of General Hawley he gained a considerable sum of money and recovered his honour to a certain degree. The Duke of Cumberland was immediately ordered to take the command of the army in Scotland and leaving London on the 25th, arrived at Edinburgh on the 30th of January.

The destruction of our battery at once terminated the siege of the Castle. The Prince was informed the same day of the arrival of the Duke of Cumberland at Edinburgh, and immediately reviewed his army at Bannockburn with the intention of advancing to meet him. But finding that a number of Highlanders were missing, whom our long stay at Stirling and the proximity of their own country had induced to return home, our army was obliged to retreat and to abandon all its artillery to the enemy, with the exception of a few field-pieces. To our eternal shame we fled with precipitation from the same army which we had completely beaten sixteen days before.

How fortunate the army which has an able general at its head! How distressing the reflection, that the existence of thousands of men depends upon a single individual! an error in judgment of whom may render them in an instant the victims of misfortune, by occasioning a chain of calamities without remedy, the necessary consequences of a first fault. The absurd wish to possess an insignificant castle, which could be of no real utility to us, produced a series of effects, which ruined the Prince's enterprise and brought a great number of his partisans to the scaffold. The bulk of mankind are only capable of seeing at one time a part of an important, extensive and exalted project, and very few indeed view it in all its extent, with the events which ought naturally to occur in its execution. If the basis of an operation is false, the bad consequences which flow from it give rise, in their turn, to other bad consequences, and the evil increases every day.

We left Stirling on the 31st to proceed to Inverness, the capital of the Highlands, situated a hundred and fifty-six miles to the north-west of Edinburgh, and having crossed the river Forth, at the ford of the Frew, we passed the night at Crieff. On the morning of our leaving Stirling, the church of St Ninians, where we had fifty barrels of powder, accidentally blew up with a terrible explosion. On the 1st of February, our army left Crieff, in two columns; one, conducted by Lord George Murray, took the road along the sea-coast, passing through the towns of Perth, Dundee, Montrose, Aberdeen, and Peterhead; the other column, with the Prince at its head, went straight across the mountains by Blair Athol, which is the shortest road to Inverness. The Prince's column, in passing through Badenoch, took a little fort at Ruthven, and another at about five leagues from it, called Fort Augustus,* which King George had constructed to restrain and awe the Highlanders. They were immediately razed, and the garrisons made prisoners of war.

On the 16th, the Prince slept at Moy, a castle belonging to the chief of the clan of Mackintosh, about ten miles from Inverness. As Lord Loudon, a lieutenant-general in the service of King George and colonel of a regiment of Highlanders, was at Inverness with about two thousand regular troops, the Prince intended to wait the arrival of the other column before approaching nearer to that town. In the meantime, Lord Loudon formed the project of seizing by surprise the person of the Prince who, conceiving himself in perfect security at Moy, could have no suspicion of any attempt of the kind. His Lordship would have succeeded in this design but for the intervention of that invisible Being who frequently chooses to manifest his power in overturning the best contrived schemes of feeble mortals. His Lordship, at three o'clock in the afternoon, posted guards and a chain of sentinels all round Inverness, both within and without the town, with positive orders not to suffer any person to leave it, on any pretext whatever, however high the rank of the person might be. At the same time, he ordered fifteen hundred men to hold themselves in readiness to march at

*The capture of Fort Augustus took place after that of Inverness.

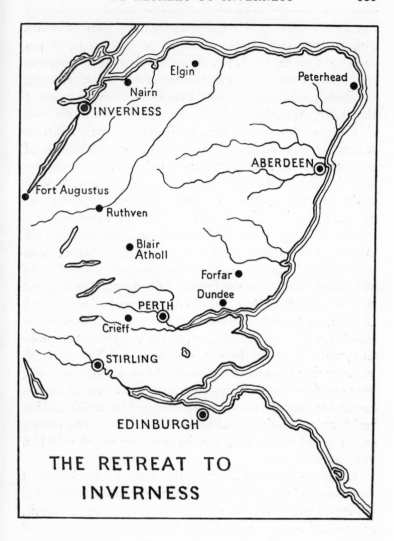

THE RETREAT TO
INVERNESS

a moment's warning. Having assembled this body of troops without noise and without alarming the inhabitants, he put himself at their head and instantly set off, planning his march so as to arrive at the castle of Moy about eleven o'clock at night.

Whilst some English officers were drinking in the house of Mrs Bailly, an innkeeper in Inverness, and passing the time till the hour of their departure, her daughter, a girl of thirteen or fourteen years of age, who happened to wait on them, paid great attention to their conversation and, from certain expressions dropped by them, she discovered their designs. As soon as this generous girl was certain as to their intentions, she immediately left the house, escaped from the town, notwithstanding the vigilance of the sentinels, and immediately took the road to Moy, running as fast as she was able, without shoes or stockings (which to accelerate her progress she had taken off) in order to inform the Prince of the danger that menaced him. She reached Moy, quite out of breath, before Lord Loudon, and the Prince, with difficulty, escaped in his robe-de-chambre, night-cap and slippers, to the neighbouring mountains, where he passed the night in concealment. This dear girl, to whom the Prince owed his life, was in great danger of losing her own, from her excessive fatigue on this occasion; but the care and attentions she experienced restored her to life, and her health was at length re-established. The Prince, having no suspicion of such a daring attempt, had very few people with him in the castle of Moy.

As soon as the girl had spread the alarm, the blacksmith of the village of Moy presented himself to the Prince and assured His Royal Highness that he had no occasion to leave the castle, as he would answer for it, with his head, that Lord Loudon and his troops would be obliged to return faster than they came. The Prince had not sufficient confidence in his assurances to neglect seeking his safety by flight to the neighbouring mountains. However, the blacksmith, for his own satisfaction, put his

project in execution. He instantly assembled a dozen of his companions and advanced with them about a quarter of a league
from the castle on the road to Inverness. There he laid an ambuscade, posting six of his companions on each side of the highway, to wait the arrival of the detachment of Lord Loudon,
enjoining them not to fire till he should tell them, and then not
to fire together, but one after another. When the head of the
detachment of Lord Loudon was opposite the twelve men,
about eleven o'clock in the evening, the blacksmith called out
with a loud voice, 'Here come the villains, who intend carrying
off our Prince; fire, my lads, do not spare them; give no
quarter!' In an instant muskets were discharged from each side
of the road, and the detachment, seeing their project had taken
wind, began to fly in the greatest disorder, imagining that our
whole army was lying in wait for them. Such was their terror
and consternation that they did not stop till they reached Inverness. In this manner did a common blacksmith, with twelve of
his companions, put Lord Loudon and fifteen hundred regular
troops to flight. The fifer of his Lordship, who happened to be
at the head of the detachment, was killed by the first discharge,
and the detachment did not wait for a second.

Next morning the Prince assembled all his column, who had
passed the night in the villages and hamlets some miles from
Moy, and advanced to Inverness with the intention of attacking Lord Loudon and taking revenge for the attempt of the
preceding night. But, as he approached the town, his Lordship
retreated across the arm of the sea to the north of Inverness,
after collecting and taking along with him to the other side, all
the boats, great and small, and other vessels, that could aid us
in pursuing him.

The castle of Inverness was fortified in the modern manner,
being a regular square with four bastions, and it was advan-
tageously situated on the top of an eminence which commanded the town. It was built in the time of Oliver Cromwell

and had ever since been kept in good repair with the view of enforcing the subjection of the Highlanders, who are naturally brave and faithful and generally attached to the house of Stuart.* Since the Revolution of 1688, the keeping up of this fortress had cost, it is said, above fifty thousand pounds sterling. The governor of the castle, who was in a situation to stand a siege, at first refused to comply with the summons of the Prince, but two hours after the trenches were opened, he surrendered himself with his garrison which consisted of two companies of Lord Loudon's regiment. The Prince immediately gave orders to raze the fortifications and blow up the bastions. Monsieur L'Epine, a sergeant in the French artillery, who was charged with the operation, lost his life on the occasion. This unfortunate individual, believing the match extinguished, approached to examine it, when the mine sprung, which blew him into the air, with the stones of the bastion, to an immense height.

Our cavalry, which had taken the same road as the column of Lord George Murray, arrived on the 16th at the river Spey; a detachment forded this river and slept at Elgin, the capital of Morayshire. On the 17th, the column of Lord George arrived at Elgin; on the 18th, part of it advanced to Forres, and part of it as far as Nairn, escorting the cargo of two ships, which had landed at Peterhead (one from France and the other from Spain), consisting of money, arms and military stores. The vessel from France had on board a picket of the cavalry regiment of Fitzjames. On the 19th, the whole army formed a junction at Inverness.

The *Hazard*, a sloop of war of about eighteen guns which had been taken by the Highlanders in a very singular manner and sent into France with news of our victory at Falkirk, was

*The fort built by Cromwell was in ruins long before 1745. The castle of Inverness, which was destroyed by the rebels, stood on a hill to the south-west of Cromwell's fort.

retaken by the English on the 25th of March. Having been chased the whole of the 24th by the English ship of war the *Sheerness*, it threw itself on the coast of Lord Reay's country, in the northern extremity of Scotland. The *Hazard* conveyed a hundred thousand crowns, and stores from France, but the vassals of Lord Reay, who were attached to the house of Hanover, pillaged the cargo and made prisoners of the crew, who had lost thirty-six men in the engagement with the *Sheerness*, a vessel of sixty guns.

The Highlanders had taken the *Hazard* without any premeditated design. For some time it had been cruising before Montrose and had annoyed the Highlanders very much, firing on them continually whenever any of them made their appearance on the shore. The Highlanders were quite indignant at seeing it anchored so near to the land. One day, when there happened to be a very thick fog, they embarked in fishing-boats, and the officers who were with them induced them to approach nearer and nearer, as if from curiosity to examine a ship of war which they had never before seen. As soon as the crew of the *Hazard* perceived them through the fog, the sailors, seized with panic, threw themselves on their knees, on the deck and asked quarter with uplifted hands, being afraid that the Highlanders would board them and put the whole of them to the sword. The Highlanders immediately climbed up the vessel, and took possession of it, but knowing nothing of navigation, they compelled their prisoners, with pistols at their breasts, to steer the vessel into the port of Montrose.

The Duke of Cumberland arrived at Stirling, with his army, on the 2nd of February, where he remained till the 5th. He passed the night of the 5th at Crieff, and arrived at Perth on the 6th. From this place he sent a detachment to seize the Duchess of Perth in her castle, because her son was with the Prince, and also the Viscountess of Strathallan, whose husband and son were both of them in our army. These two ladies were conveyed to Edinburgh Castle, where they were shut up for nearly a whole year in a small and unhealthy prison. This trait of the Duke of Cumberland was quite unexampled. Who ever before heard of rendering a mother responsible for the opinions of her son, or a wife for those of her husband?

On the 8th of February, the Prince of Hesse, son-in-law of King George, landed at Leith with five thousand infantry and five hundred hussars in the pay of England. He remained at Edinburgh till the 23rd, when he left it to proceed to Perth with his troops, to replace his brother-in-law the Duke of Cumberland, who had gone to the north of Scotland against us. The Prince of Hesse, during his stay at Edinburgh, was beloved and esteemed by everybody, on account of the moderation of his conduct and the propriety of his behaviour to the partisans of the Prince, mingling indifferently in all circles, without appearing to take any personal interest in the quarrel between the houses of Hanover and Stuart. The Hessians, imitating the example of their Prince, were equally well liked.

As all the male vassals of the Duke of Athol were in our army with his brother Lord George, the Duke of Cumberland sent a detachment of his troops into their country, where they committed the most unheard-of cruelties—burning the houses of the gentlemen who were with the Prince, and turning out their wives and children in the midst of winter, to perish in the mountains with cold and hunger, after subjecting them to every species of infamous and brutal treatment. As soon as these proceedings were known at Inverness, Lord George set off instantly with the clan of Athol to take vengeance for this treatment, and he conducted his march so well, passing through bye-ways across the mountains, that the enemy had no information of his approach. Having planned his march so as to arrive at Athol in the beginning of the night, the detachment separated, dividing itself into small parties, every gentleman taking the shortest road to his own house, and in this manner all the English were surprised in their sleep. Those who found their wives and daughters violated by the brutality of these monsters, and their families dying from hunger and the inclemency of the season, made no prisoners. All the English received, while they slept, the punishment which their inhumanity merited. Thus they were all either put to the sword or made prisoners, except two or three hundred men, who barricaded themselves in the castle of the Duke of Athol, which could not be forced without cannon.*

The Prince of Hesse was then at Perth, which is thirty-five miles from the castle of the Duke of Athol at Blair, and as soon as he received information of this adventure, he immediately dispatched a body of Hessian troops to the support of the English, and to oblige Lord George to raise the siege of the castle of which he had already formed the blockade. These hussars having attacked Lord George, the Highlanders fell upon them with rapidity and impetuosity, sword in hand, and running after them as fast as their horses, they killed five or six Hessians and took one lieutenant prisoner. Next day, Lord George sent back the officer, with a letter to the Prince of Hesse, in which he demanded, in the name of Prince Charles, a cartel for the exchange of prisoners on both sides, adding that if he would not grant it, all the Hessians who might fall into our hands should be put to the sword. The Prince of Hesse communicated the letter of Lord George to the Duke of Cumberland, representing the demand as reasonable and just, but the Duke would not hear of any cartel. The Prince declared instantly, that, 'without a cartel, no Hessian should stir from Perth'; and he added, that he was not so much interested in the quarrel between the houses of Stuart and Hanover as to sacrifice his subjects in combating with men driven to despair. The

*Some excesses may have been committed at this time by government troops, but the picture here is exaggerated.

Prince kept his word, always remaining at Perth with his Hessians, and refusing to advance to the north of Scotland to join the English army, as the Duke of Cumberland wished him to do.

The Duke of Cumberland, on his arrival at Aberdeen, a considerable city about ninety miles from Inverness, distributed his army in quarters in that city and its neighbourhood, with the intention of remaining there till the commencement of the fine weather in the spring. The little town of Keith in Strathbogie, where he had part of his troops, was almost in the centre of the places occupied by him. Mr Glasgow, an Irish officer in the service of France, proposed to the Prince to carry the post at Keith, and pledged himself to effect this with a detachment of only two hundred men. The Prince at first hesitated, having great doubts of the success, but at length he gave his consent.

The enterprise of Glasgow was both bold and dangerous, but he conducted himself like a prudent and skilful officer and succeeded in the most complete manner. He arrived at Keith at one o'clock in the morning without being discovered and exactly at the termination of the time he had calculated his march would occupy. On the sentinel before the guard-house calling out, 'Who goes there?' Mr Glasgow replied, 'A friend,' and advanced himself to the sentinel, whom he killed with his dirk. The Highlanders immediately rushed on the guard, who at first made some resistance but were soon disarmed. Then, without losing a moment, they flew through the town, making prisoners of the soldiers who were quartered in the houses of the inhabitants. Mr Glasgow managed matters so well that, in less than an hour, he accomplished his object and retired with a hundred and eighty prisoners whom he presented next day to the Prince. This bold enterprise had a very good effect, and made such an impression on the English that, conceiving themselves insecure everywhere, they were obliged to redouble their service in the midst of winter. The consequent fatigues in that cold and mountainous country occasioned so much disease, that the hospitals of Aberdeen, the headquarters of the Duke of Cumberland, were continually filled with their sick.

Lord Loudon with his corps frequently harassed and annoyed us and he sent detachments across the arm of the sea between himself and us, keeping us continually on the alert. When we attempted to attack them, they re-embarked and crossed immediately to the other side, and as we could not pursue them for want of shipping, we were obliged to put up with their insults. This position of Lord Loudon was the more alarming to us as we were assured the Duke of Cumberland only waited for favourable weather to attack us, and his Lordship might cross this arm of the sea or firth whilst we were engaged with the English, and thus place us between two fires. It was, therefore, deemed an object of the highest importance that we should attack Lord Loudon, and disperse his detachment.

The Prince ordered all the fishing-boats, large and small, to be found at Speymouth and the other little ports of our side of the firth, to be brought to Findhorn, and during the night between the 19th and 20th of March, we embarked as many men in them as they could contain under the orders of the Duke of Perth, who was appointed to command this expedition. The Duke took with him about eighteen hundred men, and a very thick fog which came on in the morning, having greatly favoured the enterprise, he landed his detachment very near the enemy, who did not perceive our troops till they were within fifty paces of them, advancing rapidly sword in hand. The enemy were so much confounded on seeing the Highlanders ready to fall on them, that the greater part threw down their arms and surrendered themselves prisoners of war. A few escaped by flight, and Lord Loudon was of the number. The Duke of Perth returned the same day to Inverness with some hundred prisoners, without having fired a single shot or shed one drop of blood.*

On the 19th, after the detachment had been assigned to the Duke of Perth, Mr Macdonald of Scothouse came to pass the day with me. He was about forty years of age, had a fine countenance, and to his agreeable exterior he added a noble and commanding figure. He had all the qualities which usually distinguish a worthy and gallant man: brave, polished and obliging, he possessed at the same time a cultivated mind and a sound judgment. Although our acquaintance had only commenced with the Prince's expedition, I soon learned to appreciate his merit and the charms of his society, and notwithstanding the disproportion of our ages, we were united together in the closest friendship. He entertained for me all the affection of a father. As he was naturally of a gay disposition, the grief in which he appeared on his entrance attracted my notice. On enquiring the cause, this worthy man replied, with tears in his eyes, 'Ah! my friend, you know not what it is to be a father. I am one of the detachment which is to set out this evening to attack Lord Loudon. You are ignorant that a son whom I adore is an officer in his regiment. I thought myself fortunate in being able to procure such a situation for this youth, being unable to anticipate the landing of the Prince in Scotland. Perhaps, tomorrow, I may be so unfortunate as to kill my son with my own hand; and thus the same ball which I fire in my defence may give to myself the most cruel death! However, in going with the detachment, I may be able to save him, and if I do not go, he may fall by the hands of another.'

The recital of poor Scothouse distressed me very much, and I could not refrain from mingling my tears with his, although I had never seen the young man, the subject of such painful

*The boats were assembled at Tain, whence they crossed to Dornoch. The only force they met was one of 200 men of Loudon's regiment under Majors Mackenzie and Mackintosh, and this promptly surrendered.

anxiety to an affectionate father. I kept him with me the whole day, endeavouring by every means in my power to divert his attention from so melancholy a subject, and I made him promise, on his taking leave of me, to visit me immediately on his return from the expedition. Next evening, I heard a loud knocking at my door, and running to it, I perceived this good father holding a handsome young man by the hand. He instantly called out with eyes sparkling with joy, 'Here, my friend, here is he, who caused me yesterday so much anxiety. I took him prisoner myself, and, having secured him, I troubled myself very little about taking others.' He then shed tears of joy, very different from the tears of the preceding evening. We supped all three together in my apartment, and I scarce ever enjoyed more satisfaction than in witnessing this tender scene between the father and son.

Mr Cameron of Lochiel departed with his clan for his own country on the 18th of March, in order to lay siege to Fort William which greatly harassed his vassals. He took with him Mr Grant, and a few field-pieces which we found in the castle of Inverness on its surrender. He began the siege on the 20th, and it lasted only a few days. It was the last of the Highland forts that remained to be taken, and when it came into our possession it was immediately razed like the rest.*

Having taken a greater number of English soldiers prisoners since the commencement of our expedition than that of all the Highlanders in our army, it became extremely difficult to know how to dispose of them. As our ambulatory army was always in motion, they continually escaped, so that at last very few remained with us. What was still worse, they rejoined their different regiments, so that we had always to encounter the same men whom we had vanquished before, and whose lives we had spared. It was a very considerable advantage to the English to gain in this manner thousands of soldiers for their

*Fort William was besieged, but never taken.

army to whom they had no longer any right. There were two ways of avoiding this inconvenience; either to send them to France, which was not an easy matter from the difficulty of obtaining transports; or to make no prisoners, but put all the enemy to the sword, which might be deemed fighting on equal terms, as every Scotsman who was made a prisoner was sure to perish on the scaffold. The latter alternative appears extremely harsh to those who are as humanely disposed as we were, and yet it was but consonant to justice. Indeed this was the only kind of warfare that we ought to have adopted to infuse more terror into the enemy, and to prevent us from having to combat the same individuals over and over again. Besides, the English soldiers, when once dispersed, would not have been so anxious to join their colours as they actually were, nor to expose themselves, by escaping from us, a second time to the swords of the Highlanders, when they knew they would receive no quarter. But they perceived that our humanity bordered upon weakness, and that they only ran the risk of being once more taken prisoners.

Mr Peter Smith, of whom I have already spoken, and who had always very singular ideas, suggested to the Prince a means of extricating ourselves from this dilemma, which was to cut off the thumbs of their right hands to render them incapable of holding their muskets. But the excessive attachment of the Prince for the English nation, the executioners of his family, prevented him from adopting any expedient which could give them the smallest umbrage.

We had from four to five hundred officers prisoners, to whom the Prince gave permission to go wherever they pleased, on their parole not to serve against him for the space of eighteen months. The Prince obliged those who were taken prisoners at Falkirk to add their oath to their parole, to bind them more effectually. But the Duke of Cumberland, on leaving Edinburgh, sent circular letters to all the English officers, our prisoners of war, to absolve them from their parole and their oath, declaring that they could not be bound by any parole given to rebels, and he added that, unless they immediately joined their respective regiments, he would punish their disobedience by disposing of their commissions to others. To the eternal disgrace of the English officers, there were only four who refused to accept of the absolution of the Duke of Cumberland: Sir Peter Halket, lieutenant-colonel of Lee's regiment, taken at the battle of Prestonpans, Mr Ross, son of Lord Ross, and two other officers, all of whom replied, 'That he was master of their commissions, but not of their probity and honour.'

We learned at Inverness that the Duke of Cumberland, having assembled his army, had set out from Aberdeen on the 8th of April, and had taken the road by Old Meldrum and Banff. The Prince immediately dispatched Lord John Drummond to Elgin, with his regiment of Royal Scots, five pickets of the Irish brigade, Lord Elcho and our cavalry, and the picket of Fitzjames's regiment. The last-named had recently landed at Peterhead with saddles, bridles and other cavalry equipment but without horses, and were hastily mounted on such as could be got.

Lord John was instructed to throw up entrenchments along the banks of the Spey and to dispute the passage of that river with the Duke of Cumberland. Relying on the resistance of Lord John, who, he supposed, would have recourse to every possible device to defend the ford and who, if he could not render it altogether impassable, would at least, by fortifying it with strong entrenchments, retard the approach of the Duke of Cumberland, the Prince expected to have had sufficient time to assemble his whole army, of which nearly the half had gone home to see their families, along with the chiefs who intended to order out every vassal capable of bearing arms. Besides, the excessive scarcity of provisions at Inverness was an additional

H

motive for permitting them to return home, as the Prince was convinced that they would cheerfully rejoin his army the moment they received orders for that prupose.

The astonishment which prevailed at Inverness, when the information came upon us like a clap of thunder that the Duke of Cumberland had forded the river Spey without experiencing the least opposition, may be easily conceived. Lord Elcho, who always distinguished himself, alone appeared at the ford, with the life-guards, and exchanged a few shots with the English whilst they were in the river; but they were immediately obliged to fall back and had much difficulty in effecting their retreat, being hotly pursued by the English cavalry. Lord John Drummond had remained at Elgin, with the corps of infantry under his command, without taking any steps to oppose the passage of the river.

Mr Hunter of Burnside, an officer in the life-guards, narrowly escaped being made a prisoner. On firing his pistol at the enemy, he accidentally wounded his horse in the neck, who threw him; but at the moment the English were on the point of seizing him, he sprung up behind a life-guardsman and they both saved themselves. The ignorance of Lord John Drummond in the art of war appears the more extraordinary as he was a general officer in the service of France. It is astonishing that persons of illustrious houses, destined by their birth to command armies, to fill the highest offices in the state, and to act the first parts in the kingdom, should not apply themselves with keenness and assiduity to the study of military affairs, in order to enable them to discharge their duty with honour and distinction, to the advantage of their king and country. Especially is this so as the shame and disgrace which necessarily attach to the military blunders they are continually liable to commit from their ignorance in the art of war, can never be effaced during the rest of their lives.*

*Since the government forces crossed the Spey at three places

As the Duke of Cumberland advanced, our out-posts fell back upon Inverness. The Prince ordered all the chiefs who had leave of absence to join him with the utmost diligence. In the meantime, he had the mortification to learn that the Earl of Cromarty and his son Lord MacLeod, having been surprised in the castle of the Countess of Sutherland by a detachment commanded by Mr Mackay in the service of King George, had been made prisoners and sent on board the *Hound* ship-of-war, to be transported to London. This misfortune deprived the Prince of the clan of Mackenzie, amounting to about five or six hundred men.

For some time provisions had become very scarce at Inverness and our army suffered very much from want of food. Our military chest, too, was empty, as the Prince had not at most above five hundred Louis and, from the extreme indigence of the inhabitants, we were without hope of obtaining any pecuniary supplies in the Highlands, into which we had blindly precipitated ourselves. Everybody felt the distress more or less. We were shut up in the mountains and our communication with the Lowlands was entirely cut off by the English army. Even the richest lords in our army were very much embarrassed to find means to defray their daily expenses, as they were unable to obtain any money from their tenants.

simultaneously, it would have been impossible for Lord John Drummond to prevent them. He might, however, have made such a crossing far more difficult.

VII

THE Prince left Inverness on the 13th of April, to occupy a position which he had chosen for the field of battle at the distance of half a league from that town, and we continued there day and night, sleeping on the bare ground in the open air, without tents or any shelter from the inclemency of the weather. The Highlanders had no other nourishment than some biscuits and water. I never quitted my friend Scothouse, who shared with me all the provisions that he could find, giving me, at the same time during the very cold nights, the half of his covering and a part of the straw which the Highlanders of his regiment had procured for him.

The 15th of April was the birthday of the Duke of Cumberland, and the Prince, conceiving that the English would on that day be intoxicated and might therefore be taken by surprise, formed the project of attacking the Duke in the night-time in his camp at Nairn, which was from three to four leagues from the place near the Castle of Culloden, where we had remained since the 13th. For this purpose, he immediately ordered our army to set out without noise about eight o'clock in the evening, marching in two columns. Lord George, as usual, was at the head of the first, which served as a guide to the Prince, who commanded the second himself. This march across the country, in a dark night which did not allow us to follow any track, had the inevitable fate of all night-marches. It was extremely fatiguing and accompanied with confusion and disorder. The Highlanders, who could not keep together from the difficulty of the roads, were more or less dispersed and we had many stragglers. As there were a great many bad places to cross, it would have been impossible for the best disciplined troops to have preserved anything like order.

When Lord George, at the head of the first column, was at

the distance of about a quarter of a league from the English at the entrance into a meadow which led to their camp, he halted his column and immediately acquainted the Prince that it was absolutely necessary to wait a little and to form the Highlanders in order of battle as they came up, with the view of presenting a front and attacking the enemy together and without confusion. This advice of Lord George was highly approved of by Mr Hepburn of Keith and Mr Cameron of Lochiel, who were with him at the head of the first column, and has always appeared to me sensible and correct. But the Prince, who did not see the necessity of waiting to form the men in order of battle and attacking in a body, instead of advancing confusedly and unconnectedly, sent an aide-de-camp to Lord George with orders to fall upon the camp of the Duke of Cumberland as soon as he should reach it, whatever number of men might be with him. As soon as Lord George received the answer of the Prince, he instantly retrograded by a road to the left, instead of continuing to advance against the English. He observed to Mr Hepburn that it was too late, that the day would begin to appear before they could arrive at the camp of the Duke of Cumberland, and that the enemy, being aware of our approach, might take advantage of our situation and attack us while disordered and dispersed. Mr Hepburn replied that there would be no great harm if we had a little daylight to assist the Highlanders in using their swords to advantage, but Lord George would not listen to him and was immoveable in his resolution of returning to the Castle of Culloden immediately, without attempting anything. As the Prince was unacquainted with the retreat of Lord George, he imagined that the first column was still before him, and nearly entered the camp of the enemy. But as soon as he perceived his mistake he turned back, and our army arrived at Culloden about seven o'clock in the morning, worn out with fatigue and enraged at having attempted nothing.

I could never comprehend why the Prince wished to attack the English army, so much superior in number to his own, with only a part of his men, without waiting till the rest should come up, and without forming them in order of battle. A shameful repulse would have been the inevitable consequence of such an attack. A surprise ought not only to be judiciously planned, and all the measures which it may naturally lead the enemy to adopt be foreseen, but it ought to be conducted and executed at the same time with wisdom and attention to all the means necessary to ensure success. An enemy surprised is, no doubt, half conquered; but the case is altered if he have time to recover from his confusion. Then he may not only contrive to escape, but even to destroy his opponent.

I do not mean to justify the conduct of Lord George in retiring with the first column, contrary to the express orders of the Prince, and without informing him of it. Had he waited at the entrance into the meadow for the arrival of the whole army, he might have insisted on the absolute necessity of forming in order of battle in order to begin the attack like people in their senses, and have convinced the Prince of the absurdity of acting otherwise. The Irishmen, whom the Prince had adopted as his only counsellors on all occasions, and who were men of the most limited capacities, endeavoured, by all manner of clandestine reports, to cause it to be believed that, in acting as he did on this occasion, Lord George had betrayed the Prince. But, knowing him perhaps better than any other person, I can only attribute his disobedience of the Prince's orders to the violence and impetuosity of his character.

Exhausted with hunger and worn out with the excessive fatigue of the three last nights, as soon as we reached Culloden I turned off as fast as I could to Inverness, where, eager to recruit my strength by a little sleep, I tore off my clothes, half asleep all the while. But when I had already one leg in the bed and was on the point of stretching myself between the sheets, what was my surprise to hear the drum beat to arms and the trumpets of the picket of Fitzjames sounding the call to boot and saddle. I hurried on my clothes, my eyes half shut, and mounting a horse, instantly repaired to our army on the eminence on which we had remained for three days, and from which we saw the English army at the distance of about two miles from us. They appeared at first disposed to encamp in the position where they then were, many of their tents being already erected; but all at once their tents disappeared and we immediately perceived them in movement towards us. The view of our army making preparations for battle probably induced the Duke of Cumberland to change his plan. Indeed, he must have been blind in the extreme to have delayed attacking us instantly in the deplorable situation in which we were, worn out with hunger and fatigue, especially when he perceived from our manoeuvre that we were impatient to give battle under every possible disadvantage, and well disposed to facilitate our own destruction. The Duke of Cumberland remained ignorant, till it was day, of the danger to which he had been exposed during the night and, as soon as he knew it, he broke up his camp and followed us closely.

The Prince, on his return to Culloden, enraged against Lord George Murray, publicly declared that no one in future should command his army but himself.* As soon as the English army began to appear, the Prince, who was always eager to give battle without reflecting on the consequences, was told that, as the Highlanders were exhausted with fatigue, dispersed, and buried in deep sleep in the neighbouring hamlets and enclosures, many could not possibly be present in the battle from the difficulty of finding them. Besides, what could be expected

*Had Prince Charles slept during the whole of the expedition, and allowed Lord George to act for him, according to his own judgment, there is every reason for supposing he would have found the crown of Great Britain on his head, when he awoke. *Author's note.*

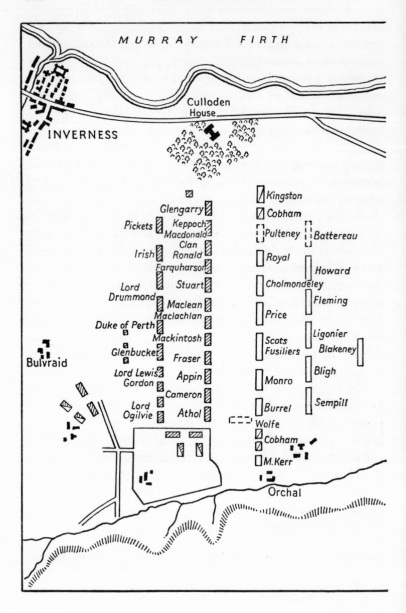

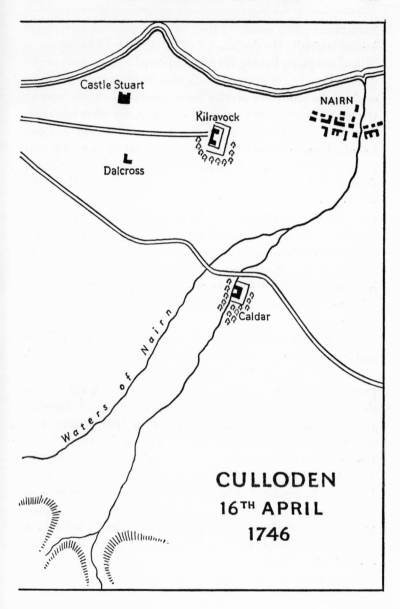

Castle Stuart

Kilravock

NAIRN

Dalcross

Caldar

Waters of Nairn

CULLODEN
16TH APRIL
1746

from men in their situation; they were not possessed of supernatural strength. He was advised to fall back on the high ground
behind the plain, having his left supported by the ruins of the
castle where he could place his cannon to advantage, whilst he
could at the same time occupy Inverness and allow his army to
refresh themselves and obtain some sleep. By allowing them
twenty-four hours' repose, it was said, they would be quite
recruited and altogether new men. In such an advantageous
position, by throwing up an entrenchment to cover Inverness,
there was no reason to fear an immediate attack from the Duke
of Cumberland, should he examine our position with attention;
but if the Duke ventured to attack us notwithstanding, he could
not fail to pay dear for his temerity. We might, therefore, cal-
culate on remaining tranquil in this position for some days, and
the delay would give time to those who were absent on leave to
join the army. The Prince, however, would listen to no advice,
and resolved on giving battle, let the consequences be what
they might.

The ground in the hollow, between the Castle of Culloden
and an enclosure on our right, being marshy and covered with
water which reached half-way up the leg, was well chosen to
protect us from the cavalry of the enemy. The English were
drawn up in three lines, but we had much difficulty in forming
two. Our second line was composed of the Irish pickets, with
the regiments of Royal Scots, Kilmarnock, Lord Lewis
Gordon, the Duke of Perth, Lord Ogilvie, Glenbucket, and
John Roy Stuart, of which the two last, and that of Lord
Kilmarnock, consisted only of from two to three hundred men
each. When the English army was on a line with the enclosure,
about six or eight hundred yards from the eminence behind the
swamp, our army descended with great rapidity into the marshy
ground and charged the enemy sword in hand. The Prince,
who remained on the eminence with the picket of Fitzjames,
out of reach of the musketry of the enemy, observed them

employed in throwing down the walls of the enclosure to attack us in flank, and immediately sent repeated orders to Lord George Murray, whilst he was at the head of the first line and ready to fall upon the enemy, to place some troops in the enclosure and prevent the manoeuvre of the English, which could not fail to prove fatal to us.* Lord George paid no attention to this order, and the English, having finished throwing down the walls of the enclosure, entered with two regiments of cavalry and four pieces of artillery, which they fired with grape-shot on our right wing. Their fire, from the circumstance of their being quite close to our right, was so terrible that it literally swept away whole ranks at once.

From the inequality of this marshy ground, our right and centre came first up with the enemy, our first line advancing a little obliquely; but, overpowered by a murderous fire in front and flank, our right could not maintain its ground and was obliged to give way, whilst our centre had already broken the enemy's first line and attacked the second. The left wing, where I was with Scothouse, was not twenty paces from the enemy, who gave their first fire at the moment the flight began to become general, which spread from the right to the left of our army with the rapidity of lightning. What a spectacle of horror! The same Highlanders, who had advanced to the charge like lions, with bold, determined countenances, were in an instant seen flying like trembling cowards in the greatest disorder. It may be said of the attack of the Highlanders, that it bears great resemblance to that of the French; that it is a flame, the violence of which is more to be dreaded than the duration. No troops, however excellent, are possessed of qualities which will render them constantly invincible.

It was evident our destruction would become inevitable, if the English got possession of the enclosure. The Prince saw

*A few troops were stationed in the enclosure but they were soon overcome.

this from the eminence where he was posted, and sent his aide-de-camp six or seven times, ordering Lord George to take possession of it. He saw that his orders were not executed, but yet he never quitted his place on the eminence. This was a critical moment when he ought to have displayed the courage of a grenadier, by immediately advancing to put himself at the head of his army, and commanding himself those manoeuvres which he wished to be executed. He would never have experienced disobedience on the part of his subjects who had exposed their lives and fortunes to establish him on the throne of his ancestors, and who would have shed for him the last drop of their blood. There are occasions when a general ought to expose his person, and not remain beyond the reach of musketry, and surely there never was a more pressing occasion for disregarding a few shots than the one in question, as the gain or loss of the battle depended on it. In the desperate expedition on which he had entered, though it was proper that he should guard against danger, he ought to have done so in a manner which showed that life or death was equally indifferent to him, conducting himself with valour and prudence, according to circumstances. But he was surrounded by Irish confidants, whose baseness of soul corresponded to the obscurity of their birth. The natives of Ireland are generally supposed, in England, to have a great confusion of ideas, and they are in general very bad counsellors. But the Prince blindly adopted their opinions.

As far as I could distinguish, at the distance of twenty paces, the English appeared to be drawn up in six ranks, the three first being on their knees, and keeping up a terrible running fire on us. My unfortunate friend Scothouse was killed by my side, but I was not so deeply affected at the moment of his fall as I have been ever since. It would almost seem as if the Power that presides over the lives of men in battles marks out the most deserving for destruction and spares those who are more unworthy. Military men, susceptible of friendship, are much to be

The Battle of Culloden

pitied. The melancholy fate of my friends has often cost me many a tear, and left on my heart an indelible impression of pain and regret. Mr Macdonald of Keppoch, who had been absent on leave with his clan, having made great haste to join the Prince, arrived at the moment of the charge, in time to take his station in the first line with his clan, where he was instantly killed. He was a gentleman of uncommon merit, and his death was universally lamented.*

As the Highlanders were completely exhausted with hunger, fatigue and the want of sleep, our defeat did not at all surprise me; I was only astonished to see them behave so well. If our right could only have maintained its ground three minutes longer, the English army, which was very much shaken, would have been still more so by the shock of our left wing, which was yet at the distance of from fifteen to twenty paces from the enemy, when the disorder began on the right. And if our centre, which had pierced the first line, had been properly supported, it is highly probable that the English would have been soon put to flight. There were about twelve hundred men killed† upon the field of battle, and of that number there were as many of the enemy as of the Highlanders. Thus our loss was by no means considerable.

The right wing of our army retreated towards the river Nairn and met in their way a body of English cavalry, which appeared as much embarrassed as the Highlanders; but the English commander very wisely opened a way for them in the centre and allowed them to pass at the distance of a pistol-shot, without attempting to molest them or to take prisoners. One

*The Macdonalds considered themselves bitterly insulted when they were stationed on the left of the army rather than in their usual position on the right. This may have been partly the cause of their turning tail before they even came to grips with the enemy. Their commander was so mortified that he advanced alone.

†The rebel losses were 1,000 killed and 500 taken prisoner. On the government side the total loss was about 300.

officer only of this body, wishing to take a Highlander prisoner, advanced a few paces to seize him, but the Highlander brought him down with his sword and killed him on the spot. Not satisfied with this, he stopped long enough to take possession of his watch, and then decamped with the booty. The English commander remained a quiet spectator of the scene, renewed his orders to his men not to quit their ranks, and could not help smiling and secretly wishing the Highlander might escape, on account of his boldness, without appearing to lament the fate of the officer who had disobeyed his orders. If this body of cavalry had not acted so prudently, they would instantly have been cut to pieces. It is extremely dangerous in a defeat to attempt to cut off the vanquished from all means of escape.

Our left, which fled towards Inverness, was less fortunate. Having been pursued by the English cavalry, the road from Culloden to that town was everywhere strewed with dead bodies. The Duke of Cumberland had the cruelty to allow our wounded to remain amongst the dead on the field of battle, stripped of their clothes, from Wednesday, the day of our unfortunate engagement, till three o'clock in the afternoon of Friday, when he sent detachments to kill all those who were still in life. A great many, who had resisted the effects of the continual rains which fell all that time, were then dispatched. He ordered a barn, which contained many of the wounded Highlanders, to be set on fire and the soldiers stationed round it drove back with fixed bayonets the unfortunate men who attempted to save themselves, into the flames, burning them alive in this horrible manner, as if they had not been fellow-creatures.

This sanguinary Duke was obliged to have an act of indemnity from the British Parliament, for these and a number of similar acts which he had committed in violation of the laws of Great Britain. Cruelty is a proof of a base and cowardly disposition.

As soon as the Prince saw his army begin to give way, he made his escape with a few horsemen of Fitzjames's picket. Some hours after the battle, Lord Elcho found him in a cabin, beside the river Nairn, surrounded by Irish and without a single Scotsman near him, in a state of complete dejection, without the least hopes of being able to re-establish his affairs. He had given himself altogether up to the pernicious counsels of Sheridan and the other Irish, who governed him as they pleased, and had abandoned every other project but that of escaping to France as soon as possible. Lord Elcho represented to him that this check was nothing, as was really the case, and exerted himself to the utmost to persuade him to think only of rallying his army, putting himself at its head, and trying once more the fortune of war, as the disaster might be easily repaired. But he was insensible to all that his Lordship could suggest, and utterly disregarded his advice.

However critical our situation, the Prince ought not to have despaired. On occasions when everything is to be feared, we ought to lay aside fear; when we are surrounded with dangers, no danger ought to alarm us. With the best plans we may fail in our enterprises, but the firmness we display in misfortune is the noblest ornament of virtue. This is the manner in which a Prince who, with an unexampled rashness, had landed in Scotland with only seven men, ought to have conducted himself.

We were masters of the passes between Ruthven and Inverness, which gave us sufficient time to assemble our adherents. The clan of Macpherson of Clunie, consisting of five hundred very brave men, besides many other Highlanders who had not been able to reach Inverness before the battle, joined us at Ruthven. Our numbers increased every moment, and I am thoroughly convinced that, in the course of eight days, we should have had a more powerful army than ever, capable of re-establishing without delay the state of our affairs and of avenging the barbarous cruelties of the Duke of Cumberland. But the Prince was inexorable and immoveable in his resolution of abandoning his enterprise, and terminating in this inglorious manner an expedition, the rapid progress of which had fixed the attention of all Europe.

Our separation at Ruthven was truly affecting. We bade one another an eternal adieu. No one could tell whether the scaffold would not be his fate. The Highlanders gave vent to their grief in wild howlings and lamentations; the tears flowed down their cheeks when they thought that their country was now at the discretion of the Duke of Cumberland and on the point of being plundered, whilst they and their children would be reduced to slavery and plunged, without resource, into a state of remediless distress.

An accident which took place at Inverness, some days after the battle, might have proved very advantageous to us if the Prince had joined us at Ruthven. A young gentleman of the name of Forbes, related to Lord Forbes and a cadet in an English regiment, having abandoned his colours to join the Prince, had the misfortune to be taken prisoner and was hanged at Inverness without any distinction, amongst the other deserters. Whilst the body of Forbes was still suspended from the gibbet, a brutal and vulgar English officer plunged his sword into his body, and swore that 'all his countrymen were traitors and rebels like himself'. A Scots officer, who heard the impertinence of this Englishman, immediately drew his sword and demanded satisfaction for the insult done to his country, and, whilst they fought, all the officers took part in the quarrel and swords were drawn in every direction. At the same time, the soldiers, of their own accord, beat to arms and drew up along the streets, the Scots on one side and the English on the other, beginning a very warm combat with fixed bayonets. The Duke of Cumberland happening to be out of town, information was immediately conveyed to him, and he hastened to the scene of action before this warfare had made much progress. He addressed himself immediately to the Scots, whom he endeavoured to mollify by the high compliments he paid them. He told them that whenever he had had the honour of commanding them, he had always experienced their fidelity and attachment to his family, as well as their courage and exemplary conduct; and at length he succeeded in appeasing them.

Thus did Prince Charles begin his enterprise with seven men and abandon it at a moment when he might have been at the head of as many thousands. He preferred to wander up and down the mountains alone, exposed every instant to be taken and put to death by detachments of the English troops, sent by the Duke of Cumberland in pursuit of him—who followed him closely, often passed quite near him, and from whom he escaped as if by miracle—to putting himself at the head of a body of brave and determined men, of whose fidelity and attachment he was secure, and all of whom would have shed the last drop of their blood in his defence. Indeed this was now the only means of saving themselves from the scaffold and their families from being slaughtered by a furious, enraged and barbarous soldiery.

The Highlands are full of precipices and passes through mountains, where only one person can proceed at a time and where a thousand men can defend themselves for years against a hundred thousand, and as it abounds with horned cattle, of which they sell above one hundred thousand yearly to the English, provisions would not have been wanting. But it would only have been necessary to adopt this partisan-warfare as a last resource, for I am morally certain that, in the course of ten or twelve days, we should have been in a condition to return to Inverness and fight the Duke of Cumberland on equal terms. Whenever I reflect on this subject, I am always astonished that Lord George Murray and the other chiefs of clans did not resolve to carry on this mountain-warfare themselves, for their

I

own defence, as nothing can be more certain than what was
said by a celebrated author, that in a revolt, 'when we draw the
sword we ought to throw away the scabbard'. There is no
medium; we must conquer or die. This would have spared
much of the blood which was afterwards shed on the scaffold in
England, and would have prevented the almost total extermina-
tion of the race of Highlanders which has since taken place,
either from the policy of the English government, the emigration of their families to the colonies, or from the numerous
Highland regiments which have been raised, and which have
been often cut to pieces during the last war.*

For several months Prince Charles was hotly pursued by detachments of English troops, and they were frequently so very
near to him, that he had scarcely quitted a place before they
arrived at it. Sometimes he was wholly surrounded by them.
The Duke of Cumberland never failed to say to the com-
manders of these detachments, at the moment of their departure, 'Make no prisoners: you understand me.' They had
particular instructions to stab the Prince if he fell into their
hands, but Divine Wisdom frustrated the atrocious and barbarous designs and pursuits of the sanguinary Duke, whose
officers and their detachments—his executioners—inflicted
more cruelties on the brave but unfortunate Highlanders than
would have been committed by the most ferocious savages of
Canada. The generous and heroic action of Mr Roderick
Mackenzie contributed greatly to save the Prince from those
blood-thirsty assassins.

Mr Mackenzie, a gentleman of good family in Scotland, had
served during the whole expedition in the life-guards of Prince
Charles. He was of the Prince's size and, to those who were not
accustomed to see them together, might seem to resemble him a
little. Mackenzie happened to be in a cabin with the Prince and

*The Seven Years War (1756–63).

two or three other persons when, all of a sudden, they received information that they were surrounded by detachments of English troops advancing from every point, as if they had received positive information that the Prince was in this cabin. The Prince was asleep at this moment and was awakened for the purpose of being informed of his melancholy fate, namely that it was morally impossible for him to save his life. He answered, 'Then we must die like brave men, with swords in our hands.' 'No, my Prince,' replied Mackenzie, 'resources still remain. I will take your name and face one of these detachments. I know what my fate will be, but whilst I keep it employed, Your Royal Highness will have time to escape.' Mackenzie darted forward with fury, sword in hand, against a detachment of fifty men, and on falling covered with wounds, he exclaimed aloud, 'You know not what you have done! I am your Prince, whom you have killed!' after which he instantly expired. They cut off his head and carried it without delay to the Duke of Cumberland, nobody doubting that it was the head of Prince Charles. The barbarous Duke, having now, as he thought, obtained the head of the Prince, the great object of his wishes, set off next day for London with this head packed up, in his post-chaise.

The depositions of several persons in London, who affirmed that this was the head of Prince Charles, had the good effect of rendering the English less vigilant and less active in their pursuits. Before that event, they had formed a chain from Inverary to Inverness, and the Prince had frequently escaped with great risk, having been obliged to cross the chain between their detachments. Mr Morison, his valet-de-chambre, was then in the prison of Carlisle, condemned to death, and the government dispatched a messenger to suspend the execution of the sentence and bring him to London to declare, upon oath, whether this really were the head of Prince Charles. But Mr Morison, having been attacked on the road with a violent fever accompanied with delirium, remained in bed at the messenger's house, where he continued a prisoner for fifteen days after his arrival in London. When he began to recover, the head was in such a putrid state that it was judged unnecessary to examine him, as it was no longer possible to distinguish any of the features. Mr Morison obtained his pardon and repaired immediately to France, where he still lives.

At length the Prince embarked on the 17th of September, on board a vessel which Mr Welsh of Nantes had fitted out and sent to Scotland for the express purpose of saving him. In the month of October he landed at Morlaix, having escaped death a thousand times during the space of five months, and having exposed himself to a thousand times more danger than if he had supported his cause with courage and perseverance, at the head of his faithful Highlanders, as long as he could hope to make head against the English. He should only as a last resource have embraced the resolution of skulking and running about the Highlands without attendants, after the passes had been forced and all possibility of opposing the enemy was destroyed. But our situation was not desperate. All that we can say is that this Prince entered on his expedition rashly and without foreseeing the personal dangers to which he was about to expose himself; that in carrying it on he always took care not to expose his person to the fire of the enemy; and that he abandoned it at a time when he had a thousand times more reason to hope for success than when he left Paris to undertake it.

The battle of Culloden (which was lost on the 16th of April rather from a series of mistakes on our part than any skilful manoeuvre of the Duke of Cumberland), by terminating the expedition of Prince Charles, prepared a scene of unparalleled horrors for his partisans. The ruin of many of the most illustrious families in Scotland immediately followed our defeat. The scaffolds of England were, for a long time, deluged every day with the blood of Scottish gentlemen and peers, whose executions served as a spectacle for the amusement of the

English populace, naturally of a cruel and barbarous disposition, whilst the confiscation of their estates reduced their families to beggary. Those who had the good luck to make their escape into foreign countries were consoled for the loss of their property in escaping from a tragical death by the hands of the executioner. They considered themselves as very fortunate withal, for His Most Christian Majesty did not merely grant an asylum to the unfortunate Scots who were the victims of their attachment to their legitimate Prince, but set apart a fund for their subsistence of forty thousand livres a year, which was distributed to them in pensions. These pensions have always been regularly paid, but the intentions of His Majesty, who destined this fund exclusively for the Scots who were followers of Prince Charles, have not been attended to in its distribution.

As soon as the Duke of Cumberland was certain, from the total dispersion of the Highlanders at Ruthven, that he had no reason to fear their re-appearance with arms in their hands, he divided his army into different detachments which were ordered to scour the Highlands in order to pillage the houses and take prisoners. These detachments, acting as executioners of the Duke of Cumberland, committed the most horrible cruelties, burning the castles of the chiefs of clans, violating their wives and daughters and making it their amusement to hang up the unfortunate Highlanders who happened to fall into their hands.

Orders were at the same time transmitted to all the towns and villages along the two arms of the sea between Inverness and Edinburgh, to stop any person without a passport from the Duke of Cumberland or the magistrates of Edinburgh. They were also sent to all the seaports of Great Britain, prohibiting all masters of merchant vessels from receiving any person on board without a passport, or contributing in any manner to the escape of a rebel (a name they had given to us as we were vanquished, while we should have been heroes had we succeeded) under pain of high-treason and of being liable to the same punishment as those who had taken arms. The Duke of Cumberland at the same time detached his cavalry into the Lowlands to seize all those who might present themselves without passports to cross the first arm of the sea, with orders to send out continual patrols along the coast and to search all the towns and villages in the neighbourhood of the sea. In consequence of all these arrangements, it was almost impossible to escape the fury of this sanguinary Duke who, on account of his excesses and cruelties, unheard of among civilized nations, was held in contempt by all respectable persons in England, even by those who were in no manner partisans of the house of Stuart. Ever afterwards he was known in London by the appellation of 'the Butcher'.

VIII

AS for myself, my friendship for the unfortunate Macdonald of Scothouse, who was killed by my side at the battle of Culloden, had induced me to advance to the charge with his regiment. We were on the left of our army and at the distance of about twenty paces from the enemy, when the rout began to become general. Almost at the same instant that I saw Scothouse fall—to add to the horror of the scene—I perceived all the Highlanders around me turning their backs to fly. I remained for a time motionless, and lost in astonishment; then, in a rage, I discharged my blunderbuss and pistols at the enemy and immediately endeavoured to save myself like the rest. But having charged on foot and in boots I was so overcome by the marshy ground, the water on which reached to the middle of the leg, that instead of running I could scarcely walk. I had left my servant, Robertson, with my horses, on the eminence about six hundred yards behind us where the Prince remained during the battle, with orders to remain near the Prince's servants, that I might easily know where to find my horses in case of need. My first object on retreating was to turn my eyes towards the eminence to discover Robertson; but it was to no purpose. I neither saw the Prince, nor his servants, nor anyone on horseback. They had all gone off and were already out of sight. I saw nothing but the most horrible of all spectacles; the field of battle, from the right to the left of our army covered with Highlanders dispersed and flying as fast as they could to save themselves.

Being no longer able to keep myself on my legs, and the enemy always advancing very slowly but redoubling their fire, my mind was agitated and undecided whether I should throw away my life or surrender a prisoner, which was a thousand times worse than death on the field of battle. All at once I perceived a horse without a rider about thirty paces before me. The idea of being yet able to escape, gave me fresh strength and served as a spur to me. I ran and laid hold of the bridle which was fast in the hand of a man lying on the ground, whom I supposed dead. What was my surprise, when the cowardly poltroon, who was suffering from nothing but fear, dared to remain in the most horrible fire to dispute the horse with me at twenty paces from the enemy? All my menaces could not induce him to quit the bridle. Whilst we were disputing, a discharge from a cannon loaded with grape-shot fell at our feet and covered us with mud, without, however, producing any effect upon this singular individual, who obstinately persisted in retaining the horse. Fortunately for me, Finlay Cameron, an officer in Lochiel's regiment, a youth of twenty years of age, six feet high, and very strong and vigorous, happened to pass near us. I called on him to assist me. 'Ah! Finlay,' said I, 'this fellow will not give me up the horse.' Finlay flew to me like lightning, immediately presented his pistol to the head of this man and threatened to blow out his brains if he hesitated a moment to let go the bridle. The fellow, who had the appearance of a servant, at length yielded and took to his heels. Having obtained the horse, I attempted to mount him several times; but all my efforts were ineffectual as I was without strength and completely exhausted. I called again on poor Finlay, though he was already some paces from me, to assist me to mount. He returned, took me in his arms with as much ease as if I had been a child and threw me on the horse like a loaded sack, giving the horse at the same time a heavy blow to make him set off with me. Then, wishing that I might have the good fortune to make my escape, he bounded off like a roe, and was in a moment out of sight. We were hardly more than fifteen or twenty paces from the enemy when he quitted me. As soon as I found myself at the distance of thirty or forty paces, I endeavoured to set myself right on the horse, put my feet in the stirrups and rode off as fast as the wretched animal could carry me.

I was too much indebted to Finlay Cameron not to endeavour continually to ascertain his fate; but all my enquiries
were in vain. His conduct on this occasion was the more noble
and generous as I never had any particular intimacy with him.

There is every probability that I also saved the life of the
poltroon who held the horse, in rousing him out of his panic-
fear, for in less than two minutes the English army would have
passed over him. The cowardice of this man has often furnished
me with matter for reflection, and I am thoroughly convinced
that for one brave man who perishes in routs there are ten
cowards. The greatness of the danger is increased in the eyes of
a coward; it blinds him, deprives him of reflection and renders
him incapable of reasoning with himself respecting his position.
He loses the faculty of thinking and the presence of mind which
is necessary in great dangers and, seeing everything through a
false medium, his stupor costs him both his honour and his life.
The man who is truly firm, brave and determined, sees all the
dangers which surround him, but his presence of mind enables
him to see at the same time the means of extricating himself; and
thus, if any resource remains, he will turn it to account.

As soon as I was out of the reach of the dreadful fire of the
infantry, I stopped to breathe a little and to deliberate as to the
resolution I should adopt and the route I should follow. Whilst
our army lay at Inverness, I had frequently been on parties of
pleasure at the castle of Mr Grant of Rothiemurchus, which is
situated in the midst of the mountains about six leagues from
that town. This worthy man, who was then about fifty years of
age and a delightful companion, took a strong liking for me and
frequently assured me of his friendship, as did also his eldest
son with whom I had been at school, but who was in the service
of King George. The father was a partisan of the house of
Stuart, but from prudential motives, did not openly declare
himself; and both he and his vassals remained neutral during
the whole of our expedition. This castle is situated in one of the

most beautiful valleys imaginable, a valley which equals any thing in the most romantic descriptions of the poets. It is on the banks of a very beautiful river, the Spey, which winds through a plain about a quarter of a league broad and two leagues long. Round this plain the mountains rise behind each other in the form of an amphitheatre, the tops of some of them being covered with wood while others are covered with the most beautiful verdure. It seemed as if nature had exhausted herself in forming this charming retreat, for every conceivable description of rural beauty has been lavished on it with the utmost profusion. It enchanted me more than any place I ever saw.

During the two months that our army remained at Inverness on our return from England, I passed as much of my time as I possibly could at this delightful place, which I always quitted with regret. I happened to be there when we received information that the Duke of Cumberland had crossed the Spey in the direction of Elgin, and that he was advancing to Inverness. Immediately I set off to join our army, but not without regret at quitting so pleasant a place and the agreeable society of Rothiemurchus, a most amiable, mild, honourable and accomplished gentleman, possessed of an even temper, great natural gaiety and wit, and a great fund of good sense and judgment. On taking leave of him, he clasped me in his arms, embraced me tenderly with tears in his eyes and said, 'My dear boy, should your affairs take an unfortunate turn, which may be the case, come straight to my house as a hiding-place, and I will answer for your safety with my life.' His mountains being, in reality, a secure asylum against all the researches of the English troops, I resolved, without hesitation, to take the road to Rothiemurchus, which was on our right from the field of battle, but I had not advanced a hundred paces when I saw a body of English cavalry before me which barred the way. I then turned back, taking the road to Inverness, which I followed till I saw from an eminence that the bulk of our army were throwing them-

selves in that direction; from which I judged that the principal
pursuit of the enemy would be along that way. I therefore
quitted that road also and proceeded straight across the fields,
without any other design than that of getting as far from the
enemy as possible.

On reaching the banks of the river Ness, a quarter of a
league higher up than the town of Inverness and nearly the
same distance from the field of battle, I stopped to consider
what route I should take, as the cavalry of the enemy on the
road to Rothiemurchus had totally disconcerted me. Whilst I
was agitated and tormented from my uncertainty, never having
been in this part of the mountains, I suddenly heard a brisk
firing in the town which lasted a few minutes. As in misfortune
the imagination is often filled with delusive hopes, I at first
thought that it might proceed from the Highlanders who were
defending the town against the English, and I bitterly regretted
that I had quitted the Inverness road. I recollected that there
was a footpath which led to the town by the banks of the river
along which I had several times passed in fishing excursions.
Having discovered this road, I immediately took it without
giving myself time to reflect that the place was not capable of
any defence, being merely surrounded by a wall proper only
for an enclosure. I had not proceeded a hundred paces before
I met a Highlander, coming from the town, who assured me
that the English had entered without meeting with any resistance. He informed me at the same time that the whole road
from the field of battle to Inverness was covered with dead
bodies, and that the streets were likewise covered with dead,
as the bridge at the end of the principal street had been immediately blocked up by the fugitives. I was not sorry to find that
my first conjectures were unfortunately but too true, for, in
following the road to the town, I should have been of the
number of these bodies. I returned then, with my heart more
oppressed than ever and plunged in the greatest grief.

As all my hopes were vanished I thought only of removing as far as possible from the fatal spot. The Highlander informed me that he was going to Fort Augustus, a small place about thirty miles from Inverness, which our army had demolished some time before, so I took the high road under his guidance and proposed that we should proceed together to that place. We reached Fort Augustus at midnight without finding a single hut on our way, and I alighted at a very small cottage, which had the name of a public-house, and the landlady of which had nothing to give me but a piece of oaten bread and some whisky, with a little hay for my horse. This last gave me the most pleasure, for although I had tasted nothing during the last twenty-four hours, the terrible vicissitudes which I had experienced in the most cruel and unfortunate day I had yet known, completely took from me all appetite and all disposition to eat. Being very much fatigued in body and mind, I slept for two or three hours on a seat near the fire, for as to beds there were none in the house.

I never ceased, however, from looking upon Rothiemurchus as my only resource, but his castle being situated to the south of Inverness, when I was at Fort Augustus, I was at a greater distance from it than when I left the field of battle. I quitted the cabin, therefore, before day, having found another guide who conducted me to Garviemore, twelve miles south from Fort Augustus. The next day I proceeded to Ruthven in Badenoch, which is only two leagues distant from Rothiemurchus.

Hitherto I had fallen in with no person who could give me any news, and I was therefore agreeably surprised on finding that this little town had by chance become the rendezvous for a great part of our army, for no place had been fixed on as a rallying-point in case of a defeat. In an instant I was surrounded by a number of my companions, who eagerly announced to me that a great part of our army was at Ruthven and its neighbourhood; that the Highlanders were in the best disposition for

taking their revenge, and waited with impatience the return of
an aide-de-camp whom Lord George Murray had sent to the
Prince to receive his orders, expecting to be led to battle. I
never felt more intense joy than on this occasion, and can only
compare my situation to that of a sick person who, after languishing for a long time, suddenly finds himself restored to a
state of perfect health. Having learned that there was no ac-
commodation at Ruthven—the greater part of our people being
obliged to sleep in the fields—I did not alight from my horse,
but after making every possible enquiry for Finlay Cameron, to
express my gratitude to him, without obtaining any information as to what had befallen him, I proceeded on to Killihuntly,
about a quarter of a league from Ruthven.

When our army retreated to the north of Scotland, I had
stopped at the mansion of Mr Gordon of Killihuntly, where I
passed several days very agreeably and received many civilities.
This amiable family now received me in the most friendly
manner, and I found Lord and Lady Ogilvie there with several
other friends. As I had tasted nothing for forty hours but a crust
of oaten bread and some whisky, I did great honour to the
good cheer of the lady of the house; and as I had been a stranger
to a bed since we left Inverness to meet the enemy, I went immediately to rest with a mind at ease, and slept eighteen hours
without waking. Next day, after dinner, I went to Ruthven, but
as the aide-de-camp had not yet returned, there was nothing to
be learned there and I returned to sleep at Killihuntly. I was de-
lighted to see the gaiety of the Highlanders, who seemed to
have returned from a ball rather than from a defeat.

As I passed the night impatiently and with uneasiness, I rose
early next morning and went again to Ruthven. On entering
the place I was immediately struck with the gloom and melancholy painted on the countenance of every person I met, and I
soon learned that the cause of it was but too well founded. The
first officer I fell in with told me that the aide-de-camp had

returned and that the only answer he had brought from the Prince was, 'Let every one seek the means of escape as well as he can.' A sad and heart-breaking answer for the brave men who had sacrificed themselves for him.

I returned immediately to Killihuntly with a sad and heavy heart to take leave of my friends and thank them for their civilities. The lady offered me an asylum in their mountains, which are very solitary and difficult of access, telling me that she would cause a hut to be constructed for me in the most re- mote situation where she would take care to lay in every kind of provisions, that I should not want for books, and that she would give me a flock of seven or eight sheep to take care of. She added that, the place proposed being at a mile's distance from the castle on the banks of a stream abounding in trout, I might amuse myself by fishing, and she would often take a walk in that direction to see her shepherd.

The project pleased me very much at first, for my misfor- tunes had suddenly metamorphosed me into a philosopher, and I should have consented to pass the whole of the rest of my days in solitude, if my mind had been at ease and free from anxiety. Besides, it was now the beginning of summer, and the natural beauties of the country, the water-falls, the mountain-glens, the rivers, lakes and woods, everything in short, had irresistible at- tractions. Indeed, the grandeur and magnificence which nature there displayed could hardly fail to produce a strong impres- sion on the most insensible minds. A thousand wild graces left all the beauties of art far behind them. A poet or painter would have selected such a spot as an inspired abode calculated to give birth to those ideas which never can be effaced from the mind of man.

Besides, the amiable society of Mr and Mrs Gordon who then showed so much friendship for me, led me to think I could not do better. But before coming to a decision, I wished to see my good friend Rothiemurchus and consult with him as to the possibility of finding means of embarking for a foreign country, that I might not remain eternally between life and death. After dinner I went, therefore, to Rothiemurchus, which is situated at the other extremity of this beautiful valley and nearly two leagues from Killihuntly, but the father was not at home. He had gone to Inverness as soon as he heard the news of our defeat, to pay his court to the Duke of Cumberland, rather from fear of mischief which this barbarous Duke might do to him than from any attachment to the house of Hanover. However I found his son there, as also Gordon of Park, lieutenant-colonel of Lord Lewis Gordon, Gordon of Cobairdie, his brother and Gordon of Abachie.

Young Rothiemurchus advised me very much to surrender myself a prisoner to the Duke of Cumberland on account of the difficulty, or rather impossibility, of effecting my escape, alleging at the same time that those who first surrendered could hardly fail to obtain their pardon. He added that he had just returned from Inverness, whither he had conducted Lord Balmerino who followed his advice in surrendering himself a prisoner. I by no means relished the perfidious advice of my old school-fellow, who was of a very different character from that of his father. I replied that I trembled at the very idea of seeing myself ironed in a dungeon, that I should preserve my liberty as long as I could, and when I could no longer avoid falling into the hands of the Duke of Cumberland, he might then do with me whatever he liked and I should then meet my fate with resignation. The unfortunate Lord Balmerino was beheaded at London during the time I was concealed there, and died with an astonishing constancy and bravery, worthy of an ancient Roman.

The servant of Rothiemurchus told us that, having gone over the field of battle, there appeared among the dead as many English as Highlanders, and it gave us some consolation to think that they had not obtained an easy victory.

Gordon of Park, his brother and Abachie, having resolved to go to their estates in Banffshire, about ten or twelve leagues to the south of Rothiemurchus, proposed that I should accompany them. I consented the more willingly, as my brother-in-law Rollo, now a peer of Scotland, was settled in the sea-port of Banff, where he had the inspection of merchant-ships, in virtue of an office lately obtained by him from the government. I hoped, through his means, to find an opportunity of escaping abroad. Thus situated, I abandoned without difficulty the project of becoming a shepherd to Mrs Gordon, which would have kept me too long in a state of uncertainty as to my fate. Besides, as I was a stranger in the Highlands and totally unacquainted with the language of the country, I was the more induced to place myself under the auspices of Gordon of Park.

After staying two or three days at Rothiemurchus, we all set off and, having proceeded some miles, slept at the house of one of their friends, near a mountain called Cairngorm.

These gentlemen yielded to the entreaties of their friend to stay a day at his house, and I was not displeased at it. Forgetting our disasters for a moment, I rose at an early hour and flew immediately to the mountains among the herdsmen, where I found some pretty and beautiful topazes, two of which, sufficiently large to serve for seals, I afterwards presented to the Duke of York,* at Paris. When I returned to dinner, my friends seeing me enter with a large bag of flints, burst into a loud laugh, and Gordon of Park exhorted me very seriously to think rather of saving myself from the gallows than of collecting pebbles. My mind was, however, as much occupied as theirs with our unfortunate situation, and the scaffold was as deeply imprinted on my imagination. But I knew, at the same time, that the possession of a few stones could not hasten my destiny, if it were my fate to be hanged, whilst the search after them

*Prince Charles's brother.

dissipated, for a moment, those ideas which entirely engrossed my companions in misfortune.

We reached Banffshire on the fourth day after our departure from Rothiemurchus, when it became necessary for us to separate, as the people were all Calvinists and declared enemies of the house of Stuart. We had lodged the preceding night at the house of a Mr Stuart, a Presbyterian minister but a very respectable man and secretly in the interest of Prince Charles. On rising in the morning, I exchanged my laced Highland dress with his servant for an old labourer's dress, quite ragged and exhaling a pestilential odour. This, according to all appearance, had for several years only been used when he cleaned the stables of his master, for it smelt so strongly of dung as to be absolutely infectious at a distance. Having made a complete exchange with him, even to our shoes and stockings, each of us found our advantage in it—particularly myself, as these rags were to contribute to save my life. Thus metamorphosed, we took leave of each other, everyone following a different road. Gordon of Park advised me to pass the night at his castle of Park, and I accepted his offer the more readily as, being only a league and a half from Banff, it was conveniently situated for an interview with my brother-in-law Rollo. I was not, however, without fear of meeting some detachment sent out to surprise Mr Gordon who was nearly related to the Duke of Gordon, and which might have made me a prisoner in his stead. I found in this mansion his cousin Mrs Menzie, a very amiable, sprightly and sensible lady, with whom I had passed some time very delightfully at the house of Mr Duff, provost of Banff, whose family was one of the most agreeable and respectable I ever knew in the whole course of my life, and whose charming society I had quitted with the greatest possible regret to rejoin our army at Inverness.

Mrs Menzie informed me that there were four hundred English soldiers in the town of Banff and strongly advised me

K

not to expose myself by going there; but as I placed all my hopes of effecting my escape to a foreign country on an interview with my brother-in-law, I determined to go, and set out next day on foot about nine o'clock in the evening, leaving my horse till my return. On entering the town I met a number

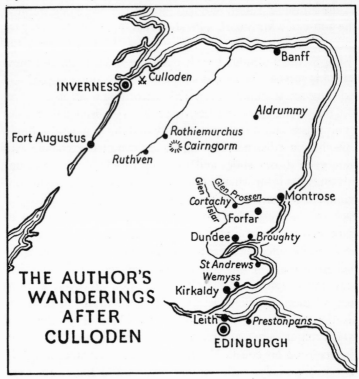

THE AUTHOR'S
WANDERINGS
AFTER
CULLODEN

of soldiers who paid no attention to me, which was a very favourable omen of the success of my disguise as a beggar. Indeed, my clothes were so bad that the lowest peasant would have been ashamed to wear them. My blood boiled in my veins at the sight of the soldiers, whom I considered the authors of all the trouble and distress which I began to feel, and I could hardly prevent myself from casting at them looks expressive of rage and indignation. I proceeded, however, on my way, invoking the Supreme Being with much earnestness to favour us with one single opportunity of taking vengeance on them for their cruelties at Culloden. I should then die tranquil and satisfied.

I went straight to the house of Mr Duff, where I had been so agreeably entertained a short time before. He was a secret partisan of the Prince but, being prudent and discreet, he only avowed his principles to his particular friends. He was one of the most amiable men in the world, endowed with every possible good quality and possessed of true merit: he was of an equal mind, of a gay and sprightly disposition and had a great share of good sense, judgment, talents and discernment. Mrs Duff resembled her husband in everything, and their two daughters, the youngest of whom was a great beauty, were the exact copies of their father and mother. There was but one way of thinking in Mr Duff's house, and I shall regret the loss of their delicious society as long as I live. As the servant-maid who opened the door did not know me on account of my disguise, I told her that I was the bearer of a letter to her master which I was charged to deliver into his own hands, and I therefore desired her to inform him of it. Mr Duff came down stairs and did not recognise me at first any more than his maid had done, but having fixed his eyes on me for some moments, his surprise was succeeded by a flood of tears. He strongly exhorted the maid to fidelity and secrecy. As Mrs Duff and her daughters were in bed, he conducted me into a room and immediately sent his maid in quest of my brother-in-law who happened to be from home and who could not be found, notwithstanding every search was made for him. As the neighbourhood of soldiers was too alarming to allow me to remain tranquil, it had not been my intention to sleep in Banff, if I could have seen my brother-in-law without delay, and ascertained if I had anything to hope from his services at a moment so critical for me. I therefore resolved to leave Banff before day and to return to Mr Gordon's house, and when, after Mr Duff had retired to rest at one o'clock in the morning, I went to bed, I was unable to close an eye.

I rose as soon as day began to appear and put on my rags. Whilst I was seated in an arm-chair, with my eyes fixed on the fire, pensive, melancholy, and absorbed in a train of reflections which my situation suggested to me in abundance, the servant-maid suddenly entered my chamber and told me that I was undone, as the court-yard was filled with soldiers come to seize me. Less important intelligence would have been enough to rouse me out of my reverie. I immediately flew to the window, when I saw in reality the soldiers which the maid had told me of. Having thus ocular demonstration of my misfortune, I returned to my chair perfectly resigned, and considered myself as a man who was soon to end his days. I instantly conjectured that the maid must have betrayed me, having some soldier for her sweetheart, a common enough circumstance. One feeble ray of hope alone remained, which was to open a passage for myself through the soldiers with a pistol in each hand, and I kept my eyes steadfastly fixed on the door of my chamber in order to spring on the soldiers *like a lion* the moment they should appear. A melancholy resource! I had little hopes of success, but I had no alternative.

Having passed about a quarter of an hour in the most violent agitation, the door of my chamber at length opened and I sprang forward with precipitation to the attack. But what was my surprise when, in place of the soldiers, I saw the beautiful and adorable Miss Duff the younger burst in out of breath to tell me, like another guardian angel, to be no longer uneasy; that the disturbance was occasioned by some soldiers fighting among themselves who had entered into the court to elude the observation of their officers, and who, after settling their quarrel by a boxing match, had all gone off together. Miss Duff the younger was very beautiful, and only eighteen. I seized her in my arms, pressed her to my bosom and gave her, with the best will in the world, a thousand tender kisses. In an instant the whole family were in my room to congratulate me on my happy deliverance, for the noise of the soldiers had raised every person in the house, though it was hardly six o'clock. Fully convinced of the sincere friendship and esteem of this respectable family, my greatest uneasiness during this adventure was lest, from their excessive anxiety for me, some of them should have innocently betrayed me. Mr Duff was the only person on whose coolness and presence of mind I could fully rely.

My brother-in-law called on me a few minutes after the alarm was over and made me many protestations of friendship, whilst he excused himself at the same time from contributing in any manner to assist me in procuring a passage for some foreign country, as all the vessels at Banff were strictly searched by different officers of government before their departure. He advised me strongly to return to the Highlands, as the only measure that I could adopt. I own that I felt indignant at his conduct—the more so as he was under numberless obligations to me—and I returned for answer that I did not want his advice, but his assistance. He took his departure after remaining a quarter of an hour with me, during all which time he seemed as if on thorns, and from that moment to this I have neither seen him nor heard from him. He knew all the masters of trading ships at Banff and, had he been disposed to serve me, he could certainly have found some one of the number who would have taken me on board disguised as a sailor, which would have saved me from the infinity of troubles and sufferings to which I was subjected before I effected my escape. But he would not expose himself to the least risk for a brother-in-law who on all occasions had given him the most essential proofs of his friendship. He was of such a character that I do not believe he would have put himself to any inconvenience for his own father or for any human being on the face of the earth.

Adversity is the touchstone of man, and I have learned from mine how little reliance ought to be placed on friendship in general. All those from whom I hoped for assistance in my misfortunes, threw off the mask and displayed nothing but falsehood and dissimulation, and it was only those from whom I did not expect any services, who acted as sincere friends. From having been deceived my whole life, experience has at length taught me to know mankind.

Having passed the whole day at Mr Duff's, in as agreeable a manner as was compatible with the unfortunate situation in which I was placed, I took my final leave of that amiable family about nine o'clock in the evening to return to the castle of Gordon of Park, and our tears at parting were reciprocal and abundant. I spent the night without going to bed in conversation with Mrs Menzie, not without fears of a visit from some detachment sent in pursuit of Mr Gordon, for the mistake would not have been to my advantage. After a great deal of discussion with this lady as to the measures which I ought to adopt, I at length determined to gain the Lowlands and try by every means to approach Edinburgh, that I might be in the way of receiving assistance from my relations and friends (as I knew nobody in the Highlands but those who were plunged in the same distress with myself) or perish in the attempt. I resolved to consider myself in future as a lost man, against whom there were a thousand chances to one that he would end his days on a scaffold, but in favour of whom there was still one chance remaining. I determined, therefore, to abandon myself wholly to Providence and trust rather to accident than to any certain resource; to preserve, on all occasions, the coolness and presence of mind which were absolutely necessary to extricate me from the troublesome encounters to which I should be exposed, and which would enable me to avail myself of the favourable opportunities which might present themselves. Such were my resolutions: I was determined to carry them into execution and to think of nothing which might divert me from my purpose.

Mrs Menzie did everything in her power to induce me to change my plan by representing the insurmountable difficulties which I should have to encounter at every step; the counties I had to pass through, where all the peasants were fanatical Calvinists, who assembled with their ministers at their head, to go out on expeditions to take such unfortunate gentlemen prisoners as made their escape from the Highlands and the pursuits of the soldiers; the great distance from the castle of Park to Edinburgh; and the impossibility of crossing the two arms of the sea without a passport from the government, as the English cavalry were constantly patrolling along the shore and searching the different villages to examine and arrest all persons without passposts. But nothing could shake my determination of proceeding to the south.

About five o'clock in the morning I took leave of Mrs Menzie who gave me a letter of recommendation to Mr Gordon of Kildrummy, one of her relations who then resided about twelve miles from the castle of Park, and she gave me a servant by way of guide, whom I sent back as soon as we were in sight of the mansion in question. Upon asking for Mr Gordon, I was told that he had just gone out but that he would return to dinner; and the servant added, with a tone of indifference, that if I were cold, I might in the meantime go into the kitchen and warm my self. As it was very cold, I accepted his offer and entered the kitchen where I found a number of servants assembled around the fire. Believing themselves of a class above mine, they allowed me to remain standing a long time before inviting me to sit down and join their company, which I did very respectfully. They embarrassed me very much by their incessant questions. One lackey asked me if I had been long in the service of Mrs Menzie? I answered, with an air of the utmost humility and submission, that I had not yet been two months.

A chambermaid whispered to a lackey sufficiently loud to allow me to hear her, that Mrs Menzie ought to be ashamed to send so shabbily dressed a servant with commissions to her master. Their jargon, stupidity and impertinence wearied me to death and irritated me for two long hours until Mr Gordon at length arrived to relieve me.

I delivered to him Mrs Menzie's letter before his servants and continued following him to his apartment. As soon as I saw an opportunity, I informed him who I was and begged him to procure me a guide to conduct me to the first arm of the sea, as I was unacquainted with the country. He appeared greatly affected with my situation, showed me every possible kindness and immediately sent a servant with an order to one of his gamekeepers to procure me a guide to his estate of Kildrummy, sixteen miles distant. Whilst we were waiting the return of the servant he contrived to bring some provisions into the room, of which, from pure precaution, I ate a great deal without any appetite, not knowing whether I should get any supper at Kildrummy. The guide being arrived, I took my leave of Mr Gordon and reached the village of Kildrummy at an early hour.

As there are only a few cottages there, I passed the night in one which went by the name of a public house, where I slept very uncomfortably on a bed of straw. But to make amends for my bed, my landlady gave me an excellent young fowl for supper, and surprised me next morning by only demanding threepence for my supper and bed. This public house, it is true, was a very extraordinary one, for it contained no liquor of any description. This outset gave me pleasure, as I perceived that I should not have hunger, in addition to my other sufferings, to encounter in my journey to the south. Mr Gordon had sent an order to Kildrummy to furnish me with a guide to Cortachie, a village belonging to Lord Ogilvie, at the foot of the mountains to which I had kept very close since my departure from Banff. Before leaving, I ordered my landlady to roast another fowl for me, which I put in my pocket by way of precaution, for I was uncertain if I should find anything to eat in the course of the day; and on giving a sixpence to the good woman of the house, she seemed to be as well pleased as myself. These good people have very little money among them, and indeed they have little want of it as they possess the necessities of life in great abundance.

As soon as my guide had conducted me so far on the road that I could not go wrong, I sent him back again and reached Cortachie in the evening. In traversing the moor of Glenelion,* I wished much to have fallen in with the minister of that parish, a sanguinary wretch who made a practice of scouring this moor every day with a pistol concealed under his great coat, which he instantly presented to the breasts of any of our unfortunate gentlemen whom he fell in with, in order to take them prisoners. This iniquitous interpreter of the word of God considered it as a holy undertaking to bring his fellow-creatures to the scaffold, and he was the cause of the death of several whom he had thus taken by surprise. Mrs Menzie had cautioned me to be upon my guard, but I was not afraid of him as I always had with me my English pistols which were of excellent workmanship, loaded and primed, one in each breeches pocket. I desired, indeed, nothing so much as to fall in with him for the good of my companions in misfortune, being confident that I should have given a good account of myself in an engagement with pistols, for I have all my life remarked that an unfeeling, barbarous, and cruel man is never brave. But the punishment of this inhuman monster was reserved for Mr Gordon of Abachie.

When we had separated, four days after our departure from Rothiemurchus, Abachie had resolved to go to his own castle. The minister of Glenelion, having been informed of his return, put himself at the head of an armed body of his parishioners, true disciples of such a pastor, and proceeded with them to the

*Probably Glenisla.

castle of Abachie, in order to take Mr Gordon prisoner. He had only time to save himself by jumping out of a window in his shirt. As we seldom pardon a treacherous attempt on our life, Mr Gordon assembled a dozen of his vassals some days afterwards, set out with them in the night and contrived to obtain entrance into the house of this fanatical minister. Having found him in bed, they immediately performed the operation upon him, which Abelard formerly underwent, and carried off * * * * * as trophies, assuring him at the same time that if he repeated his nightly excursion with his parishioners, they would pay him a second visit which should cost him his life. In this adventure his wife alone was to be pitied; as for himself, his punishment was not so tragical as the death on the scaffold which he had in view for Mr Gordon of Abachie. It is to be hoped that this chastisement completely cured him of his lust for inhuman excursions.

As most of the vassals of Lord Ogilvie had been in the army of Prince Charles, I ran no risk in applying to the people of the first house in Cortachie which I came to.* Having entered a public house and informed the landlady that I belonged to the army of the Prince, she immediately told me that two of our gentlemen were concealed in Glen-Prossen, a large ravine between two mountains, at the bottom of which there is a small rivulet. This glen lies at the foot of the mountains and is a most picturesque and retired spot. Having enquired my way to them and received the necessary directions, I proceeded immediately to the house of a peasant, named Samuel, who dwelt at the head of the glen about half a league from Cortachie, and there found the two gentlemen in question. They were Messrs Brown and Gordon, officers in the service of France who had escaped from

*In Scotland, the vassals were always of the party to which their chief belonged, whether it was that of the house of Stuart, or that of the house of Hanover. *Author's Note.* Not generally true except in the Highlands.

Carlisle after the capitulation. They were very glad to see me and strongly urged me not to attempt proceeding any farther to the south, where I should infallibly be taken. They had received certain information that all the towns and villages on the banks of the first arm of the sea (the Firth of Tay) were searched with the utmost strictness and vigilance by patrols of cavalry, who were constantly riding up and down the coast and examining the passports with the utmost rigour. They added that it had been their intention to go to Edinburgh, but that they had altered their mind from the impossibility of carrying their plan into execution, and they mentioned the names of several of our comrades who had been made prisoners within the last few days in attempting to pass the nearest ferry, about twenty miles from Cortachie. They earnestly entreated me to abandon my intentions and to remain with them for some time in Glen-Prossen. However desirous I was to reach Edinburgh, I did not wish to throw away my life with blind precipitancy. My situation was then so critical that the least false step or error of judgment was sure to cost me my life. I therefore followed their advice and consented to remain with them at Samuel's.

Samuel was a very honest man but extremely poor. We remained seventeen days in his house, eating at the same table with himself and his family, who had no other food than oatmeal and no other drink than the water of the stream which ran through the glen. We breakfasted every morning on a piece of oatmeal bread, which we were enabled to swallow by draughts of water; for dinner we boiled oatmeal with water, till it acquired a consistency, and we ate it with horn-spoons; in the evening, we poured boiling water on this meal in a dish for our supper. I must own that the time during which I was confined to this diet appeared to pass very slowly, though none of us seemed to suffer in our health from it; on the contrary, we were all exceedingly well. We might have had some addition to our sorry cheer by sending for it to Cortachie, but we were afraid

(as Samuel's mode of living was well known and as any alteration in it would lead to a suspicion that people were concealed
in his house) lest some ill-disposed person should give information of the circumstance to one of the numerous cavalry detachments that passed through Cortachie, which would lead to our
being made prisoners.

Honest Samuel and his family had scarcely any other food
than this the whole year through except, perhaps, during summer, when they mixed a little milk with their oatmeal instead of
water. Their manner of living placed them beyond the reach of
fortune; they had nothing to fear but bad health, and to this
they were less exposed as their frugal and simple mode of life
does not fill the body with gross humours so much as a more
luxurious diet. As their wants were few, their labour could
always supply them with the means of subsistence, and they
enjoyed a degree of health unknown to those who live in ease
and abundance. Their desires were confined to the preserva-
tion of their existence and their health, without any ambition to
change the state in which fortune had placed them, or the wish
to ameliorate their condition. Content with what they possessed, living without care, sleeping without anxiety, and dying
without fear, they desired nothing more.

Besides the poverty of our fare, to which I had a good deal of
difficulty to accustom myself, we were frequently alarmed by
detachments of English cavalry making their appearance in our
neighbourhood. Samuel had a married daughter who lived at
the entrance into the glen, and she served as a sentinel to inform
us when there were any English detachments at Cortachie. This
tranquillised us during the day, for our sentinel was very exact
in acquainting us with everything that passed; but when the
troops arrived in the evening, we were obliged to consult our
safety by escaping to the neighbouring mountains, where we
frequently passed nights in the open air, even during dreadful
tempests of wind and rain.

One day our sentinel, who was always attentive and alert, came to inform us that various detachments were hovering round our quarters, and that they had taken Sir James Kinloch, his brothers and several other persons who were in his castle, prisoners. Mr Ker, formerly a colonel in the service of Spain and an aide-de-camp of Prince Charles, had been likewise taken about four miles from us, near the little town of Forfar. She added that a party had searched all the castle and environs of Cortachie in hopes of finding Lord Ogilvie, who was not then far from us (as his Lordship has since informed me) without our knowing it at the time; that the same party had received information of our retreat in Glen-Prossen, and that we ran great risk of being soon taken prisoners. We immediately held a council and, as there was no longer any safety for us in Glen-Prossen on account of the detachments with which we were continually surrounded, we unanimously agreed to quit Samuel's next morning at three o'clock, to return to the Highlands and fix our abode for some time amongst the rocks. In consequence of our decision we went to bed at eight o'clock in the evening, in order to lay in a stock of sleep before our departure, as we could have no hopes of sleeping under a roof for some time to come.

I never gave credit to the stories of supernatural interference which abound in every country and with which men are deceived from their infancy. These stories are generally the creation of over-heated imaginations, of superstitious old women or of disordered intellects. This night, however, I had so extraordinary and so incomprehensible a dream, that if any other person had related it to me, I should have treated him as a visionary. However, it was verified afterwards to the letter, and I owe my life to the circumstance of my having been so struck with it, incredulous as I was, that I could not resist the impressions which it left upon my mind. I dreamed that—having escaped the pursuits of my enemies and being at the end of my troubles and sufferings—I happened to be at Edinburgh in the company of Lady Jane Douglas, sister of the Earl of Douglas. I was relating to her everything that had occurred to me since the battle of Culloden and detailing all that had taken place in our army since our retreat from Stirling, with the dangers to which I had been personally exposed in endeavouring to escape a death on the scaffold.

When I awoke at six o'clock in the morning, this dream had left such a strong impression on my mind that I thought I still heard the soft voice of Lady Jane Douglas vibrating in my ears. All my senses were lulled in a state of profound calm while I felt, at the same time, a serenity of soul and tranquillity of mind to which I had been a stranger since the fatal epoch of our misfortunes. I remained in my bed, absent and buried in all manner of reflections, my head leaning on my hand and my elbow supported on my pillow, recapitulating all the circumstances of my dream, regretting that it was only a dream, but wishing to have such dreams frequently to calm the storms and agitations with which my soul was devoured from the uncertainty of my fate. What situation can be more cruel than that of a continual oscillation between hope and a despair a thousand times worse than death itself? In the certainty of a visible and inevitable punishment we make up our minds to it with firmness and resignation.

I had passed an hour in this attitude, motionless as a statue, when Samuel entered to tell me that my companions had set out at three o'clock in the morning, and to acquaint me with the place in the mountains where I should find them. He added that he had been twice at my bed-side to awaken me before their departure, but seeing me fast asleep, he could not find in his heart to disturb me, convinced of the need I had of fortifying myself by repose for the fatigues I must undergo in the mountains. He told me to rise without delay, as it was time to depart and his daughter, who would suppose we had already left his house, might not be exact in informing us of the arrival of detachments. I answered in a composed and serious tone, 'Samuel, I am going to Edinburgh.' Poor Samuel stared at me, and with a foolish and astonished air exclaimed, 'My good Sir, excuse me, are you right in your head?' 'Yes,' replied I, 'my head is perfectly sound. I am going to Edinburgh and I shall set out this very evening. Go and inform your daughter that I am still here, that she may continue her usual watch and let me know if any military arrive at Cortachie in the course of the day.' Samuel began to tire me with his remonstrances, but I imposed silence by telling him once for all that it was a thing decided upon and that it was useless to speak to me any more on the subject.

No day ever seemed so long to me. My mind was a prey to all manner of reflections, and impatience and fear agitated me by turns. A thousand gloomy ideas crowded on my mind: the detachments of soldiers; the fanatical zeal of the peasantry (an evil still greater than that of the soldiers); the towns and villages I had to pass through, all filled with Calvinists, bitter enemies of the house of Stuart; and the risk which I should be obliged to run in applying to the boatmen to cross the arm of the sea. The dangers were magnified in my eyes, and I trembled at the idea of the dreadful difficulties which I had to overcome. But still nothing could shake my resolution of going to Edinburgh or perishing in the attempt. I always concluded with saying to myself, as if I had been in conversation with somebody, 'Well, then, I must perish! But it is the same thing to me, whether I am taken in going to the south or in the Highlands; there is danger everywhere. If I can only reach Edinburgh, I shall be safer there than in the Highlands where I have neither relations nor friends, and where all my acquaintances are of recent date. If I am taken, my fate will be soon decided and I shall not be obliged to languish a long time in the utmost misery, as I would if I betook myself to the mountains; and after all, perhaps that will not save me from ending my days on the scaffold.' Such were my reflections and I could assign no better reasons for the resolution I had adopted of advancing southward, for it must be confessed that all appearances were against me. But my head was so filled with my dream that if all the world had endeavoured to dissuade me from my purpose, it would have been unavailing.

At length the night which I had so impatiently waited for arrived. I mounted on horseback with Samuel behind me, for he consented to be my guide to the first arm of the sea, twenty miles from Cortachie. On our way there was a small town called Forfar, one of the most famous for presbyterian fanaticism, whose inhabitants had lately signalized their holy zeal by contributing to arrest Colonel Ker. Samuel informed me that we should be obliged to pass through this infernal town as there was no other road to Broughty, a village on the shore of the first arm of the sea, where all the roads to the south centre. Late in the evening, therefore, I started to pass through that execrable town whilst its worthless inhabitants were buried in sleep. The moment we entered this abominable place a dog began to bark and frightened poor Samuel, who was at bottom an honest man, though naturally a coward and poltroon. Seized with a panic terror, he lost his senses and endeavoured by every possible means to throw himself from his horse and take to his heels; but I seized fast hold of the skirts of his coat and kept him on horseback in spite of all his efforts to disengage himself, lest the terror which had deprived him of the use of his reason should actually induce him to run away and leave me in the most perplexing of all situations. I was totally unacquainted with the country, and should not even have been able to find my way back to Cortachie without asking at every village and thus exposing myself to be taken prisoner by a vile rabble.

He was continually struggling to get down, but I prevented

him by the hold I had of his coat. I exhorted him to be quiet, I reproached him, I alternately entreated and menaced him; but all in vain. He no longer knew what he was about, and it was to no purpose I assured him that it was only the barking of a dog. He heard nothing that I said and was completely beside himself, perspiring at every pore and trembling like a person in an ague. Fortunately I had an excellent horse. The day after the battle of Culloden, when I was opposite the castle of Macpherson of Clunie, the jade which had saved me from the field of battle being ready to sink under me and no longer able to stand upon its legs, I met Lady Macpherson in the high-road, who told me that seven or eight gentlemen had just abandoned their horses near the place where we were, in order to escape on foot to the mountains. I had taken one of the best of them, and clapping spurs to it, I now galloped through Forfar at full speed, to extricate myself as soon as possible from this troublesome crisis. As soon as we were fairly out of the town, and as no persons had come out of their houses, poor Samuel began to breathe again. When he came to himself, he made a thousand apologies for his fears and promised me, upon his word, that he would never allow himself to get into such a plight again, whatever might happen.

When day began to appear I alighted from my horse which I offered as a present to Samuel, being no longer able to keep him on account of the passage of the ferry from which we were still about four miles distant. But Samuel refused to take him, saying that his neighbours, seeing him in possession of a fine horse, would immediately suspect that he had received it from some rebel whom he had assisted in effecting his escape; that they would immediately inform against him; that he would in consequence be prosecuted and, the horse being an evidence, he would infallibly be sentenced to be hanged. I took off the saddle and bridle, which we threw into a draw-well, and then we drove the horse into a field at some distance from the road, in order

L

that those who found him might take him for a strayed horse. We had great difficulty in getting quit of this animal, for he followed us for some time like a dog.

We had not walked a quarter of an hour after giving liberty to my horse, when we fell in with a friend of Samuel who questioned him a great deal as to the place to which he was going, what his business was, and who I was. Samuel answered without the least hesitation (which I hardly expected, after the adventure of the dog at Forfar), 'I am going to bring home a calf which I left to winter in the Lowlands last autumn. I am taking this young man with me out of charity, as he was without bread and he serves me for his victuals. I intend sending him back with the calf, whilst I go myself to Dundee to buy a cow to help to support my family with during the summer.' As there happened to be an ale-house very near, the two friends agreed to have a bottle of beer together, and I was obliged to accompany them. I showed such respect for my new master that I did not venture to sit down beside him till he invited me. The friend of Samuel pressed me to partake of their small-beer, which tasted for all the world like physic, but Samuel excused me, extolling so much my sobriety and good character that his friend was incessantly showing me a thousand little attentions, expressing a wish, from time to time, to find a lad like me on the same terms. I thought I could perceive a secret desire in him to entice me from Samuel's service to his own. After they had swallowed a considerable quantity of beer, they left the ale-house and separated, to my great pleasure, for I was not only frequently very much embarrassed in playing the part which Samuel had assigned me, but also tired to death of their stupid jargon. Scarcely had this man left us, when Samuel whispered in my ear that he was one of the greatest knaves and cheats in that part of the country and famous for his villainy; that if he had found out who I was he would have undoubtedly sold me; and that the mere wish to obtain possession of my watch and purse would have been a sufficient inducement for him to have betrayed me and brought me to the gallows. I was the more astonished at what Samuel told me as, from their conversation which was full of assurances of mutual esteem, I had not a doubt on my mind that they entertained for each other the most sincere friendship. I bestowed great praise on this occasion on the prudence and discretion of my new master.

Artifice, hypocrisy and the art of deceiving, which has been very improperly called policy, are commonly supposed to be found only in the courts of princes, the only schools for learning falsehood and dissimulation; but I saw as much finesse and duplicity in the false assurances of friendship and compliments of these two peasants whilst they were drinking their beer, and I was as completely a dupe in this case, as I was afterwards in a conversation at which I happened to be present between two noblemen of the first rank.* The one was my particular friend, and the other ambassador at a court where he had promised, and where he had it in his power if he had been so inclined, to be of essential service to my friend, then outlawed and exiled from his native country. These two personages embraced each other with an air of cordiality, said a thousand flattering things to each other and repeatedly expressed the strongest assurances of mutual friendship; but the moment the ambassador had terminated his visit and taken his departure, my friend informed me that they cordially detested each other. When I reproached him with having acted a part unworthy of a man of honour and a gentleman, he replied that he only wished to pay the ambassador in his own coin. Still, however, the pantomime of these two lords would have less easily deceived me, from the opinion generally entertained of the duplicity of courtiers, than that which was acted by these two peasants.

*The Duke de Mirepoix, then ambassador at the court of London, and Lord Ogilvie, now Earl of Airly. *Author's Note.*

IX

ABOUT nine o'clock in the morning, being within a distance of half a league from the ferry, without knowing as yet how I could pass it, to whom I should apply for assistance, or where to find an asylum till a favourable opportunity should present itself for crossing over, I asked Samuel if he knew of any gentleman in the neighbourhood of Broughty, not hostile to the house of Stuart, but who had not been in our army. 'That I do,' said Samuel. 'Here is the castle of Mr Graham of Duntroon, who answers precisely to your description. His two nephews were in your army, but he remained quiet at home without declaring himself.' I did not know Mr Graham, never having seen him, but I had frequently heard my sister Rollo speak of him, his niece having been the companion of Lady Rollo, her mother-in-law. Mr Graham was of a very ancient family, and one of those who had taken up arms in favour of the house of Stuart in the year 1715. After that unfortunate adventure, he entered into the service of the English East India Company and attained to the command of one of their ships, by which means he acquired a considerable fortune and raised his family.

I immediately dispatched Samuel to inform him that he had brought an unfortunate gentleman near his house who wished very much to speak to him. Samuel soon returned and told me that Mr Graham had ordered him to conduct me into one of his enclosures where there was very high broom and where the would soon join me. Mr Graham joined me accordingly without delay. I told him who I was and earnestly entreated him to procure me a boat in order to pass the ferry at Broughty as, from his vicinity to it, he must certainly be acquainted with all the inhabitants on whom any reliance could be placed. He replied that it would give him the greatest pleasure to have it in his power to be useful to me; that he knew my sister Rollo, whom he had even very lately seen at the castle of Lord Rollo; and after a thousand apologies for not daring to take me to his castle on account of his servants, of whose fidelity he was not assured, he told me that he would instantly send to Broughty for a boat. He asked me at the same time what I wished for breakfast. I answered that, after passing seventeen days with Samuel upon oatmeal and water, he could send me nothing that could come amiss and to which I should not do justice from my appetite. He left me and soon after sent me his gardener, in whose fidelity he could confide, with new-laid eggs, butter, cheese, a bottle of white wine and another of beer. I never ate with so much voracity, and devoured seven or eight eggs in a moment, with a great quantity of bread, butter and cheese.

Mr Graham returned to the enclosure, but finding me drowsy he soon left me with an assurance that he would immediately send to Broughty to engage boatmen to transport me to the other side of the Firth in the course of the night. Having dismissed Samuel with a gratification beyond his hopes, I lay down among the broom, which was at least four feet high, and slept till one o'clock, when I was agreeably woken by Mr Graham with the pleasing intelligence that he had engaged boatmen to carry me across the Firth about nine o'clock in the evening.

Mr Graham asked me what I wished to have for dinner, enumerating to me the various good things in his house, all of which appeared exquisite to one who had undergone such a rigorous Lent at Samuel's. Among other things, he mentioned a piece of beef, and I begged he would send me nothing else. Although it was not more than three hours since I had eaten plentifully, I felt my stomach already empty and the beef seemed more delicious to me than anything I had ever before tasted. I was well entitled to make an ample repast on this occasion as I was uncertain whether I should have an opportunity of making such another for a long time. Mr Graham returned immediately after dinner, bringing with him a bottle of excellent old claret, which we drank together, and after which I felt myself sufficiently strong and courageous to attempt anything. He then communicated to me the arrangements which he had made. At five o'clock precisely I was to climb over the wall of the enclosure at a place which he pointed out to me, where I should see the gardener with a sack of corn upon his back, whom I was to follow at some distance, till he entered a windmill. Then an old woman would take the place of the gardener and I was to follow her in the same manner to the village of Broughty. Mr Graham kept me company till four o'clock, when he took his leave after embracing me and wishing me success. I regulated my watch by his, that I might be exact in the appointment with the gardener.

I had still an hour to remain in the enclosure, which, in my impatience, appeared extremely long and tedious. I kept my watch constantly in my hand, counting every minute till the hand touched five, when I began to follow the directions of Mr Graham. I had no difficulty in discovering the gardener with the sack of corn on his back, but I was very much at a loss to distinguish the right old woman among three or four who happened to pass by the mill at the very moment the gardener entered it, and I did not know, therefore, whom I ought to follow till mine, seeing my embarrassment, made a sign with her head, which I understood perfectly well. As soon as we arrived at the top of the hill above the village of Broughty, she stopped to inform me that she would go by herself to see if all was ready, and enjoined me to wait for her return in the road where she left me.

Broughty is situated on the sea-side and was not visible till we reached the top of that hill from which the road descends obliquely to the village. The sun was just going down when the good woman left me, and having waited more than half an hour for her in the road, my impatience induced me to quit it and advance five or six paces into a ploughed field to approach the brink of the hill, where I lay down in a furrow in order that I might perceive her as soon as she began to ascend the hill on her return. I had not been above five minutes there, watching for the old woman, when I heard a movement and saw a head, which I took at first for hers. But having distinguished the head of a horse, I lay down, as before, flat on the ground, with my face towards the road, where I saw eight or ten horsemen pass in the very place which I had quitted. They had scarcely passed when the old woman, who followed them closely, arrived quite out of breath. I immediately rose and approached her. 'Ah!' said she, in a transport of joy, and trembling as if she had a fit of the ague, 'I did not expect to find you here.' I begged her to calm herself and take breath, not knowing at first what she alluded to; but as soon as she had somewhat gained her composure, she explained to me the cause of her alarm. The horsemen whom I had seen pass were English dragoons who had been searching the village with such strictness, and making use of such threats, that they had so frightened the boatmen whom Mr Graham had engaged to carry me over, that they absolutely refused to perform their engagement. I censured her a little for her imprudence and thoughtlessness in not acquainting me that the dragoons were in the village, for I had not only run the risk of being carried off by this detachment, but I was tempted several times, from my impatience at her stay, to go down to the village. If I had known the situation of the ale-house in Broughty, or could have found it without asking for it from door to door, I would certainly have done so and would thus have thrown myself into the lion's mouth, through the folly and stupidity of this woman who nearly brought me to the scaffold. What situation is so distressing as that in which our lives depend on the discretion of weak people! She told me that on entering the public-house to find the boatmen, she was so much alarmed on seeing it filled with soldiers, that she lost all presence of mind and no longer knew what she was about.

At a time when I began to think my escape half secured by the certain passage of this arm of the sea, the refusal of the boatmen was a dreadful disappointment to me. I entreated the old woman to conduct me to the house where the boatmen were, but she had no inclination to return and excused herself by saying that it was quite useless to go as the boatmen had been so intimidated by the menaces of the soldiers that they would not carry me over that night for all the money in the world. She concluded by informing me that my wisest plan was to return to Mr Graham, who would find means to conceal me till the following night when the boatmen would have recovered from their alarm. I could not endure the idea of measuring back my steps, and when I reflected that I was now on the shore of that very arm of the sea which had caused me so much uneasiness, that it was the most difficult to pass, on account of its proximity to the mountains and the detachments of dragoons who were constantly patrolling in its vicinity, and that if I were so disposed I could overcome this difficulty, I became more and more determined to advance, hoping to gain the boatmen over either by money or by fair words. I therefore assured the old woman that a more favourable opportunity than the present could never occur, as the dragoons, having discovered no trace of any rebels, would not think of examining the village a second time the same night. At length she yielded to my entreaties and consented, though with some repugnance, to conduct me to the village.

As soon as I entered the public-house, the landlady, who was called Mrs Burn, whispered in my ear that I had nothing to fear in her house as her own son had been in our army with Lord Ogilvie. This I considered as a very good omen. She immediately pointed out to me the boatmen who had promised Mr Graham to transport me to the other side of the Firth. I applied to them immediately, but found them trembling and alarmed at the threats of the soldiers, and all my offers, prayers and solici-

tations were of no avail. Having employed half an hour in endeavouring to persuade them to no purpose, I perceived that
the two daughters of Mrs Burn, who were as beautiful as Venus,
were not objects of indifference to the boatmen from the glances
they bestowed upon them from time to time. I therefore quitted
the stupid boatmen and attached myself to these two pretty
girls, with the view of gaining them over to my interest and
availing myself of their influence with the boatmen, as a mistress is naturally all-powerful with her lover. I caressed them, I
embraced them, the one after the other, and said a thousand
flattering and agreeable things to them. Indeed, it cost me very
little to act this part, for they were exceedingly beautiful, and
the compliments I paid them were sincere and flowed from the
heart. As I had resolved to sleep at Mrs Burn's in case I did not
succeed in crossing the Firth, I dismissed the old woman.

In less than half an hour my two beauties were entirely in
my interest and each of them made a vigorous assault on her
sweetheart, making use of all manner of prayers and entreaties,
but with as little success as I had had. The fear of these stupid
animals was more powerful than their love. The beautiful and
charming Mally Burn, the eldest of the two, disgusted at
length, and indignant at their obstinacy, said to her sister, 'O,
Jenny! they are despicable cowards and poltroons. I would not
for the world that this unfortunate gentleman was taken in our
house. I pity his situation. Will you take an oar? I shall take
another and we will row him over ourselves, to the eternal
shame of these pitiful and heartless cowards.' Jenny consented
without hesitation. I clasped them in my arms and covered
them by turns with a thousand tender kisses.

I thought at first that the generous resolution of these girls
would operate upon their lovers, but the unfeeling cowards
were not in the least moved. They preserved their phlegm and
allowed the charming girls to act as they pleased, without being
in the smallest degree affected by their conduct. Seeing the

obstinacy of the boatmen and wishing to take advantage of the offer of my female friends, I immediately took the two oars on my shoulders and proceeded to the shore accompanied by my two beauties. I launched the boat, pushed it into deep water as soon as we had all three entered, and taking one of the oars myself gave the second to one of the girls, who was to be relieved by the other when she found herself fatigued. I experienced on this occasion the truth of the maxim that every kind of knowledge may be useful. While I was in Russia, where parties of pleasure on the water are frequent, I used sometimes to amuse myself with rowing, little thinking then that I should one day be obliged to row for my life.

We left Broughty at ten o'clock in the evening and reached the opposite shore of this arm of the sea, which is about two miles in breadth, near midnight. The weather was fine and the night was sufficiently clear from the light of the stars, to enable me to distinguish the roads. My two beauties landed with me to put me on the highway that leads to St Andrews, and I took leave of them, deeply affected with their generous sentiments and heroic courage, experiencing a sensible regret on quitting them, when I thought that perhaps I should never see them more. I embraced them a thousand times by turns, and as they would not consent to receive any pecuniary gratifications, I contrived to slip ten or twelve shillings into the pocket of the charming Mally, who was one of the most perfect beauties nature ever formed. Under any other circumstances, they would have tempted me to prolong my stay in their village, and if fortune had ever permitted me to return to my native country, I should certainly have gone to Broughty for the express purpose of visiting them.

I could never form beforehand any fixed plan with respect to what I should do, or what road I should take. A thousand obstacles, difficult to surmount, sprang up at every step, whilst, at the same time, unforeseen circumstances operated in my favour. During my passage I had been unable to recollect any person of my acquaintance in the whole extent of country between the two arms of the sea, as most of the gentlemen of Fifeshire had taken up arms in favour of Prince Charles,* and were in the same situation with myself. At length I thought of applying to my relation, Mrs Spence, who had an estate in the neighbourhood of St Andrews and generally resided in that town. But St Andrews was always the most fanatical town in all Scotland, famous on account of the assassination, in former times, of Cardinal Beaton, its archbishop. It was full of the accursed race of Calvinists, hypocrites who cover over their crimes with the veil of religion, are fraudulent and dishonest in their dealings, and carry their holy dissimulation so far as to take off their bonnets to say grace when they take even a pinch of snuff. They have the name of God constantly in their mouths, and hell in their hearts, and no town ever so much deserved the fate of Sodom and Gomorrah. However, I resolved to go there as it was a sea-port, and the hope of being able to find a passage to a foreign country through the means of Mrs Spence, was a strong inducement.†

I travelled all night, and when day began to appear I sat down on the banks of a stream to ease my feet, as my toes were bruised and cut to the very bone by my coarse peasant's stockings and shoes. When I pulled off my shoes to bathe my feet, I found them filled with blood, but the bathing rendered

---

*Though a number were Jacobites, few of them actually joined in the rising.

†Cardinal Beaton was assassinated in 1546 by John Leslie in revenge for the cardinal having sent the reformer George Wishart to the stake. Almost certainly, however, Johnstone is confusing Beaton with James Sharp who was also Archbishop of St Andrews and who was assassinated on Magus Muir in 1679, his conversion from presbyterianism to episcopacy and his subsequent repressive zeal having aroused the extreme hatred of the covenanters.

the pain less violent and intolerable. I remained two hours with my feet in the stream, during which time I felt a sweet serenity pervade my whole frame, though I was worn out with fatigue and in a condition to excite compassion in the hardest heart. I was perfectly prepared for death and I invoked the Supreme Being with great fervour to take pity on my sufferings and put an end, at once, to my miserable existence. The aspect of death, however alarming at another time, was then nothing terrible to me; on the contrary, I looked upon my dissolution as the greatest good that could befall me. I bitterly regretted that I had not met my fate in the battle of Culloden, where I escaped so narrowly, and envied the fate of my comrades who remained dead on the field of battle. The horrible idea of the hangman, with a knife in his hand, ready to open my body whilst yet alive, to tear out my heart and throw it into the fire, still palpitating— the punishment inflicted on all those who had the misfortune to be taken and condemned—always haunted my imagination. I could not get rid of the impression that I should also be taken, and the prospect of perishing in this manner on a scaffold, in presence of a cruel and brutal populace, almost tempted me to abridge my days upon the banks of this stream. My life had become a burden to me and, in such circumstances, the pleasure of existing seemed to me of very little value. But, fortunately, the wretched are never slow to embrace the illusions of hope. They see nothing in their projects except the termination of their misfortunes: on that all their calculations are founded. I implored the Almighty, that if it was my fate to perish by the executioner, he would, at least, prevent me from languishing any longer between life and death, in a cruel state of uncertainty.

I put on my stockings and shoes and rose to proceed on my way, but I found I could scarcely stand upright. My stockings and shoes being hardened with blood, I felt a pain that cut me to the heart as soon as I attempted to stir. I took them off again and put my feet once more in the water, and having soaked my stockings and shoes in the stream for half an hour to soften them, I found myself in a condition to walk and proceeded on my journey. After an hour I met a countryman who told me that I was still four miles from St Andrews. I flattered myself that he was mistaken, but I found in the end that these four miles were as long as the leagues in the environs of Paris. I arrived at St Andrews about eight o'clock in the morning, very much fatigued. It was Sunday and the streets were filled with people who stopped me continually to learn news of the rebels. I always answered that I knew nothing of them as I had only come from Dundee, a town almost as fanatical as St Andrews itself. I enquired for Mrs Spence's house on entering the town, and having found it, I told her maid-servant that I had a letter for her mistress which I must deliver into her own hands. She conducted me to her chamber, where she was still in bed, and immediately retired. My cousin did not at first recollect me under my disguise, but having examined me for a moment, she exclaimed, shedding a flood of tears, 'Ah! my dear child, you are inevitably lost! How could you think of coming to St Andrews, and particularly to a house so much suspected as mine?' 'The mob yesterday,' added she, 'arrested the son of my neighbour Mr Ross, who was disguised like you as a country-man, before he had been a quarter of an hour in his father's house. He is now loaded with irons in the prison of Dundee.'

I did not expect such a reception, but I was sensible of the false step I had taken and very anxious to extricate myself from it. I therefore entreated her to calm herself, as a contrary con-duct would be the sure means of ruining me by exciting sus-picion in her servants. As soon as she had recovered herself a little, she wrote a letter to her farmer who lived a quarter of a league from the town, requesting him to give me a horse and conduct me to Wemyss, a village on the shore of the arm of the sea which I had yet to cross before reaching Edinburgh, and about ten miles' distance from St Andrews. This was precisely what I most desired, for I was overcome with fatigue and with the deplorable state of my feet. She stated in the letter to the farmer that she was sending me to Edinburgh with papers which were urgently wanted, nay, absolutely necessary, for a law-suit which was to be decided in that city in the course of a few days. I took leave immediately of my cousin, without sitting down in her house, and set off with a little girl whom she sent to conduct me to her farmer, taking bye-roads through gardens to avoid appearing in the streets of this execrable town. As soon as I was fairly out of the town, the flattering idea of obtaining a horse to Wemyss gave me new force and courage to support my sufferings.

I delivered the letter to the farmer and the answer I received from this brute petrified me. 'Mrs Spence,' said he, 'may take her farm from me and give it to whom she pleases, but she cannot make me profane the Lord's day by giving my horse to one who means to travel upon the Sabbath.' I represented to him, with all the energy of which I was master, the necessity of having his horse on account of the law-suit of Mrs Spence, and the great loss with which any delay in transmitting her papers to her advocate might be attended; but all that I could urge had no effect upon him, and he obstinately persisted in his refusal.

This holy rabble never scrupled to deceive and cheat their neighbours on the Lord's day, as well as other days, nor to shed the blood of such unfortunate gentlemen as they made prisoners in their infernal excursions, though they had done them no harm and were even unknown to them. These hypocrites, the execration and refuse of the human race, with their eyes continually turned towards heaven, avail themselves of everything that is sacred, as a mask by which they may deceive more easily; and, unfortunately, the spirit of hypocrisy is to be found in all religions.

Frustrated in my hopes of obtaining a horse, I immediately

quitted the house of the farmer and took the road to Wemyss. What a dreadful situation! The wounds in my feet were so painful as almost to deprive me of respiration. Not knowing anyone to whom I could apply in the village of Wemyss, if I should be able to walk these ten miles; foreseeing the risk I should run of being seized in the public-house where I might pass the night; in short, not knowing what to do, nor what to make of myself, I fortunately came to a stream half a league from the infernal town. I went about a musket-shot from the road, and having taken off my shoes and stockings, I found the wounds in my feet considerably augmented and the blood flowing from them in torrents. I bathed my feet as before, and soaked my shoes and stockings, which were full of blood, but my lameness was not the greatest of my misfortunes. My mind was as much lacerated and tormented as my body. The hopes, in which I had fondly indulged, of receiving an asylum and assistance from my cousin Spence, were vanished into air, and the twelve long miles from Broughty to St Andrews had been travelled in vain.

In vain I tortured my imagination to find out some resource: I could find none. The castle of Lord Rollo was on the same side of the arm of the sea, but it was twenty-five miles to the westward of St Andrews. I was convinced of the friendship of his lordship and the good wishes of the whole family, but how was it possible, exhausted with fatigue and lame as I then was, to get there? It was several days' journey for me. Besides, supposing I should be able to reach it, it was still farther from Edinburgh than the place where I then was. I knew not what to do. However, as I saw no other feasible project, I determined at length to embrace it and to go there by short journeys, sleeping always in the fields, and avoiding the towns and villages that lay in my way as much as possible.

Whilst my body was worn out with pain and fatigue, and my mind was cruelly agitated and lost in a labyrinth of reflections, I recollected all of a sudden a chamber-maid of my mother, married two years before to George Lillie, gardener to Mr Beaton of Balfour, whose mansion was about half a league from the village of Wemyss. As this woman had taken great care of my mother during a long illness, my father, as a reward for her attachment, was at the expense of the wedding. I knew that Lillie was a Calvinist and the most furious and extravagant fanatic in that part of the country, but in consequence of the kindness which had been shown to him by my family, I was not afraid of any treachery on his part, even if he should refuse to render me any service. If he received me into his house, I knew I should be quite secure with him. The recollection of Lillie and his wife produced such an instantaneous effect on me that I immediately jumped up to walk, without thinking of my stockings and shoes, and without perceiving that I had not sufficiently reposed myself. Although it was not above a quarter of an hour since I had sat down, I felt no longer either uneasiness or pain.

I had eaten nothing since my repast in the enclosure at Duntroon, and though Mr Graham had made me fill my pockets with bread and cheese, my mind had been too much agitated to allow me to feel hunger. My appetite, however, now returned with my hopes of finding refuge with Lillie, and drawing my bread and cheese from my pocket, I made a hearty meal of it whilst my stockings and shoes were soaking in the water. My strength and courage returned at the same time, and having rested for a couple of hours, and put paper over the wounds of my feet to prevent the friction of my coarse stockings and shoes, I proceeded on my journey and walked six miles without stopping.

I had now gone half the way from St Andrews to Wemyss, and had only to walk four miles to reach Balfour. The impatience of my desire to arrive there made me feel less acutely my fatigue and my pain. I found on my way another stream, where I rested myself and repeated my former operations with respect to my feet. My toes were now in a most wretched condition, bruised and cut to the very bone, and the marks of these wounds and bruises will remain on them as long as I live. Indeed, the second toe of my left foot was put quite out of joint by this cruel day. However, my sufferings, poignant as they were, did not prevent me from finishing the remaining four miles to Balfour, and I arrived there about nine-o'clock in the evening, with a joy and pleasure surpassing all imagination.

When I found myself within a step of Lillie's house, I eagerly seized the door with both hands to prevent my falling on the ground. My strength was totally exhausted and I could not have proceeded one step farther to escape even the scaffold. What an additional strength is given to us by necessity and the desire to preserve our existence in such a case as mine, and what incredible efforts they enable us to make! Having knocked, Lillie opened the door, but did not recognise me in my disguise of a beggar. He said to me several times with impatience and evident alarm, 'Who are you? What is your business? Whom do you want?' I made no reply, but advanced inside of the door lest he should shut it in my face. This added to his alarm, and it was evident that he took me for some robber or housebreaker, for he trembled from head to foot. I asked him if there were any strangers in the house? His wife, who was sewing near the fire, knew my voice, and perceiving my dress, called out immediately to her husband, 'Good God, I know him; quick— shut the door!' Lillie obeyed without farther examining me, and following me to the light, also recognised me. I could scarce suppress a laugh, notwithstanding my pain, at his look of amazement. Confounded, lost in astonishment and petrified, he clasped his hands and with uplifted eyes exclaimed, 'O, this does not surprise me! My wife and I were talking about you last night, and I said that I would bet anything in the world that you were with that accursed race.' I answered that he was in the

M

right to conclude I was, from the principles of attachment to the house of Stuart in which I had been educated. 'But, at present, my good George,' continued I, 'you must aid me in escaping the gallows!'

It was a severe and humiliating trial for Lillie to be obliged, from gratitude, to give an asylum to a rebel, and to find himself under the necessity of succouring one of those very men whom he had so loudly condemned! No one in that neighbourhood had, on all public occasions, held forth with more zeal and eloquence against the Pope and the Pretender, who were always coupled together. He was, however, an honest man, notwithstanding his fanatical principles. He assured me that he was deeply affected with my situation and would do everything in his power to save me and to procure me a passage to the other side as soon as possible. Finding that I was utterly helpless and incapable of stirring either leg or arm, Lillie and his wife took off my shoes and stockings, and as all the gardeners in Scotland have an empirical knowledge of medicine, Lillie first bathed my feet with whiskey, which made me suffer the most excruciating pain, and afterwards applied a salve to them. They then drew on a pair of Lillie's stockings and slippers, after which I found myself relieved and quite a new person.

I sent Lillie with my compliments to Mr Beaton, his master, begging him not to take it amiss if his gardener should not be at his work at the usual hour as I was concealed in his house and had need of his services. Mr Beaton sent back Lillie immediately to tell me that he was exceedingly sorry that he could not wait upon me in person as he had been unwell for some time past, and was just then going to bed; that it was also out of his power to offer me a bed in his house, where I would have been more conveniently lodged than at Lillie's; but that he begged me most earnestly to send freely to him for whatever I might have occasion for. He wished that Lillie should take with him some wine, fowls and other articles, but whatever desire Lillie might have that I should fare well in his house, he very prudently refused this offer, lest, as he told me, it should have excited a suspicion amongst the servants of Mr Beaton that he had some person concealed in his house. I praised Lillie very much for his prudence and discretion.

Mrs Lillie soon prepared a dish of steaks for my supper, which I devoured in haste, as I had more inclination to sleep than to eat, having been two days and nights on my legs without any sleep, except during the few hours I passed in the enclosure of Mr Graham. Lillie having undressed me, carried me to bed in his arms, as it was utterly impossible for me to put a foot to the ground. I slept without waking from ten o'clock that evening till half past nine on the following evening, and Mrs Lillie took particular care not to make the least noise, nor would she even wake me to receive a visit from Mr Beaton.

As nothing restores an exhausted frame so much as sleep, I found myself greatly refreshed and in all respects well, excepting that I suffered greatly from my feet. Mrs Lillie had a fowl ready to put to the fire as soon as I awoke and I ate it in bed. Lillie took off the dressing which he had applied to my feet and replaced it by another. He told me that his mother-in-law kept a public-house in the village of Wemyss, much frequented by fishermen, and perhaps she would be able to procure some person of her acquaintance to carry me across the arm of the sea. He proposed that I should accompany him to her house if I were in a condition to walk. I was not sorry that in his desire to get rid of me he was as eager that I should escape as I was myself. He offered me a horse on the part of Mr Beaton but, before accepting it, I wished to try my strength and see whether I could perform the journey on foot. Having risen, I walked round the room supported on his arm, and found I could do without the horse. Mrs Lillie had, while I slept, been so good as to cut off the feet of my coarse stockings, and to put stuff soles to them, but I still suffered much from my feet.

We set out about half past ten o'clock at night. Suspended rather than resting on the arm of Lillie, I walked with difficulty, the hope of finding an opportunity to cross this arm of the sea and of reaching Edinburgh making me endure a pain which, at any other time, would have appeared insupportable. Whilst we were on the road, I said to him, jocularly, 'My good Lillie, if I should actually be taken in your company, what a figure you would cut! You would never dare to show your face again in any of your holy assemblies. Your reputation as a good Calvinist would be blasted for ever.' He heaved a deep sigh, and exclaimed, 'Ah! Sir, do not speak of that.' I burst into a laugh, and continued: 'It is true, Lillie, you would not be embowelled alive like me, but your character would be lost for ever with your brethren.' I amused myself during the road with similar observations, and I had the pleasure of remarking that he considered his honour as every way engaged, and that he would try every means to procure me a passage, as much from the fear of my being discovered along with him, as from the wish of making a merit of it with my family.

When we arrived at the house of his mother-in-law, she told us that of all the fishermen of Wemyss, she knew no one on whom we could rely except a person of the name of Salmon. She added that he was a very zealous Calvinist and a violent enemy of the house of Stuart, but in other respects an honest man and much distinguished in the village for his probity and good conduct. She thought we might apply to him with perfect safety as, in case he should not be disposed to serve us, he was too honest a man to do us any injury.

We went immediately to Salmon's. It was about midnight, and we found him already up and preparing his nets to go out fishing. As he knew Lillie's voice he opened the door to us. Lillie, after considerable struggles with himself, at length broke silence and, in a plaintive tone of voice and with an air of humility, shame and embarrassment, said: 'My friend Salmon, this is the only son of the mistress of my wife. He has been imprudent and foolish enough to join that accursed race who seek to destroy our religion and enslave us. You see, my friend, the dreadful situation to which he has brought himself! Everybody knows the kindness which his family showed to my wife and me at our marriage. I honour and respect them, and I am much afraid, if he should be taken, that he would cause the death of both mother and father, for they are greatly attached to him. I come, my friend Salmon, to entreat you with uplifted hands to give him a passage tomorrow in your boat, when you go to Leith to sell your fish.'

The pathetic manner in which Lillie spoke to Salmon gave me much pleasure, but the answer, pronounced in a rough tone, by no means pleased me, and left me little hopes of success. 'You deserve, indeed,' said Salmon, 'to have your life saved! you, who wished to abolish our holy religion, destroy our liberties and make all of us slaves! No, Lillie, he applies to the wrong person when he comes to me. I will do him no harm: I am not capable of informing against him, he is in perfect safety in that respect; but he must not expect that I should ever do any service to him or any other of the accursed race of rebels.' I offered him all the money which I still possessed, about six guineas, to convey me over next morning in his boat, but he would hear no more on the subject. Seeing that he was not to be gained over by money, as he was by no means interested, and that he bore on his countenance the stamp of an honest man—a much more expressive mirror than his gesture, his language, or even his accent—I could not think of abandoning my enterprise. I had offered him all my money without producing the least impression on him. I hoped, however, to gain him over through his feelings. As he kept an ale-house, I asked him to do me at least the pleasure of drinking a bottle of beer with us. He consented and I did not spare the beer, taking glass for glass with them without, however, speaking a single word about my passage, but always attentive to insinuate myself into his good graces to render him favourable to my wishes.

After passing an hour in this way, he turned towards Lillie and said to him, 'What a pity, that this poor young man should have been debauched and perverted by this worthless rebel crew! He is a fine lad!' Lillie artfully took advantage of this favourable indication to drop a word or two in my favour, and observed that by that time I heartily repented of what I had done. I pretended not to hear them, but I saw that my affairs were in an excellent train and did not fail to push about the small beer, which was as weak as water. At length I played my part so well and gained the friendship of Salmon so completely, that this honest man offered me, all of a sudden, a passage in his boat next morning and would not hear of any money, being actuated merely by a pure and noble feeling of generosity. I had not, indeed, a difficult part to play with poor Salmon, who was a truly virtuous man, highly respected by the whole village for his pure and upright conduct, as the mother of Mrs Lillie had represented him to me; and a virtuous man is never hardhearted, but always susceptible of compassion and humanity for the unfortunate. Virtue always pleases us in whatever class of men we find it, and we are involuntarily predisposed in favour of the possessor. Hence we are not obliged to do violence to our own feelings in saying flattering and obliging things to a worthy man, however low his situation in life may be, as we are when obliged to say them to a nobleman of the first rank without merit, whose elevation is the effect of chance.

Salmon was only part-owner of the boat, which he shared with several other fishermen, and it was necessary for him to manage matters with his associates. He advised me to conceal myself in a cavern, which looks towards the sea at the distance of a gunshot from Wemyss, till the break of day. It was agreed that then, as soon as the fishing-boats returned into the harbour, I should come down to the boat in which Salmon was and ask if they would give me a passage to Leith for money. He would answer in the affirmative and then settle with his associates as to the price. If anyone in the boat should make objections, he would endeavour to overcome them. At the same time Salmon and Lillie taught me the peculiarities of the dialect of that part of the country, in which I should speak on the occasion. When I quitted Salmon I slipped a guinea into his hand, telling him that this was only earnest-money, but he made some difficulty in taking it, observing that I ought to know that it was not interest that induced him to render me this service. Lillie having accompanied me to the cavern, took leave of me to return home, after offering me an asylum in his house in case this opportunity should fail. Although I looked upon my passage as certain, I was by no means displeased at the idea of a safe retreat at Lillie's, as it was impossible to foresee what unfortunate accidents might happen.

The cavern was one of the most remarkable of the antiquities of Scotland and according to tradition was, in former times, a heathen temple. It is dug under a hill, with an entrance about five feet high and three wide, and the foot of the hill is about thirty paces from the sea-shore. It is very high and spacious within and appears to be of an immense depth. An adventure, which happened in this cavern to King James the Fourth of Scotland, has given celebrity to it. The King, who used to amuse himself in wandering about the country in different disguises, was overtaken by a violent storm on a dark night, and obliged to take shelter in the cavern. Having advanced some way in, he discovered a number of men and women ready to begin a roasted sheep by way of supper. From their appearance he began to suspect that he had not fallen into the best company, but as it was too late to retreat, he asked hospitality from them till the tempest was over. They granted it and invited the King, whom they did not know, to sit down and take part with them. As soon as they had finished their supper, one of them presented a plate on which two daggers were laid in form of a St Andrew's cross, telling the King at the same time that this was the dessert which they always served to strangers, and that he must choose one of the daggers and fight him whom the company should appoint to attack him. The King did not lose his presence of mind, but instantly seized the two daggers, one in each hand, plunged them into the hearts of the two robbers who were next him, and running full speed to the mouth of the cavern, escaped from pursuit through the obscurity of the night. Next morning he ordered the whole of this band of cut-throats to be seized and they were all hanged.

I went a little into the cavern and, having thrown myself on the ground, had dozed for about an hour when I was awakened by the most horrible and alarming cries that ever were heard. I began at first to suspect the fidelity of Salmon, notwithstanding the very favourable opinion that I had formed of him, imagining that this was a detachment of soldiers whom he had sent to take me prisoner. I buried myself in the interior of the cavern, holding a pistol ready cocked in each hand, advancing always till I could place my back against the wall, in order that I might be the better able to defend myself. I then began to examine the noise with attention, and from the velocity in the movement of the object which caused the noise, I soon became convinced that it did not proceed from men, and men alone I dreaded at that time. Sometimes the object was about my ears and nearly stunned me; then, in an instant, at a considerable distance, moving with an incredible swiftness and rapidity. At length I ceased to examine any more this horrible and incomprehensible phenomenon, which made a noise and confusion like that of a number of trumpets and drums, with a mixture of different sounds altogether unknown to me.

I approached the entrance of the cavern without any further inclination to sleep, and when day began to appear I fixed my eyes on the sea to observe the movements of the fishing-boats, which were about a quarter of a league from land. As soon as I saw them enter the harbour, I left the cavern and followed exactly the lesson that Salmon had given me. Unfortunately for me, his boat had been very unsuccessful, and his associates had obliged him to sell their fish to another boat, having caught so few that it was not worth their while to go to Leith to sell them. I asked if they would give me a passage to Leith for money. Salmon replied, 'Very willingly', and joined his companions to settle the price with them. They all agreed to take me over for half-a-crown, upon which I felt an inexpressible pleasure.

Having concluded our agreement, I was proceeding to enter the boat when, that moment, Salmon's wife arrived, swearing and bawling that she would not allow her husband to go that day to Leith where he had nothing to do, especially with a stranger. There appeared to her something mysterious in the business, which she could not comprehend. What a terrible disappointment! I cursed this mischievous vixen in my heart, but that availed me nothing, and Salmon, who was the weaker party, was obliged to submit to his wife. I was prudent enough to take no part in their dispute, fearing from the suspicions she threw out, lest she might have overheard our conversation in the night whilst we were drinking our beer, for I had not been aware that Salmon was married and that his wife was sleeping in the room in which we were. I therefore yielded with a good grace and with an air of indifference. Salmon proposed our drinking a bottle of beer together, I consented, and as we mounted the stairs, he slipped the guinea which I had given him into my hand saying, 'You see, Sir, I am not the master. I wish, with all my heart, that you may have the good fortune to escape, and I am extremely sorry that I have not the means of contributing to it.' I admired the honesty of Salmon, for he might not only have kept the guinea but, by informing against me, have got my purse and watch, and also the considerable reward which the government paid for every rebel taken prisoner. His generous conduct was so much the more meritorious as he was a decided enemy of the house of Stuart and totally unacquainted with me. Humanity alone, and a noble soul, made him act towards me with an elevation of sentiment superior to his condition in life.

I did not wish to proceed directly to the house of Mrs Lillie's mother for, as the cursed fishwoman had told her suspicions of me before everybody, I was afraid of being followed. I therefore proceeded along the sea-shore to return to the cavern, and when I came opposite to the mouth, I looked about me in every direction, and seeing no-one, immediately threw myself into it. I felt a strong desire to discover the cause of the extraordinary noise which had disturbed me so much the preceding night, and of which I could form no idea. I advanced about thirty or forty paces in the dark, having even lost sight of the entrance, when the same loud noise was renewed. On clapping my hands and shouting, the noise increased a thousandfold and absolutely stunned me. I even felt the wind caused by the rapid movement of these unknown objects which incessantly approached quite close to me as if with an intention to attack me. I drew back till I could see the light from the entrance of the cavern, began to clap my hands again and redouble my shouts, and then saw numberless owls and other birds fly out. The terrible noise of these birds cannot be compared to any sounds which I have ever heard. Their screams, and the noise of their wings while flying, were confounded together by the echo of the cavern, and formed together a noise that pierced my very ears, whilst the impetuosity of their flight resembled a tempest. If I had not coolly and thoroughly examined into the cause of so singular an effect, I should never have known what to think of it, and I have no doubt that if a pious hermit had been in my place he would have placed the adventure to the account of supernatural agency, and would have given as romantic an account of the

miracles and ghosts seen by him as that of the good Saint
Anthony.

After remaining half an hour in the cavern, I returned to the
house of Mrs Lillie's mother-in-law and told her how I had lost
the most favourable opportunity for crossing the arm of the
sea through the wickedness of Salmon's wife after I had made
the proper arrangements with the husband, and I earnestly entreated her to endeavour to procure some person who would
carry me over as soon as possible, at any price. She immediately
introduced a person into my room, without previously giving
me any information respecting him, merely announcing him
as an officer of the customs in the service of King George. I
imagined she had either lost her senses or wished to betray me,
but I was still more astonished when she began to tell him that
I had been with Prince Charles. The officer, perceiving my
uneasiness, begged me not to be alarmed, adding that he had
been himself in a similar situation in the year 1715; that, having
lost his property, he was reduced to the cruel necessity of
accepting a mean employment under the Usurper in order to
procure a livelihood, but that his attachment and wishes for the
prosperity of the house of Stuart were still the same.

Having recovered from my alarm, I asked him if he could
recommend me to any honest man who would undertake to
convey me across the Firth. He replied that there was one
David Cousselain, sexton of the meeting of Non-jurors in the
village of Wemyss, a very honest man and zealously disposed
to render any service to all who belonged to the party of Prince
Charles, and that I could not apply to a better person than to
him. He immediately went out in quest of him and returned
with him in a few minutes. Cousselain said that he would very
willingly take one oar if he could find anyone who would join
him, and he proposed conducting me to the house of Mr
Robertson in the village of Dubbieside, half a league from

Wemyss, in order to borrow his boat. He informed me that
Mr Robertson was secretly attached to the Prince's party and
would do everything in his power to oblige me.

We set off immediately for Dubbieside. Cousselain cautioned
me, as we had two bad villages to pass through in our way and
in case any questions were put to me, to call myself John
Cousselain, weaver in Culross, the name and trade of his
brother whom nobody knew in that neighbourhood. If they
should suspect me for a rebel, he would claim me and maintain
against all and sundry that I was actually his brother. I was
dreadfully afraid of my new trade of a weaver. When I was
merely a servant it was easy for me to act my part, as I had done
in the service of Mrs Menzie and Samuel, but if I were arrested
on suspicion and obliged to show that I could work at my new
trade of weaver, I knew I should immediately be discovered
and ruined without remedy. However there was no trade which
suited me better on this occasion. Mr Robertson told me with a
smile that he would not lend me his boat, but that he would
willingly permit Cousselain to carry it off if he could find
another person to assist him in rowing me to the other side,
though for himself, he did not know one single person in
Dubbieside in whom he could confide. He advised me to call on
Mr Seton, a gentleman living in Dubbieside, whose eldest son
had been in our army. I did not know the father, but I had been
an intimate friend of the son. I had not, however, been aware
that his father lived in Dubbieside and I was quite charmed at
this discovery.

Having found Mr Seton at home, I acquainted him with my
name and my intimacy with his son. He immediately desired
me to walk into the parlour, where he tired me to death with a
thousand questions which I knew not what to make of, with a
number of abrupt and disjointed observations, receiving me in
the coldest manner possible, which I could not possibly account
for. After harassing me in this manner for half an hour, all of

a sudden his son entered the parlour and clasped me in his arms. He told me that they had suspected me of being a spy sent to take him prisoner, and that, though he had examined me for half an hour from head to foot through a hole in the partition of the room, it was only that instant that he had been able to recognise me under my disguise. I was very glad to see young Seton again, particularly as I knew nothing of his fate since the battle of Culloden, and our pleasure at meeting was reciprocal. There is always a friendship between persons involved in the same misfortunes. He invited me to remain with him at his father's house, and his offer was the more agreeable to me as Dubbieside was conveniently situated for my obtaining an opportunity of crossing the arm of the sea.

After a stay of eight days with my friend, at the end of which I was not one whit nearer my object than the first day of my arrival, we experienced a great alarm, which interrupted the happiness that I began to enjoy in the amiable society of Mr Seton's family. Miss Seton having asked a fishwoman, whilst she was cheapening her fish at the door, if there were any news, the fishwoman answered that the general talk was of a rebel seen hovering every day along the coast as far as Wemyss who offered a great deal of money to the fishermen for a passage. She added that he would certainly be caught some day in his excursions. The alarm which this piece of news occasioned us may easily be conceived, especially as I might have been followed as far as Mr Seton's without my perceiving it. As there was every reason for fearing that Mr Seton's house would be searched immediately, my companion in misfortune resolved to quit his father's house the same evening and take refuge in the house of some friend, whilst I made up my mind to return to Lillie's. But, before I left Dubbieside, I was determined to make a last effort to cross the arm of the sea that very night. I sent for Cousselain who came immediately and informed me that, notwithstanding his utmost endeavours, he had not been able to find a single person who would join him. What a deplorable situation! To be so near Edinburgh, where all my wishes centred, and yet, at the same time, to be on the point of being obliged to remove farther from it, in order to bury myself in the heart of the country and to abandon all thought of crossing the arm of the sea. The idea of retreating instead of advancing threw my mind into the most cruel agitation and chagrined me beyond measure.

Mr Seton, a younger brother of my friend, a youth of eighteen years of age who had made some voyages, seeing my distress and touched with my situation, generously offered to take an oar with Cousselain to row me across the Firth which, from Dubbieside to Leith, is about three leagues in breadth. I accepted his obliging offer with gratitude, and at the same time with a determination to avail myself of it, my position excluding everything like ceremony. His whole family encouraged him in his good and generous resolution, and we agreed to set out about nine o'clock in the evening.

Everything seemed to favour me, and the passage of this arm of the sea, which had cost me so much trouble and anxiety, seemed to be placed beyond the reach of accident. But fortune took a pleasure in raising up new obstacles to my deliverance. The noise which Seton and Cousselain made in launching the boat alarmed the inhabitants of the village, who were not yet gone to bed. A cry was immediately heard in every direction, that a rebel was attempting to escape, and Seton and Cousselain esteemed themselves fortunate in being able to escape from this hubbub without being discovered. I was quite furious on learning this unlucky accident. I durst not say anything to Seton as it was his kindness alone which had induced him to assist me, but my rage broke out against Cousselain with double fury. I reproached him bitterly for his stupidity in making so much noise in launching the boat and treated him like a Negro. However, notwithstanding this unfortunate beginning, I was still determined to prosecute the undertaking. Being present at the operations myself, and with a fortunate obstinacy, the more objections that were started against repeating the attempt that evening, the more I was determined to make it. Mr Seton and all his family entreated me to defer the attempt till next night, alleging that the inhabitants, being alarmed, would be on the look-out the whole night, and that it was, therefore, morally impossible for me to succeed. I answered that it was useless to speak to me on the subject, that my resolution was decidedly taken, and that, rather than delay another night, I would embark alone, with an oar in each hand, and commit myself to Providence. Indeed I certainly would have done so, however extravagant the attempt might appear, so bent was I on parting and so enraged at not being able to find a single honest man among the fishermen who would join Cousselain to save my life, and so convinced, at the same time, that I had no better prospect for the period to come.

An immoveable firmness in my resolutions has always been very useful to me. I reflected well before coming to any determination as to the part I should take, examining with impartiality the reasons for and against any measure, and considering the results which might naturally be expected from it. But having once decided, no person could ever succeed in making me waver in my resolution, even in cases where there was no alternative but success or death, and where everyone was against my opinion. I have always found my account in acting in this manner. Though obstinacy may, generally speaking, be a defect in a man's character, we must know our own affairs better than any other person can, and being the person chiefly interested, our mind exerts itself more to discover the resources of which we are in want. Hence, if we are endowed with good sense and discernment, our affairs will be more successfully conducted by ourselves than by the counsel of others, who frequently, by their doubts, only shake our confidence in our opinions, and lead us astray. I told Cousselain to hold himself in readiness at ten o'clock as I wished to make one more attempt, and I gave him some money to purchase the refreshment of which he might be in want for the passage.

Cousselain returned at the hour agreed on, but so drunk that he could hardly stand, having employed the intervening hour to good purpose. Everything seemed to conspire against me. I cursed and swore, but I was resolved to persevere. To the new solicitations that were made me to remain, I replied that Cousselain being required to bring back the boat, he might sleep and become sober during the passage whilst I rowed with Mr Seton; that that was the only inconvenience; and that I should certainly take my departure that night. I took Cousselain on my back and stretched him out in the bottom of the boat which Mr Seton and I launched without the least noise, and taking each of us an oar, we began to row with all our strength. As soon as we were about fifty paces from the shore and safe from any disturbance on the part of the inhabitants, I began to breathe again and felt my heart as if relieved from a heavy load.

An easterly wind arose which tossed our little boat in a dreadful manner. Seton was greatly alarmed and he had good reason to be so, for had a wave broken against our boat it would have filled it with water and sunk us. I kept encouraging him always, though in any other situation, I should have been as much alarmed as himself, for with every wave we were in the greatest danger of being swallowed up. But I was then afraid only of the scaffold, and every other danger made a slight impression on me. We had another danger to encounter besides that of the winds and waves, in the drunken Cousselain in the bottom of the boat, who wished to rise every moment, and several times nearly overset us, so that we were obliged to kick him most unmercifully in order to keep him quiet, and to threaten to throw him overboard if he made the least movement in future.

We had no other means of making him listen to reason. Seton and myself rowed like galley-slaves and succeeded in landing, about six o'clock in the morning, on a part of the coast a league and a half to the east of Edinburgh. As the Firth gradually widens towards the east, it was at least four or five leagues in breadth where we crossed. I tenderly embraced young Seton, thanking him from the bottom of my soul for the essential services he had rendered me, and I gave Cousselain, who began to become somewhat sober, a gratification much beyond his hopes. They re-embarked immediately to return to Dubbieside, whilst I made all the haste I could from the sea-shore, lest some countryman should have seen me land.

No felicity could surpass that which I felt on landing, after surmounting the greatest obstacles to my escape. I was now within reach of the assistance of my relations and friends. However, it had not been without a good deal of pain and difficulty that I had succeeded in crossing, for my hands were in nearly as bad a plight as my feet had been in ten days before, bleeding a great deal and considerably swollen. But I did not much mind being lame in my hands for a few days, as I had not so much occasion for them, and my feet were now pretty well recovered. Having landed about a musket-shot from Preston-pans, where we had obtained so brilliant a victory over the English, and not daring to approach Edinburgh till it was dark, I determined to pass the whole day on the field of battle, in order to tranquillise my mind and soften a little the rigours of our fate by reflections on the past.

That spot furnished me with a most striking picture of the vicissitudes of fortune to which human nature is subject, and I compared my situation in that glorious day—when I discharged the functions of aide-de-camp to the Prince, carrying his orders everywhere and charged with the care of thirteen hundred English prisoners—to my present state, covered with rags in order to escape the scaffold, borne down with trouble

N

and distress, and placing my only happiness in the hopes of escaping to some foreign country and abandoning for ever the land which gave me birth, my relations, and friends. How different the two conditions! I could not help thinking that Providence had so disposed matters that we should land near the field of Prestonpans (having been carried so far eastwards by the ebbing of the tide) rather than in the neighbourhood of Leith, where we had intended to land, in order to impress more strongly on my mind those lessons which will never be effaced from it. How much did I then desire to see some of the favourites of the Prince, whom the notice with which they were distinguished had rendered insolent, proud, and impertinent! I imagined I saw them, mean, servile, and cringing, in the now altered state of our affairs. I have seen them since and I find I was not deceived in my conjectures; their behaviour was precisely what I had anticipated.

The instability of fortune ought to teach men the importance of preserving consistency of character. If we do not allow ourselves to be blown up with prosperity, but conduct ourselves always with modesty and respectability, we shall not be cast down or become cringing in adversity. Arrogance and vanity are infallible marks of littleness of soul and never fail to degenerate, in reverses of fortune, into the meanest servility. A man who is modest, mild and beneficent, will never allow himself to descend so low, whatever revolutions of fortune he may experience, and however exalted the elevation from which he may fall, that fall will always be accompanied by the esteem and regret of all good men, and he will always have the public voice in his favour. When happy, everyone will rejoice at his good fortune, and when he experiences reverses, everyone will be eager to console him.

In going over the ground, every step brought to remembrance some particulars of the battle. When I reached the spot where I saw thirteen hundred English prisoners guarded by eighty Highlanders, I sat down to dine upon my bread and cheese, and a bottle of Canary wine which Mr Seton had made me take at parting. The remembrance of the glorious and inconceivable victory which we had obtained on this spot added to my extreme pleasure at having passed the arm of the sea.

X

AS I was afraid of being recognised if I went straight to Edinburgh, I resolved to seek an asylum in Leith, in the house of my old governess Mrs Blythe, who had been twenty-two years in the service of my mother and particularly entrusted with the care of me, having received me from my nurse when only a twelvemonth old.

The trouble and uneasiness which she continually experienced on my account, both from the dangerous illnesses to which I was subject in my youth and the passionate, impetuous and imprudent character which I possessed in common with most only sons, only served to increase her kindness and affection for me. She loved me as much as if I had been her own child. Mr Blythe, the master of a small coasting-vessel, who was very rich, took a liking to her when she was fifty and offered her marriage, and the match was too advantageous to Margaret to allow her to hesitate as to the accepting it. It was three years since she had left our house to reside with her husband at Leith, and they lived very happily together. Blythe was a Calvinist and the sworn enemy of the house of Stuart, but as he was a man of much probity, I had nothing to fear from him. I therefore quitted Prestonpans before sunset in order to reach his house in Leith after the night was set in.

On entering Mr Blythe's I thought the good woman would have stifled me with her caresses. She sprang to my neck, clasped me in her arms, and shed a torrent of tears of joy. No one of my family knew what had become of me since the battle of Culloden or whether I was dead or alive, for my brother-in-law Rollo had allowed them to remain in ignorance of his having seen me at Banff. As soon as the first transports of this good woman were over, I entreated her to go instantly to Edinburgh and acquaint my father and mother that I was in perfect health in her house. I was the more eager to give them this intelligence as Mrs Blythe had informed me of their great uneasiness and distress on my account. During her absence, Mr Blythe showed me all the hiding-places which he had caused to be made in the partition of a room, for concealing the contraband goods which he used to bring from foreign countries, in order, as he said, that I might take refuge in one of them in case of surprise and of his house being searched for me. I observed that I was the most contraband and dangerous commodity that he had ever had in his possession and that it was very possible they might still prove serviceable, although it was a long time since he had concluded he should no longer have occasion for them.

My impatience to give the earliest intelligence to my father had made me forget to request Mrs Blythe to bring me clothes, but I had the joy and satisfaction to see her return loaded with everything necessary for me. It was indeed full time to quit my rags for, besides a thousand other inconveniences to which this disguise had subjected me, I found that they had given me the itch. However, as this disagreeable disease had yet made but little progress, I got rid of it in the course of twenty-four hours by rubbing myself all over with butter and sulphur, and taking flower of brimstone internally. These rags had been of the greatest use to me during the six weeks I had worn them, but I felt, notwithstanding, an incredible pleasure in throwing them off and in being no longer obliged to disguise myself like a beggar. My father sent me word that he would call on me next morning and pass the day with me.

Although I ardently desired to embrace my father, whom I had not seen since the month of October when our army left Edinburgh, I nevertheless dreaded his presence and the reproaches which he might make me for having joined Prince Charles without his consent, and precipitated myself, by my own fault, into the miserable condition into which I was then plunged. As soon as it had been known with certainty at Edinburgh that the Prince had landed in the north-west Highlands, I was eager to have the merit of being amongst the first who repaired to his banners and staked their fortune on the issue of his cause, and earnestly supplicated my father to grant me permission to join him immediately. But instead of granting my request, he expressly commanded me to renounce every idea of this nature, telling me that it would be time enough to join the Prince when he should be in possession of Edinburgh; that not being able to procure me a passport, as his principles and attachment to the house of Stuart were universally known, I should be arrested in my attempt to pass the first arm of the sea, and kept a prisoner during the whole expedition. In vain I represented to him that the Prince would look more favourably on me if I joined his standard in the beginning, when he had only a few hundred followers, than when in possession of the capital of his ancient kingdom of Scotland, the principal obstacles were overcome, and he had nothing more to do than to be crowned —for this was the light in which I viewed matters, though I was sadly deceived. My father was inexorable and at last commanded me to be silent. Burning with desire to join the Prince, I went to dine next day with Lady Jane Douglas, who had been my protectress from my infancy, in order to make her acquainted with my chagrin and the conversation I had had with my father. This worthy lady highly approved of my reasons and agreed that I ought to set out immediately, without consulting my father, and she undertook to appease him in case he should be enraged at my disobedience. This was precisely what I desired, and I set out next morning without saying a word on the subject to anyone.

I found no difficulty in passing the arm of the sea between Queensferry and Dunfermline. I put a black cockade in my hat, and entered the boat with an air of authority, telling those who examined the passports, that I was an officer in Lee's regiment,

then quartered in Edinburgh, and that officers had no occasion
for passports. On leaving the boat I went to the castle of Lord
Rollo, where I remained two days waiting the arrival of the
Prince at Perth, which is two miles from it. When I returned
to Edinburgh some time after with our army, my father said
nothing about my going away without his consent, but then
we were victorious and triumphant. Now everything was
changed, and those who bestowed praises on us in our prosperity, treated us, now that we were unfortunate, as hair-
brained youths. This is the way with the world in general, who
judge of things merely by the event. If we had succeeded in
placing the crown on the head of Prince Charles, of which
there was even a great probability for some time, we should all
have been celebrated as heroes. The loss of the battle of Culloden, which put an end to the contest between the houses of
Stuart and Hanover, made us immediately rebels and madmen
in the eyes of those who are incapable of reflection, and who
unfortunately are everywhere the majority.

My father came to visit me, but instead of reproving me, the
good old man was so affected at seeing me again that his eyes
were filled with tears and, locking me in his arms, he was for
some time unable to utter a single word. As soon as we were a
little composed, I amused him with the recital of all the particulars of our expedition since our departure from Edinburgh
for England, and all that had happened to me personally since
the battle of Culloden. He remained with me till nine o'clock in
the evening and the day passed over with the rapidity of
lightning. I was deeply afflicted on learning that my mother
was very ill and had been obliged to keep her room for a long
time, and I was still more so when Mrs Blythe told me that her
anxiety for me was the cause of her illness, and that the
physicians thought her life in danger. My grief was natural and
well founded as she had always adored me with the most tender
maternal affection. I proposed several projects to my father for

going to see her but he would not hear of it, alleging that I ran a risk of being discovered, and that if unfortunately I should be arrested, it would be the death of both of them. I therefore ceased to insist on seeing her. What a cruel situation! to be so near a mother whom I had such reason for loving tenderly, without being able to embrace her!

Leith, which is about a mile from Edinburgh, was then filled with Hessian and English troops waiting for embarkation for Flanders. Two English sergeants called on Mr Blythe with billets for lodging. This was a dreadful derangement for me, but Mr Blythe contrived to get an exemption and they went away. For an hour, during which these sergeants remained in the house wrangling with Mr Blythe about their lodging, I continued watching them through a hole which I had made in the partition between two rooms, with the entry of the hiding place open to receive me in case I found they intended to search in the house for rebels. I saw poor Mrs Blythe turn pale and change colour every minute, trembling like an aspen leaf, and I was much afraid lest her anxiety should induce the sergeants to suspect that there were some rebels concealed in the house. However, my fears were groundless.

I received information that Lady Jane Douglas intended to pay me a visit *incognito* in the afternoon of the following day, accompanied by Mr Stewart who became afterwards her husband, and another lady who was related to me. This worthy and virtuous lady, who was idolised by her country, possessed every good and amiable quality that could adorn her sex. She was beloved, respected and adored by all those who had the advantage of knowing her, as well as by the public in general, who only knew her through the high character and reputation she possessed. She had been very beautiful in her youth and was still beautiful at the age of forty-five, appearing at least fifteen years younger than she really was, from the uniform, temperate, regular, frugal and simple way of living she had

always observed. She was virtuous, pious, devout and chari-
table without ostentation; her devoutness was neither affected
nor oppressive to others. Her affability, easy and engaging
manners, and goodness of heart, soon set at their ease those
who paid court to her, whom her graceful and majestic air
might at first have rendered timid. Her mind was highly cultivated. She had a decided taste for literature, a great memory,
much good sense and intelligence, a sound judgment and a
quick discernment. Her library was well stored with the best
authors, without any of those trifling novels which generally
form so large a portion of the libraries of women. She possessed
great elevation of soul and was even haughty and proud on proper occasions, supporting her illustrious birth with dignity, without arrogance and without vanity, but in a manner truly noble.

Her brother, the Duke of Douglas, was a lunatic from his
infancy, frequently breaking out into the most dreadful fits of
madness. He killed his own near relation Mr Ker, without
having ever had the least quarrel or altercation with him, by running him through the body with his sword when asleep. As
Lady Jane herself several times narrowly escaped being killed
by him in a fit of insanity, their uncle, the Marquis of Lothian,
wished to have him legally declared a lunatic and Lady Jane put
in possession of all the estates of the family, amounting to more
than sixteen thousand pounds a year. This would have met with
no opposition, as his lunacy was notorious from the fatal proofs
which he gave of it every day; but Lady Jane Douglas would
never consent to it, preferring to live retired upon an annuity of
three or four hundred a year which she drew from her brother
as interest of her portion—a very small income for a person of
her rank—to dishonouring him and her family by having recourse to such a step. If ever virtue seemed to be unceasingly
persecuted by Providence, it was in the person of Lady Jane
Douglas, the most amiable of her sex, eminent for every noble
quality and the most perfect model for imitation.

Lady Jane called on me, as she had announced, and made me
repeat all my adventures since the battle of Culloden. When I
came to that part of my story which related to my stay at
Samuel's, my dream, which I had almost forgotten from the
variety of events that had happened to me since I left Glen-
Prossen, recurred to my remembrance and, struck with the
realisation of it in every point and in all its circumstances, I
stopped short for a moment in my narrative and remained
silent and confounded. I hesitated at first whether I should
relate it or not, but it appeared so supernatural and incredible,
that I was afraid to communicate it to her, lest she should
imagine that I wished to palm fictions on her. Besides, supposing she could not give credit to me, which was very
probable, it would have appeared, as I thought, in her eyes, to
betray a littleness of mind in me, to attempt to deceive her
by artifices. I therefore proceeded with my story, omitting all
account of the dream, though nothing can be more certain than
that, in inspiring me with an obstinate determination to proceed to the south instead of returning to the mountains to join
my companions, this dream was the means of saving my life.
I shall therefore remember it as long as I live, as a matter beyond my comprehension, and on which it is impossible for me
to reason, though it had such an influence on my destiny.

Having recounted to Lady Jane the affair of the two sergeants
on the preceding evening, which had so much alarmed poor
Mrs Blythe, she observed that I was not then in a proper place,
and she offered me an asylum in her house where I should be
more safe, as no one would dare to search it upon mere suspicion. She told me to come that very night about ten o'clock,
and ordered me to collect my rags for the journey. Her house
was about half a league from Leith, in the village of Drum-
sheugh, and the disguise was absolutely necessary lest I should
meet anyone who knew me on the way. I said all that I possibly
could to be freed from wearing my old clothes for which I had

a particular repugnance, but, as I durst not venture to tell Lady Jane that they had given me the itch, I was obliged to put them on to comply with her request. I took every possible precaution to prevent my catching that odious disease a second time, by putting on two shirts, a waistcoat and gloves under my rags.

I arrived at the door of Lady Jane's house, about eleven o'clock at night, and found it half open, and the gardener, who was the only one of her servants whom she dared to intrust with the secret, waiting for me. He told me that Lady Jane had ordered him to conduct me into her Ladyship's apartment as soon as I arrived, without changing my clothes, as she wished to see me in my disguise. This was another source of uneasiness, for I dreaded the pestilential odour which they would cause in the room; but I had no alternative. With Lady Jane I found Mr Stewart and a lady who was related to me waiting to see my metamorphosis. They all agreed that it was impossible to recognise me in this dress; only Lady Jane observed, that to complete my disguise, I ought to have my eye-brows blackened with burnt cork. I made the experiment immediately and found that the alteration which it produced in my appearance was considerable. I took my leave of them about midnight and was conducted by the gardener to the chamber which was destined for me, above the room where company was received and where no one had slept for a long time past. I immediately made a bundle of my clothes, which I requested the gardener to burn in the garden that I might hear no more of them and be under no apprehension of wearing them again.

As the gardener was the only individual in the secret, and as all the servants imagined that there was no person in the room that I occupied, I was obliged, so as not to make any noise which might lead to my discovery, to remain without shoes till eleven o'clock in the evening when they went to bed, and then I went downstairs into the garden to take a walk. I soon became accustomed to the sedentary and secluded life, seldom seeing anyone but the gardener who brought me my meals. Sometimes I had the pleasure of passing a few hours in the apartment of Lady Jane, where I usually found Mr Stewart; but this was an indulgence I seldom enjoyed on account of the difficulty of keeping all the servants out of the way, especially her chamber-maid, Mrs Ker. Lady Jane did not wish to let this woman into the secret, and she became very troublesome from her extreme curiosity to clear up the mystery, the existence of which she had frequent occasion to suspect without knowing what to think of it.

I immediately acquired a taste for reading, having been, till then, too dissipated for any application to books, and her Ladyship supplied me with the best historical authors. Thus I passed my whole time with a book continually in my hand, without feeling weariness for a single moment, and I should have willingly consented to pass my whole life in the same manner, on condition of escaping the scaffold. The taste which I then contracted for reading has been subsequently of the greatest utility to me, and a great resource against *ennui* in a part of America where I lived several years, and where society is not so agreeable as in Europe.

A few days after taking possession of my lodgings in the house of Lady Jane, I read in an Edinburgh newspaper, 'That the populace of Dubbieside had arrested and conducted to prison a person of the name of David Cousselain, who, with a certain individual who was not taken, had aided in the escape of a rebel; and that they had burnt the boat, which had been made use of in crossing the ferry.' I was very glad that Seton, who had acted with such generosity, had had the good fortune to escape, and I was sorry that Mr Robertson had lost his boat; but as to Cousselain, as my hands were not yet cured, I could not pity his fate so much as if he had kept himself sober. Had it not been for his drunkenness, he might have returned to Dubbieside in better time, for being then able to relieve each other, we should have effected our passage in less time, and there is every reason for supposing he might have escaped being taken, securing his return before the inhabitants were up. I rowed as well as a man could do who was rowing for his life without knowing much of the business, but with Cousselain we should have effected the passage in half the time. I learned from Mr Seton the elder, whom I met at Paris in the year 1747, that Cousselain suffered only a few weeks' imprisonment as there was no evidence against him. Indeed, nothing would have been more unjust than to have condemned him for saving a rebel, for the brute had nothing to do with it, having slept during the whole passage, while I was fatiguing myself to death with rowing and injuring my hands in such a way as to prevent me from using them for a long time.

Lady Jane and my father were of the opinion that I should go immediately to London, as I ran no risk of being discovered in that immense city, which a multitude of strangers are entering and leaving every day. They thought, too, that there was little to fear on the road after I was once ten leagues from Edinburgh. Everything was ready for my departure, when we learned that the squadron of the Duke d'Anville had sailed from France, and that it was so formidable that Admiral Anson durst not attack it. When this news first reached Scotland, no one doubted that this squadron was destined to re-establish the affairs of Prince Charles, and the feigned route which it took on its departure confirmed us still more in that belief. It is certain that this squadron might have effected a disembarkation in Scotland without experiencing the least opposition, and even in view of the English fleets which had not dared to attack it; and the troops which were on board would have been more than sufficient to re-establish our affairs. The Scots who were still concealed in the mountains would have issued out of them like so many bees from a hive, and many of the clans who had remained neutral, seeing that the Duke of Cumberland had ravaged and laid waste the whole country without distinction of friend or foe, would have taken up arms. The army of the Prince would soon have been double in number to what it was in the times of our greatest prosperity. After waiting with extreme impatience for the landing of this squadron in Scotland, which occupied the attention of every one for several weeks, an English ship at length discovered it in a latitude which put it beyond all doubt that it was only destined for America.

It was the fate of this formidable fleet to perish on the coast of Nova Scotia, without even effecting the settlement which was the object of the expedition, at Chebuctoo, a paltry fort in the worst possible soil where the English have since built the town of Halifax. This immense armament, which might have easily effected a revolution in England from the critical state of things at that time in Scotland, was reduced to nothing by tempests, by diseases, by discord and contention between the superior officers of the land and sea services—in short, by a total want of good conduct, so that a few only of the shattered remains of it returned to France. This may be considered as the last effort of the French navy.

The policy pursued by the court of France, in threatening the English with efforts in favour of the house of Stuart as they have done for a century past, is very short-sighted. This policy, from the nature of things, could only be of limited operation: the trick has become so stale from repetition that the English are no longer alarmed, and never will be alarmed in future, as they see that France, with the best possible dispositions, is now incapable of effecting anything in favour of the Stuarts because of the destruction and emigration of their partisans in Scotland, and the coolness of those in England. This was indeed clearly proved in the last war. These pretended invasions in no manner disconcerted the English or prevented them from pursuing their enterprises, and only served to open their eyes to the necessity of forming and disciplining a hundred thousand militia to guard their coasts from surprise. If France had had seriously at heart the desire to re-establish the house of Stuart on the throne, she might have easily succeeded in effecting this, during our expedition, with three or four thousand troops. Having an ally in Prince Charles, she would have thereby avoided those eternal wars with England which never took place during the reign of the house of Stuart. On the contrary, Charles II became the ally of France in a war against the Dutch, notwithstanding the friendly sentiments which the English nation always entertained towards that republic.

After passing two months in the house of Lady Jane Douglas in the most tranquil and philosophic manner, a servant-maid, who had returned from Edinburgh with provisions, told her companions in the kitchen that, whilst she was purchasing meat in the flesh-market, the lackey of an English gentleman, a commissioner of the customs, whispered in her ear, 'That they knew very well that I was concealed in the house of Lady Jane Douglas, her mistress, and that there was every reason for supposing that her house would immediately be searched.' She added that she had openly contradicted this calumny and, in fact, she could do so with a safe conscience, for no one in the house, except the gardener, knew anything of the matter. This latter went upstairs immediately to inform Lady Jane, who came without delay into my room accompanied by Mr Stewart, to consult as to what was necessary to be done, fearing lest a detachment of soldiers should come in the course of the day to visit the house. It was then only nine o'clock in the morning.

This intelligence filled me with the utmost grief and uneasiness. I trembled lest the extreme goodness of Lady Jane in giving me an asylum in her house, should involve her in difficulties with the government, and I was a thousand times more afraid of the disagreeable consequences which my being taken in her house would entail on her, than of the fate which awaited myself. When I feelingly expressed how much I regretted the dangers to which I exposed her, she replied with her usual spirit and promptitude: 'If there were no risk, you would be under no obligation to me.' It was impossible to get out by the door into the court on account of the servants who would see me from the kitchen, and there was no place in the house, which I examined all over, where I could remain concealed. But as they were then making hay in an enclosure belonging to Lady Jane, Mr Stewart proposed that I should conceal myself in a cock of hay. In order to succeed in this it was necessary to let a footman into the secret, that he might watch the other servants and seize a favourable opportunity for my leaving the house and entering the enclosure.

I went out in my waistcoat with the footman and gardener, followed by Mr Stewart. As it was necessary to observe a number of precautions, on account of some of the windows of the village which looked into the enclosure, we began to throw down all the cocks of hay, one after another, and the footman and gardener threw each other down on the hay, with which the one who happened to be undermost was covered by the other. This pretended amusement went on for some time, when they threw me, in my turn, as a part of the same sport, and covered me with hay till the cock in which I was concealed was raised as high as the rest, leaving me only a small aperture for breathing. Then, having given me a bottle of water and another of wine, they withdrew.

I do not think it possible to suffer more than I did the whole day. The weather was fine but very warm and the excessive heat of my situation under the hay, which was like an oven, almost deprived me of respiration. Mr Stewart came to see me from time to time and exhorted me to be patient; and, indeed, I had need of patience, for my sufferings were occasionally so insupportable that I was sometimes tempted to give the hay to the devil and expose myself to whatever might happen, rather than to continue where I was. My regard for Lady Jane alone restrained me. After the most dreadful sufferings from ten o'clock in the morning till nine at night, remaining always in the same attitude without power to stir myself and bathed in sweat, I was at length relieved. But when I came out of the hay my body was so bruised and I was so weak from my excessive transpiration, that it was with difficulty I could walk leaning on the arm of Mr Stewart, for my legs could scarcely support me. I was enraged to think I had passed so disagreeable a day for nothing, no person having come to search the house. I was always of opinion that they would not dare to do so on doubtful information, and they could obtain no certain information except through the gardener, of whose fidelity Lady Jane had been assured in the considerable length of time during which he had been in her service.

The certainty that the squadron of the Duke d'Anville was not destined for Scotland, the disappointment I felt in the extinction of all my hopes of the re-establishment of our affairs, and my sufferings the whole of this day under the hay, determined me to set out for London as soon as possible, and Mr Colville, Lady Jane's man of business, purchased for me next day in the horse-market a very handsome pony at a reasonable price. I urgently entreated Lady Jane to exempt me from performing a second penance during the day I should still have the honour to pass with her, adding that I would remain sentinel at my chamber window from morning till night, with my eyes constantly fixed on the door into the court. As soon as I saw a detachment enter—if they were so impudent as to send one— I would jump from the window of the first floor into the garden, whence, by climbing the garden wall, I could soon gain the open fields and place myself beyond the reach of their pursuit. This dear and amiable lady pitied my suffering under the haycock but, at the same time, could not help bursting into a

o

loud fit of laughter on seeing the panic-terror with which the idea of returning to it filled me, and she granted me a dispensation.

Next day my father came to bid me an eternal adieu and passed the afternoon with me. I felt the utmost affliction and grief at the approach of this perpetual separation. I warmly urged my father, as well as Lady Jane, to permit me to go to Edinburgh for a few moments, to embrace for the last time the most tender and affectionate of mothers, in the bed where she was then dangerously sick; but they would not give their consent, on account of the danger I should run of being discovered either in passing through the town, or by the servants of the house. What a cruel situation! To be within a mile of a tender mother who had always fondly loved me, then dangerously ill, and yet be unable to bid her an eternal adieu!

About eleven o'clock at night, I began to disguise myself in the dress of one of the persons who travel up and down the country with goods. A stock of handkerchiefs was procured for me which I put into my portmanteau with my linen, where I had also the breast of an embroidered waistcoat, which was very beautiful and very precious to me as it was the work of a mistress. Having folded up my hair, I put on a black wig which hung down over my shoulders, and Lady Jane blackened my eye-brows; but with this disguise I was by no means so completely metamorphosed as in my beggar's dress. This amiable lady, who could not be at ease on my account till she knew I had proceeded without accident some leagues from Edinburgh, where I should be less exposed to meet any persons of my acquaintance than in the neighbourhood of that city, sent her servant on her saddle-horse to accompany me the first two leagues, that she might know how I succeeded.

I proceeded six leagues without stopping, when, having come to a village in which there was a public-house, I alighted to rest a little and take some refreshment. The landlady eagerly pressed me to join a gentleman in the next room, who had just arrived, that we might dine together. I consented, suspecting that she had it not in her power to serve us up separate dinners. I was confounded, on entering the room, to find Mr Scott, a banker in Edinburgh and a young gentleman who knew me very well by sight. This encounter was the more calculated to alarm me from his being a violent partisan of the house of Hanover. Having, however, committed this blunder, it was now too late to think of retreating and, trusting to my disguise, I supported the character of a pedlar as well as I could till, in a moment of absence, he pronounced my name. As it was impossible any longer to doubt that I was known to him, I endeavoured to deceive him with respect to the road which I intended to take. As at this village several roads joined the highway to Edinburgh, I told him that I intended sleeping at Jedburgh, the road to which turns off from the London road on the right at this village. After he had pronounced my name, I could perceive that he was at great pains to induce me, notwithstanding that circumstance, to believe that he did not know me, for which I could not discover his motive. I was not afraid of being arrested in the village, having a pistol primed and loaded in each breeches pocket, but I was very much afraid that, on his reaching Edinburgh in the evening, he would lodge an information against me, and that, in consequence, the magistrates of the different towns on the London road would be written to, in order to have me arrested.

I therefore set out immediately after dinner, taking at first the Jedburgh road; but as soon as I had proceeded about a league I came to a cross road to the left, into which I struck and soon regained the London road. In the evening I arrived at Kelso, forty-three miles from Edinburgh where, availing myself of a letter of recommendation from Mr Stewart, I slept at a private house to avoid any troublesome encounters at the inn. I never passed a more painful day. Plunged in the deepest

melancholy and oppressed with the most distressing reflections, I saw myself reduced to the dreadful alternative of either
perishing on the scaffold or, by escaping to a foreign country,
of abandoning for ever my native land, my relations, my friends,
and all that was dear to me. Next day I entered England.

On the fourth day after my departure from Edinburgh, when
within two miles of Stamford where I intended passing the
night, I came up suddenly with some covered waggons and
heard a voice in one of the waggons call out, 'See, see! if there
is not a man on horseback who resembles our rebel captain as
much as one drop of water resembles another!' and I heard
my name pronounced at the same time.

Amongst the immense number of prisoners that we took in
the different battles we gained against the English, there were
many who entered our army without any sincerity of intention;
most of them had no other view in so doing than to have the
means of escaping with the greater ease to join their old colours
in the English army.

I had been informed, whilst in the house of Lady Jane
Douglas, that several waggons, filled with soldiers wounded at
the battle of Culloden, had set off about eight days before I left
Edinburgh for Chelsea Hospital, near London; but I had supposed them too far before me for there to be any danger of my
coming up with them by the way. Not expecting to meet with
any person in England who knew me, I had taken off my large
black wig on account of the excessive heat, and had only my
hat uncocked, which covered my face as if to defend me from
the sun. I affected not to hear them, and having passed the
waggons, I kept on at the same rate till I got clear of the town
of Stamford, when I put spurs to my horse and rode eight miles
at full gallop, to get so far before the soldiers that they might
not see me again. I durst not sleep at Stamford as I was afraid
their report might induce the magistrates to arrest me.

However, this adventure proved nearly fatal to my horse,

the loss of which would have reduced me to so grievous a situation that I trembled at the very idea of it. On reaching my inn, as soon as he entered the stable he threw himself down, refusing to eat or drink, seeming to be completely cut up. I tortured my imagination in order to devise how I could continue my journey in case he should be incapable of proceeding farther, and I dreaded also the arrival of the waggons, next morning at that very inn, which was the only one in the village. Restless and chagrined beyond all description, I did nothing but pass and repass between the inn and the stable during the space of two hours. At length, after inexpressible suffering, I was agreeably surprised to see my horse on his legs eating with a good appetite and looking admirably. The landlord told me that I had nothing to fear on his account, and even offered to buy him at thrice the price which he had cost me. Nothing could exceed the joy which I felt in having my mind thus set at ease with respect to my horse, the recovery of which extricated me from the most cruel perplexity. He added that in a few hours the animal would feel nothing more of his fatigue, and that I might set off with him in the morning at any hour I pleased without the least danger of his failing me on the way. I fixed my departure at half-past two in the morning, under the pretext of avoiding the heat, but in reality to get the start of those waggons which weighed so much on my mind.

Next morning, at sunrise, a man very well dressed in the manner of the people, about forty years of age and mounted on a very beautiful bay courser, came across the fields, leaping all the hedges and ditches with an astonishing facility. As soon as he entered the highway, he came alongside of me and immediately endeavoured to enter into conversation, notwithstanding the little inclination which I discovered to continue it, as he might easily see from my always answering him in monosyllables. Having examined his physiognomy when he rode up to my left side, I observed that he had a wild and troubled air and that he turned his head every instant to look about him in every direction; in short, that he had all the appearance of one of the highwaymen with whom the great roads in England are infested. I instantly had my right hand in my breeches pocket, and whilst I held my pistol in readiness, I kept my eyes always fixed on him, determined, if he made the least movement with his hands, that my pistol should be presented as soon as his. I likewise regulated the pace of my horse by his, never allowing him to get behind me, which I perceived he was sometimes desirous to do from his slackening his pace every moment. I did not wish to surrender my purse without a battle as in my situation, the loss of my money would have ruined me irretrievably.

Having proceeded in this manner for more than half an hour, always on the alert and making a number of unconnected observations, the stranger suddenly wished me good morning and darted, in the same manner as he came, across the fields, leaping the hedges and ditches without appearing to have any other object in view than that of getting to as great a distance as possible from the highway. The determined air which I exhibited probably deterred him from demanding my purse, and I was very glad to get rid of him, for the adventure, turn out how it might, would have been fatal to me. If I had blown out his brains in my own defence, I could not have presented myself before a magistrate to make my deposition, and if he had taken my purse, I know not how I could have continued my journey without money.

Whilst I was dining in an inn at Jockey Houses, a man entered whom I took, from his conversation with the landlord, to be an excise-officer. This man rudely seated himself at the same table with me, without the least apology and without asking my leave. He remained a quarter of an hour without opening his mouth, during which time he made a very considerable breach in a piece of roasted veal. Unable, at length, to devour more, he laid down his knife and fork with much gravity, and said to me with an air of contentment and satisfaction: 'Sir, I saw you pass this morning: probably you slept at Stamford? I at once perceived from your horse—for we have none of that breed in England—that you are come from Scotland. Tell me if it be true that the rebels are entirely dispersed? It must be owned that your nation is very eager for its own destruction. Have we ever been governed with so much mildness and moderation as at present under His Majesty King George? Your nation will never be quiet till it be totally destroyed. Can nothing extirpate in your country that hereditary spirit of rebellion?' I was very uneasy, for fear this rude fellow had been sent by the magistrates of Stamford to endeavour to verify the declaration of the soldiers, and with instructions to keep sight of me till he should find an opportunity for arresting me in the first great town on the road where I might pass the night. I answered, 'That I had no news respecting the rebels, having come from a part of the country called Annandale, which is on the frontiers of England and where they generally know little or nothing of what is passing in the north of Scotland. Besides, being a dealer in linen-drapery, I concerned myself only with my trade and cared very little about state affairs.'

He immediately asked to see my goods. I told him that I had sent my linen to London by sea with other goods of Scots manufacture, and that I had only handkerchiefs with me. I immediately opened my portmanteau to show them, and sold him a piece without knowing the price, for they had forgotten to mark it. I had not, it is true, anticipated any such embarrassment on the road to London as would oblige me to sell them. On paying for the handkerchiefs, he praised my probity, telling me that I was a conscientious young man, and that all the other Scots pedlars who passed that road every day were a set of arrant knaves, having lately obliged him to pay, for the same goods, nearly the double of what I had demanded. In examining my portmanteau he saw my embroidered waistcoat and had a strong desire to purchase it, but as soon as I told him that I could not sell it for less than fifteen guineas he gave up all idea of buying it, and I was very glad that he did not torment me, for I should not have let him have it on any account. If this man was really sent after me, as I suspected, he must at least have reported that I was a pedlar, and the handkerchiefs which I had sold him apparently for much less than prime cost, gave him a high opinion of my honesty. He made me take down the addresses of his friends in London, in order that they might obtain similar goods from me at the same price.

I arrived in London at six o'clock in the evening of the seventh day after my departure from Lady Jane Douglas's, having travelled nearly four hundred miles in that time, without over-fatiguing my horse. I alighted at an inn in Greek Street, the people of which Mr Stewart had recommended to me as honest and well-behaved. As soon as I had changed my linen, I went out to deliver a letter of recommendation to a person from whom all the favour I had to demand was to procure me furnished lodgings, to which I might immediately proceed in order to avoid the inconvenience of sleeping in an inn. Having found him at home, he declined, to my great surprise, to procure lodgings for me, telling me at the same time, that the master of the inn being a Scotsman much suspected by the government, it was generally supposed that the court employed some of his waiters as spies, to give them intelligence of all the Scotsmen who arrived in London. I returned to the inn highly incensed at the rudeness of this person who would not give himself the trouble to find me a lodging and I was very uneasy, after what I had heard, at being obliged to pass the night there.

I did not close an eye the whole night, from the fear of being arrested on the information of the spies of the inn, and having risen at an early hour, I sallied out in quest of furnished lodgings, without being able to find any in a neighbourhood which suited me in respect to price. Impatient and anxious to quit the inn, I at length bethought me of a female who kept a shop, and who had had a great kindness for me when I was in London in 1740. All I had to do was to ascertain if she had adopted anyone in my place whom she loved better than me, or if, after an absence of five years, I could revive the affection with which I had formerly inspired her. However, as she possessed good sense, elevated sentiments and great gentleness of disposition, I was well assured that I ran no risk in confiding my life to her fidelity, and I therefore immediately took a coach and drove to her house. Having dismisssed the coach some paces from the door, I entered her shop under pretext of buying something, supposing that she would not recognise me, but she no sooner saw me than she called me by name, in a transport of joy at again meeting with me. As her servant-maid was present, I told her that she had forgot my name, which was Leslie. We then entered into the parlour, where I related to her my misfortunes, which drew tears from her eyes, and I soon perceived that this good and amiable woman still loved me. I told her that the convincing proofs I had received from her of her friendship and affection made me believe that my life was safe in her hands. 'Oh! yes,' replied she with great vivacity. She then embraced me, and entreated me to be assured that she loved me as much as ever and that she had often thought of me.

She immediately offered me an apartment in her house, telling me that I should be the more safe with her as she had never chosen to let her apartments, and she pressed me very much to take possession of the lodging in question without a moment's delay. I accepted her obliging offer, returned to the inn for my portmanteau and came back to dine with her, when she put me in possession of an elegant front room on the first floor. Having found a stable in the neighbourhood, I brought my horse to it myself that very evening, so that the people of the inn, if they were spies of the court, might not know the part of the town where I had gone to lodge. I ceased, therefore, to be any longer uneasy on that score. My horse was so handsome that I sold him almost immediately on such advantageous terms, that I received, over and above the price I paid for him, much more than the expense of my journey and my loss on the handkerchiefs.

I had formerly remained a year in London, in consequence of a dispute with my father, till I received an order from him in the spring of 1740 to return to Scotland, and he allowed me only three weeks to join him under pain of his never pardoning my disobedience. I was in this critical situation when, in a visit which I paid to one of my friends to announce to him my departure, I met in this house the most beautiful person that ever existed, eighteen years of age, newly come from the country. She was the niece of my friend, and an only daughter. I stopped to dine at her uncle's, where she stayed, and her engaging manners, her sweet air, her conversation seasoned with good sense, wit and modesty, and without the least tincture of affectation, conspired with her beauty to captivate me and make me feel with violence the torments of a growing passion. I had never felt anything like this before. I had often, indeed, been in love, but it was that easy kind of love which we lose without knowing how or why, when a short absence or the presence of another beauty dissolves the charm and soon makes us forget the fair one for whom we sigh. But this charming person had placed me in a dreadful situation; I was bewildered and no longer knew myself. I did not speak to her of my departure, although it was the subject of my visit, and her uncle invited me to pass the day after the next with them.

I had remained in London adoring this divine beauty, till I had no more money than was barely sufficient to defray the expenses of my journey to Scotland. Then, struggling continually between love and duty, I suddenly formed the resolution of setting off next morning without taking leave, from a distrust of my self-command and an internal conviction that a single glance of the charming Miss Peggy would instantly overturn all my resolutions, however wise and prudent they might be; that in seeing her I would no longer be master of myself and would be entangled in fresh embarrassments. I arrived at my father's: a reconciliation immediately took place, and the past was forgotten.

XI

DURING the six years that I remained in Scotland at a distance from my adorable Peggy, the uncertainty of her sentiments with regard to me, the little hopes I had of seeing her again, time, which effaces everything, and new objects, though of an inferior beauty, all conspired to make me insensibly forget her. But the instant I returned to London, her image immediately presented itself to my mind. My passion kindled at once to such a flame that the certainty of the consequence of a visit being death on the scaffold would not have prevented me from attempting to see her. I only delayed my visit till the clothes which I had ordered were ready, and my tailor favoured my impatience by bringing them, with my beautiful embroidered waistcoat, in the course of twenty-four hours.

As soon as I was dressed, I took a hackney-coach, which I discharged when I was near her uncle's, and enquired of the servant who opened the door, if his master were at home. He replied that he was not, but that he was expected to dinner. I then enquired if his niece, Miss Peggy, were in town or in the country. The bare answer of the servant, 'that she was in the house,' gave me such a palpitation at the heart and such a trembling in my nerves, that I could scarcely stand upright. I stepped into the parlour, and sent the servant to ask if she were visible. He immediately returned to announce to me that she was coming down. The presence of this charming person, who appeared in my eyes more beautiful than ever, increased my disorder and I remained motionless as a statue. In vain I attempted to speak; my mouth and tongue refused to perform their functions. As soon as I was sufficiently tranquillised, I told her that, having been engaged in the unfortunate affair of Prince Charles, I had hesitated very much whether or not I should present myself to her uncle lest I exposed him to disagreeable consequences in case of my being discovered in his house. But the remembrance of the civilities and kindness which I had received from her uncle, six years ago, had been always so deeply engraven on my mind that I could not resist the temptation of personally offering to him the assurance of my lasting gratitude.

Whilst I spoke, the adorable Miss Peggy looked at me with an eye full of compassion, pity and sweetness, and then said that her uncle, having always entertained a sincere friendship for me, would certainly feel for my misfortunes, and that he would disregard any inconvenience to which he might expose himself for the pleasure of seeing me and of being useful to me. In the meantime her uncle entered, and was much surprised at seeing me again. He embraced me very affectionately, and when I related my disasters to him, he replied that I was a pretty fellow to wish to be a king-maker; that, for his part, he did not care whether King George, King James, or the devil were upon the throne of England, provided he was left in peaceable possession of his estate, which he would not hazard for all the kings in the universe. He added that he felt very much for my situation, and advised me to shun all places where I might meet any of my countrymen. He made a hearty offer of his house till I could find an opportunity of escaping beyond sea, and begged me to avail myself of his offer immediately by remaining to dine with them.

Several persons called on them after dinner, to whom the uncle introduced me under the name of Mr Leslie, and I made a party at quadrille with Miss Peggy and two other ladies. How quickly does time glide away in the company of those we love! I passed the whole of the most delicious day with her which I had ever known, and it appeared to me but an instant. The uncle told me at supper that he had stayed at home all the afternoon on my account, and begged me to have the goodness to lay aside all ceremony, as he should no longer consider me a stranger in his house. I returned to pass the night in the house of my generous female friend with a quiet contented mind, but before taking leave, the uncle invited me to come every day to breakfast, and pass the day with them. His adorable niece joined in the invitation, adding that in going out early in the morning I should be less exposed to meet in the streets any of my countrymen who might happen to know me. He likewise offered me a room in his house, which I did not choose to accept for fear of involving him in some awkward affair should I be followed in the streets by anyone who knew me, and arrested in his house.

I passed fifteen days continually with my adorable Peggy, from nine o'clock in the morning till eleven o'clock at night. I had not yet dared to declare to her that I loved her, for fear of shocking her. How timid are we when we sincerely love! What a change in my character! I no longer knew myself. I had always been bold and enterprising with the fair sex, and when I did not succeed I made my retreat with a good grace, without being disconcerted. But in presence of this divine person, I looked down when she turned her eyes towards me, and whenever I attempted to reveal my passion I was immediately seized with trembling. She seemed to me a supreme good, which I was afraid of losing in case her sentiments with respect to me were unfavourable. Always afraid of offending her, even by the slightest word, I allowed no other signs of my excessive love and affection to escape me than an occasional sigh, or my apparent uneasiness, which she might very well attribute to my unfortunate situation, and not to the true cause.

Having passed a whole day *tête-à-tête* with her, I at length threw myself suddenly at her feet, seized her hands in a transport, and bathed them with my tears. I could only say, with a broken voice and trembling lips, that I adored her and that I wished to live only for her. She immediately desired me to rise, telling me coolly that she had always had a great esteem for me; that she was extremely sorry to see me so inconsiderate in the terrible crisis in which I then was, between life and death; that every day my companions were dragged to the scaffold; and that I might every moment expect to follow them and to undergo the same punishment. She exhorted me to think more rationally, and rather of the means of saving my life than of filling my head with chimeras. But from that moment I had a tacit permission to express all the tenderness and affection that the most violent passion could inspire; which, however, never failed to draw down on me strong reprimands from her, and advice to act more like a reasonable man.

Her cold and reserved behaviour towards me grieved and affected me beyond all endurance, while her gracious, pre-possessing and engaging manners towards other men, whom she treated so very differently, rendered me excessively jealous. I imagined that all those to whom she showed the least civility or politeness stood much higher in her opinion, and were more in her good graces than myself. One of her relations had made her a present of a handsome snuff-box of *ecaille tournée de Maubois*, lined with gold, with an exquisitely beautiful minia-ture—one of the first of these boxes which had appeared in England. Whilst I was one day *tête-à-tête* with her, I observed her absent and thoughtful, frequently taking out the box and examining the miniature. My jealousy instantly broke out against the box. I bitterly reproached her, observing that certainly her mind could not be occupied with the miniature which she had so often seen, but that she was that moment thinking of the person who had made her a present of it; that he was the happiest of mortals in possessing her heart, whilst my sad and cruel fate was truly pitiable; that I was overwhelmed with afflictions of every kind and ready to sink under my mis-fortunes; that I could support with patience her rigours and the cold indifference which she continually showed me; but that the very thoughts of her loving another, and my having a happy rival, plunged a dagger in my heart. My adorable Peggy immediately dashed the snuff-box against the marble chimney-piece, which broke it in a thousand pieces, telling me, with warmth, that I should never have any reason to fear a rival; that she loved me tenderly and would no longer conceal her sentiments towards me. She conjured me at the same time to take no improper advantage of this knowledge of her way of thinking with respect to me, and to be satisfied with her friendship, which would be constant and invariable as long as she existed.

Hearing one day in my room a noise in the street, I approached the window; but what was my surprise when I saw twelve of my companions in the hands of the officers of justice, who were conducting them for execution to the scaffold on Kennington Common! They belonged to the garrison which Prince Charles had left at Carlisle upon our retreat from England, and Messrs Hamilton and Townley, the governors of the town and castle of Carlisle, were of the number of this unfortunate party. I was the more struck on seeing them because, had it not been for my obstinacy and firmness, I should then have been undergoing with them an ignominious punishment. When the Duke of Perth, my colonel, had commanded me, on our retreat, to remain with my company in Carlisle, I answered that I would willingly shed the last drop of my blood for Prince Charles but that I should never allow myself to be marked out as a victim for certain destruction, and I had left him in a rage, without waiting for his reply. Persisting in my resolution, I set out next morning with the army. Two days after our departure, when the news of the capture of Carlisle by the Duke of Cumberland, reached us, the Duke of Perth, who was of a very limited capacity but at the same time a most worthy and gallant man, told me he pardoned my disobedience, and that he had been himself deceived as to the strength of the place, as he believed it capable of sustaining a siege. I fervently thanked the Almighty, who had watched over my destiny, for without my obstinacy, my lot at that moment must have been to end my days in the same fatal manner.

The little attention I paid my hospitable female friend with whom I lodged, began somewhat to irritate her mind, to render her uneasy and even to sour her temper. In reality she had every possible reason for being angry with me as I passed my whole time with my adorable Peggy, and when absent from her I was thoughtful, lost in reveries and little capable of showing my hostess that gratitude which she merited for the essential services she had rendered me. Frequently she reproached me on account of my coldness and indifference and I pitied her myself, for she was truly a worthy woman, who merited a better return from me for the continual attentions she showed me and the warm and tender interest she took in everything that concerned me. I always assigned my cruel situation as the cause and endeavoured to persuade her of the impossibility of my being otherwise, suspended as I then was between life and death, seeing my companions daily led to the scaffold and uncertain whether I should not immediately follow them. This good and amiable woman possessed great sweetness and good sense, and was sufficiently disposed to believe whatever I told her.

Whilst I was breakfasting one morning in my room with my landlady, I was thunderstruck at seeing my charming Peggy enter, excited by a desire to see my landlady, for some distrust that she entertained with respect to me. My poor landlady, the moment she saw my angelic Peggy, fixed her eyes on the ground, blushed and remained quite confounded. She wished to retire, but I prevented her. My Peggy having satisfied her curiosity, withdrew in about a quarter of an hour and whispered in my ear, on going downstairs, that she had nothing to fear. My landlady immediately reproached me, but without

P

bitterness, observing that she was no longer astonished at my indifference, now that she had seen the cause of it; that she could not blame me, as the lady was the most beautiful person she had ever seen, with the most engaging manners and an affable air full of goodness; and she added that she was certain no man could resist her charms. I wished to avail myself of the same arguments I had before urged, but she was no longer to be duped by them.

Whatever confidence I might have in the sweetness and honourable disposition of my landlady, it was still a matter of prudence to take precaution against the bad effects which might happen to me from this adventure, especially as she might, in a moment of irritation, have recourse to a prompt vengeance. She had nothing to do but to inform against me, when I would instantly be arrested. The resentment of women who have supposed themselves slighted has but too frequently displayed itself in this manner. I therefore resolved to look out for another lodging that very day, and I was fortunate enough to find an apartment in the house of a hairdresser, in the neighbourhood of the mansion of my dear Peggy. Having told my landlady next morning, that I had found an opportunity of effecting my escape beyond sea, I immediately quitted my lodgings, after taking leave of this amiable woman, giving her all possible assurances of my gratitude and my eternal remembrance of the services she had rendered me. She embraced me with tears in her eyes, truly afflicted at our separation, and as my heart was not sufficiently hard to resist a beautiful woman in tears, I was very sensibly touched with her sentiments for me.

One day, on returning from an evening walk, having learned that one of my relations had lately arrived from Scotland, I communicated to Peggy my anxiety to obtain some information respecting my family, and instead of supping with her as usual, I took a coach and drove to the lodgings of my relation.

As soon as I entered he began to condole with me on the loss which I had sustained, but I paid no attention to what he said, imagining he alluded to the misfortunes that were common to me with all those who had been attached to Prince Charles. However he soon gave me to understand, that my mother and my sister Rollo both died a few days after I left Scotland, and that my mother's last words were, 'I now die contented and satisfied, since I know that my poor dear son is safe.'

My relation was one of those grammatical blockheads, who thoroughly understand Greek and Latin, but who are profoundly ignorant of the human heart and of the most ordinary circumstances of life. Had he been capable of the least reflection, he would have prepared me for such an overwhelming blow. I remained a moment confounded and immoveable as a statue, then turned suddenly round and flew down stairs, without uttering one word in answer to his foolish compliments. When I got into the coach I could scarcely tell the coachman to drive me home. I was nearly suffocated in the coach, where I fainted and remained for some minutes insensible. I recovered from my fainting-fit with a torrent of tears, which were a great relief to me. The coachman, who knew nothing of my state, continued his course, and I am even disposed to believe that the rough motion of the coach was of great benefit to me. When I reached my lodgings, my landlord, who had a kind and compassionate heart, seeing me in distress, followed me into my room and, having learned the cause of it, began immediately to moralize and repeat to me all the old and hackneyed topics of scholastic consolation. I seized him in a fit of rage by the shoulders, pushed him rudely out of my room and ordered him never to set his foot in it again till I should ask him. I then locked the door and threw myself upon my bed, dressed as I was, and passed the night in tears and sighs without closing my eyes.

I accused myself as the most innocent cause of the death of

the most tender of mothers, by the pain and anxiety which she had felt for me since the battle of Culloden. I looked upon myself as a monster of ingratitude in having remained two months in the house of Lady Jane Douglas, within a quarter of a league of her, sick as she then was and on the point of death, without seeing her. I ought to have exposed my life a thousand times rather than not see her in order to embrace her, bid her an eternal farewell and receive her blessing. My father in his letters had concealed these deaths from me, from an apprehension that the intelligence would be too distressing to me, and believing that my situation was already sufficiently painful. In this, however, he acted injudiciously. By communicating the intelligence to me with precaution, he might have secured me from the danger of a surprise such as that which I experienced when it came suddenly on me like a clap of thunder, a surprise that might have been fatal to me. On entering I wrote a note to the uncle of my charming Peggy, acquainting him with the distressing news which I had received.

About ten o'clock next morning I heard a knocking at my door. I still remained in the state I was in on entering my lodgings the night before, with all my clothes on and without having even changed my attitude since throwing myself on my bed. But, oh heavens! what a relief to my sufferings when, instead of my landlord whom I supposed at my door with an intention of renewing his importunate and stupid lectures, I heard the gentle voice of my adorable Peggy, who came like a guardian angel to dispel in a moment the storms and tempests by which I had been agitated, and to restore me to life. My divine beauty had arranged this visit with her uncle who, by nature, had an aversion to the society of people in distress, in order to engage me to pass the day with her. The moment I saw her I felt as if a healing balm had at once pervaded my whole frame. My sufferings and agitation suddenly diminished; in viewing her, my soul became at once serene and tranquil.

She entered warmly into my sufferings, sharing my distress, and
the tears that fell from her lovely eyes, which I eagerly wiped
away with my lips, were a thousand times more insupportable
to me than my own pain and distress.

She insisted upon my dining and passing the day with her. I
could refuse her nothing, though I was so much disfigured
from the red and swollen appearance of my eyes that an acquaintance could hardly have known me. As soon as I had
changed my linen, I repaired to her uncle's, who entered very
warmly into my misfortunes, and my charming Peggy did
everything in her power to dissipate the sorrow and melancholy which preyed on me.

A day or two after I had treated my landlord somewhat harshly,
he sent a servant to me to say that if I were visible he wished to
have the honour of speaking to me. On entering my room he
made a number of excuses for having taken it upon him to console me, observing that his heart bled on seeing me in such deep
distress. He then proposed to me, by way of a party of pleasure,
to accompany him to the house of a friend on Tower Hill, who
had promised him a window from which he could see two rebels
beheaded, the Earl of Kilmarnock and Lord Balmerino. I
thanked him for his attention but excused myself, telling him
that he might easily see that I had too feeling a heart to take any
pleasure in spectacles of that description. He little imagined that
I was as guilty as they, and that there was no difference between
us except what fortune had made in enabling me to escape being
taken prisoner.

A friend came to inform me that the captain of a merchant
ship, whom he knew to be a man of honour and fidelity, had
undertaken, for his sake, to take me on board disguised as a
sailor; but, in order to avail myself of this opportunity, it was
necessary that I should embark next morning. The idea of
tearing myself from all that was dear to me was insupportable,

and I therefore answered that this opportunity was not without risk of discovery, for they had only to look at my hands, which were too delicate for a sailor, to discover me; and besides, as I knew nothing of the management of a vessel, the trick was quite obvious. He obviated these difficulties by informing me that the captain had foreseen them, and would make me pass for a sick person the moment I entered his ship. He urged me very much to embrace this opportunity, as he ardently wished to see me out of danger. But all his arguments were useless, and he could not conceive how I should expose myself to the danger of being beheaded on the scaffold, whilst I had the means of escaping from this danger. He knew not that I loved my Peggy more than my life.

Whilst we were dining one day *tête-à-tête*, all at once she became pale, her air became restless and embarrassed, and her eyes were continually turned to the windows that looked into the street. She kept rising every instant and was incessantly leaving the room and returning. Having several times asked her, with eagerness, if anything was the matter with her and if she felt unwell, she answered in monosyllables and equivocally. I earnestly entreated her to tell me frankly the cause of her uneasiness during the last quarter of an hour. 'Oh! my dear friend,' she exclaimed, 'you are undone! I see a person who is certainly an officer of justice, and I have observed him for some time passing and repassing before our house with his eyes incessantly fixed on the door. He is undoubtedly sent to watch you, till a detachment comes to take you prisoner. Perhaps someone, having recognised you this morning and followed you to the house without your observing him, has forthwith informed against you. I have examined the house from the cellar to the garret and there is no place where you can conceal yourself.'

I examined the man and, in reality, no police-runner could have a more villanous appearance. The adventure alarmed me, the more so as a person in the dress and with the appearance of a porter had, three days before, asked for me at her uncle's; as he would not tell whence he came, they said I had left the house. When I first lodged at the house of my good friend, my former landlady, I had imprudently told her the address of Peggy's uncle, not then foreseeing the consequences. I suspected, at first, that this must have originated in a feeling of revenge on her part, as none but she could know that I spent every day, from morning till night, in the house in question; but when I reflected on her great sweetness of temper and goodness of disposition, I could not think her capable of so much baseness. I went out every morning in a hackney-coach with the blinds up, so that it was almost impossible I could have been recognised by anyone in the street. In short, I knew not what to think of the matter.

As the man still continued to walk backwards and forwards, never losing sight of the door of the house, I knew not what course to take. I was undecided whether I should go out immediately, before the arrival of the soldiers, and trust to my sword and my heels (which would create a terrible uproar in the street) or whether I should remain quietly in the house and wait the result. My charming Peggy sprang to my neck and tenderly embracing me exclaimed, with an impassioned warmth, 'No, you shall not die on the scaffold! If I cannot succeed in saving you through the interest of my friends who are in favour at court, I will visit you in prison the evening before the day of execution with two doses of poison, and I will take one to set you an example how to make use of the other.' The idea of my adorable Peggy's dying by poison filled me with horror, but I did not in the least doubt that she was capable of keeping her word, knowing as I did the violence and determination which the fair sex in England possess in a degree not to be found in any other nation. As to myself personally, poison would have been of all things the most acceptable to me after my condemnation, and the supplying me with it would have been a most friendly action.

I entreated my Peggy to go with me and examine the house once more. In this survey I remarked a window in the garret, by which I could go out upon the roof and pass from thence to the roof of a neighbouring house. I immediately dispatched my Peggy to watch as a sentinel at the window below with a silver bell in her hand, which she was to ring as soon as she saw people approach the door to knock. It was agreed that the ringing of the bell should serve as a signal for my going out upon the roof. I took off my shoes lest they should make me slip on the slates and break my neck, and put them in my pocket, and I held the window with both hands, with the intention of springing out the instant I heard the bell. Having remained a quarter of an hour in this attitude, in the utmost uneasiness, my dear Peggy returned with a changed countenance, and immediately said, with a smile, 'Plague take them both! It is, I suppose, the sweetheart of my chamber-maid. She has just asked my permission to go out to walk, and the moment she was in the street she familiarly took hold of his arm.'

A few days after this adventure, whilst I was dining with Peggy and her uncle, the servant entered and informed me that a gentleman wished to speak with me in the anti-chamber. I immediately went out and was surprised at seeing Mr Colville, Lady Jane Douglas's man of business. He told me that she had lately formed the resolution of residing in France and that he had been sent to London to procure a passport, which she had obtained for one servant more than she actually had, in order that she might have an opportunity of taking me with her, and thus enable me to escape to Holland. He had left her at Huntingdon, about twenty leagues to the north of London, in the house of a Mr Raith, where she should wait three days for me before setting out for Harwich accompanied by Mr Stewart and Miss Hewitt.

What dreadful news! Before knowing my divine Peggy, nothing would have been so ardently wished for by me as such an opportunity for escape. But now matters were changed! I lived and desired to live only for her. I remained some moments quite confounded, not knowing what to answer. I was resolved not to avail myself of the offer of Lady Jane Douglas whilst, at the same time, I was embarrassed how I should immediately find a plausible excuse to justify my refusal, and was apprehensive lest she should imagine, from the extravagance of my conduct, that I had lost my senses. For who could ever imagine that anyone, with the prospect of execution on the scaffold every day before him in case of his discovery, would refuse an opportunity of escaping that danger? After a moment's reflection, I told Mr Colville that I should, during the whole course of my life, retain the most grateful sense of the goodness of Lady Jane towards me, but that as my friends in London had discovered several means of enabling me to escape to the Continent, without any danger of discovery, I would not for the world expose her Ladyship again to any troublesome embarrassment, having already put her kindness so much to the test. I begged Mr Colville to tell her, in his letter, not to wait for me in Huntingdon as, when I reflected on the inconveniences to which I should thereby expose her, I could not think of availing myself of her generous and obliging offer.

Mr Colville immediately took his leave and I returned to table without saying a word about what had taken place. I only mentioned that it was the man of business of Lady Jane Douglas, whom she had sent to enquire after me. During the interview I dreaded nothing so much as that the uncle, from not knowing the person with whom I was in conversation, might, from uneasiness on my account, leave the dining-room and join us, when the discovery of my inconceivable extravagance would have led him to suspect the true cause of my refusal.

As soon as the uncle went out, which he commonly did in

the afternoon, I communicated to my dear Peggy the obliging offer of Lady Jane Douglas and the difficulty which I had had in getting rid of it, adding that I had refused it, as I should certainly refuse whatever should separate me from her. 'Ah! my dear friend,' replied she, 'you have done very wrong in refusing it. I suffer continual pain and uneasiness on your account, which I conceal from you. Your situation fills me with incessant apprehension, and hardly a night passes in which I do not dream I see you in the hands of the executioner. As the last occasion which presented itself was not without danger of discovery, I imagined that it might have the effect of tearing you from me to bring you to immediate punishment, and I was therefore glad that you refused it; but this occasion is very different. Lady Jane Douglas is of so illustrious a family that the court would not dare to tease her, or to insult her by subjecting her to a rigorous examination on mere suspicion; and as there could be no positive information in such a case, you could have run no risk with her, and you would have effected your escape.'

I was penetrated with the most heart-felt grief in hearing her endeavour to persuade me to depart, and I interrupted her with accusations of inconstancy and warmly reproached her for her indifference. 'No, my dear friend,' exclaimed she, 'you wrong me. My sentiments are so little changed with regard to you, that I reserve for you a proof stronger than any you have yet received and which I wished not to communicate to you till the occurrence of a favourable moment for carrying my project into execution. I have long determined to share your fate, and to abandon for you my country, my parents and whatever is dear to me. I have only waited for a safe opportunity for your escaping without danger. An opportunity now presents itself in the offer of Lady Jane Douglas, such as I have long desired. I will disguise myself as a man and take my passage in the same packet-boat with Lady Jane, without appearing to know you.

Let us go immediately in quest of clothes among the brokers, in order that we may be ready to set off tomorrow morning. Providence,' she added, 'will give us bread, and I shall be content to live with you on rustic fare, in preference to all the riches of the universe.'

I embraced my adorable Peggy with tears in my eyes, and assured her that I loved her more than my life, and that that very tenderness and affection which I vowed to her, would never allow me to plunge her into ruin and wretchedness—by doing which, I should, at the same time, draw down upon myself the contempt and indignation of her family. If I had a certainty of our being enabled to subsist independently of others the case would be different, but I did not know what would become of me on reaching a foreign country, nor how I should subsist till I obtained employment. My dear friend, on seeing me determined not to permit her to take this precipitate step, spoke no more to me of my departure, and we passed the evening together with all the pleasure and satisfaction which two persons completely devoted to each other can feel in such a situation.

Having returned to my lodgings after supper, I went to bed; but I was unable to close an eye. A thousand different reflections crowded on my mind. I examined my situation in London which, independently of the danger to which I was continually exposed of being arrested, was such that I had no certainty of being enabled to subsist for any length of time. Having already experienced the harshness of my father, it was evident that I should, sooner or later, be in want of money. My Peggy had the prospect of being one day very rich, but she did not, any more than myself, possess an independent income. As it was my intention, as soon as I could effect my escape, to repair to Russia, where my Peggy knew I had the most powerful protection through the credit of my two uncles who were still alive, I flattered myself with the prospect of being able to obtain a regiment on my arrival or soon afterwards. I thus hoped for a change in my circumstances such as would enable me to share my fortune with her. Then I could either return to England incognito to visit her, or induce her to repair to the country to the service of which I might be attached.

I also thought that, as it was the interest of France in every sense of the word, to re-establish the house of Stuart on the throne of England, the court of Versailles might abandon the old system on which it had for eighty years acted, of making use of this unfortunate house as a scarecrow to frighten the English (a policy now worn out, and no longer productive of any effect) and at length make a serious attempt in favour of Prince Charles Edward. Then I should return to England in a brilliant situation to rejoin my Peggy. A thousand other considerations made me hesitate whether I should not yet avail myself of this opportunity of escaping with Lady Jane Douglas, but always on the supposition that my dear friend wished that I should embrace it, independently of her project of accompanying me.

I rose betimes and went to breakfast with my Peggy. As soon as her uncle left the room to dress, I communicated my nocturnal reflections to her, demanding, at the same time, her opinion, and that she would herself decide whether I should go or remain. She renewed her proposal of accompanying me, but I solemnly protested that I would never suffer this, and that it was useless to speak any more on that subject; that I would rather perish under the hands of the executioner than allow her to precipitate herself in an abyss of ruin and destruction. Seeing that I was inflexible, she told me that I must decidedly accompany Lady Jane Douglas, and that she would willingly sacrifice her own happiness and tranquillity to see me out of danger. As time pressed, and as I could not expect that Lady Jane Douglas would wait an instant for me at Huntingdon after hearing my answer to Mr Colville, she ordered me to go immediately to the coach-office and take a place in the diligence that goes in one day from London to Huntingdon, and which would set off next morning at three o'clock. I forwarded my luggage at the same time, that I might have nothing more on my mind but be able to give myself altogether up to my Peggy. Finding her uncle in the room on my return from the coach-office, I mentioned to him the offer of Lady Jane Douglas, my determination to accept it, and my intention of setting off next morning. He expressed his satisfaction at my good fortune in finding so favourable an opportunity, though he regretted that I was so soon to quit them.

I took leave of her uncle immediately after dinner and went to meet my charming Peggy at a rendezvous which we had agreed on, to pass the few precious moments that were left us in some solitary walk out of town. The afternoon, which was the most melancholy we ever knew, was spent in reciprocal vows and promises of eternal fidelity and constancy; nevertheless it passed with the velocity of lightning. A hundred times I was tempted to renounce my intention of departing, and I had occasion for all the fortitude of my charming Peggy to confirm me in my resolution. She accompanied me to the coach-office where, having remained together till half-past eight o'clock, she called a coach and entered it more dead than alive.

I followed her coach with my eyes and when it altogether disappeared my resolution became weak and wavering.

My first movement was to run to the room assigned me at the coach-office, with the intention of having my luggage carried back to my lodgings at the hairdresser's, and feeling it impossible for me to support a separation, I renounced for ever the idea of it. Fortunately reflection came to my aid before my luggage was taken away, and I became sensible that such a singular step would open the eyes of her uncle, betray us, and involve us in the most unpleasant embarrassments. I therefore returned to my room and threw myself down on my bed to wait for the departure of the diligence, giving myself wholly up to despair and ready to sink under the load of my affliction. If I could have foreseen that this was the last time I should ever see her, no consideration on earth could have torn me from her; and rather than have left her, I should have coolly awaited the ignominious death with which I was every day threatened.

The coach set off at two o'clock in the morning and we arrived at Huntingdon at eight at night. Lady Jane Douglas had left it the preceding evening for Harwich, not supposing, from the answer of Mr Colville, that there was any ground to expect me there.

I took post next morning, hoping to join her before her arrival at Harwich; but the wretched post-horses were so much fatigued by the rate at which I proceeded that I was obliged to sleep at Newmarket. Next morning I hired a curricle and arrived before sunset at an arm of the sea, about a league in breadth, from which I could see Harwich on the other side. A frigate of about forty guns was riding at anchor in the middle of this arm of the sea. I immediately applied to the owner of the boats and other craft stationed here for a passage across but, in spite of all my entreaties, threats and offers of rewarding him handsomely, he persisted in refusing me, telling me that the government had prohibited all passage after sunset on account of the smuggling, and that the frigate was stationed there for the express purpose of enforcing the prohibition. I was grieved and enraged beyond measure to think that I should lose the opportunity of accompanying Lady Jane after the painful struggle I had had before I could bring myself to determine to avail myself of it. His obstinacy was not to be overcome either by my entreaties or my threats. He told me that the captain of the frigate, who was drinking in his house with his officers, would throw him into prison if he complied with my request, and his vessel would be confiscated into the bargain.

The captain of the frigate, having heard my dispute with the owner of the boats, came out of the tavern to question me. I was not at all disconcerted, but answered at once that I was a servant of Mrs Gray (a travelling name which Lady Jane Douglas had taken) who was now at Harwich, ready to embark in the first packet-boat for Holland; that she had sent me to London to execute some commissions for her, and that I was uneasy lest she should leave Harwich before my arrival with an account of my proceedings, owing to the obstinacy of the master of the boats, whom I could not induce to give me a passage, either by my offers to pay him generously, or my threats to have him punished by complaining to the governor of Harwich. I entreated the captain, with great earnestness, to make use of his authority to compel him, assuring him that I should not fail to make a faithful report to my mistress of his kindness. He told me that he had seen Mrs Gray arrive the evening before, that she appeared to be a very amiable lady, and that he should be extremely happy to have it in his power to be of any service to her; but that he could do nothing with the owner of the boats, as he had received positive orders not to cross this arm of the sea after sunset. He added that she could not have set sail, as the wind was unfavourable, and he offered to take me in his own boat and land me at Harwich as soon as he should be put on board his frigate. I did not hesitate an instant to accept his offer and entered his boat, not only without apprehension, but boldly and eagerly, telling him that my mistress would feel grateful for his civility and kindness. I should probably have been ruined beyond remedy if I had shown the least timidity or distrust.

We were scarcely a musket-shot from the shore, when the captain pointed out to me one of his midshipmen in the boat, of the name of Lockhart, asking me if I knew his family in Scotland. I answered in the negative, telling him that I had never been in any other service than that of Mrs Gray. I was uneasy

lest Mr Lockhart should have recognized me for, as I had been a
schoolfellow of his elder brother and frequently in the house of
his father, Mr Lockhart of Carnwath, he might very possibly
have known me. He was about eighteen years of age and had
been four years in the navy. His eldest brother, the heir to a
considerable estate, had been foolish enough, like so many
others, to join the standard of Prince Charles.

I suffered cruelly from the thought that the captain of the
frigate had had no other object in view by his civility in offering me his boat, than to get me quietly on board his ship, where
he would immediately make me his prisoner. Supposing even
young Lockhart not to know that I had been in the army of the
Prince, there was still something very mysterious and equivocal
in my being disguised in the dress of a servant. It was necessary,
however, to submit to my destiny.

As the boat approached the ship, I began to reckon the
minutes which were to elapse before I should be handcuffed and
in irons. My heart beat dreadfully, although I always preserved
a calm exterior and answered a thousand questions which the
captain asked me with coolness and presence of mind, without
being in the least disconcerted. I expected, nevertheless, every
moment, that this politeness would cease, that the mask would
be dropped, and that the sailors would receive orders to lay
hold of me by the neck. Of all my adventures since the battle of
Culloden, this caused me the most cruel suffering and agitation.
I could not, however, foresee it, nor could I have avoided it
without abandoning the project of escaping to Holland with
Lady Jane Douglas. In all my other sinister encounters I had
always had some ray of hope of escape in the possibility of my
defending myself or of my taking to my heels; but here I was
caught like a fish in a net. At length, on reaching the ship, the
captain invited me on board to drink a glass to the health of my
mistress. I looked on this as the *denouement* of the piece. I replied that I was afraid my mistress would be gone to bed before

my arrival in Harwich and that I had to communicate to her some very important intelligence. He immediately put an end to my sufferings, calling out to the sailors to land me in the town and not to forget to present his compliments to Mrs Gray.

I found Lady Jane Douglas at the inn, and immediately told her the obligation I lay under to the captain of the frigate and the purgatory in which I had been during the passage. She praised my firmness, but laughed at the same time at the singularity of my having made the officers of King George accomplices in saving a rebel who had attempted to tear the crown from the brow of their sovereign to place it on the head of Prince Charles Edward.

As the wind was contrary, we remained two days at Harwich before embarking. During our stay the governor of the town, to whom Lady Jane Douglas had been recommended, became our tormentor from his excessive politeness and civility. He had received orders from London to show her every attention and he came twenty times a-day, and at all hours, to ask if she had any occasion for his services. I always bolted the door of the room to prevent my being surprised at table with my mistress. Whilst we were at dinner the governor knocked at the door, and he could not be admitted till I had removed my plate and the table was arranged for three persons. Having opened the door to the governor, I took my station of servant behind the chair of Lady Jane, and when she asked the governor to taste her wine, I presented a glass to him. It was easy to see from his countenance that he suspected some mystery, but to have lightly insulted a person of Lady Jane's illustrious birth without being certain of the fact, might have been attended with inconvenience.

The first letter which I received from my charming Peggy informed me that there was a report in London that Prince Charles had escaped to Holland with Lady Jane Douglas,

Q

disguised as her servant. There is every reason for supposing, that the governor had informed the court of his suspicions, and it was fortunate for us that we set sail next morning, before he could receive any answer authorising him to act on these suspicions.

We arrived at Helvoetsluys in twenty-four hours. During our passage, I had a whimsical enough scene. Sir ———— Clifton, who happened to be on board the packet-boat, was an acquaintance of Mr Stewart, and he was invited into the cabin which Lady Jane had engaged for herself and suite, whilst his servant and myself remained in a little anti-cabin where we were very uncomfortably situated and a source of annoyance to each other. This rendered us both very cross and ill-tempered. When we were in bed our legs were continually striking against each other from the smallness of the space in which we were cooped up. We suffered the more as there were a great many passengers on board, and the weather being rainy prevented them from going on deck, so that this little place was always literally crammed and it was hardly possible to breathe in it. Each believing the other to be a footman, our respective observations were delivered in an insulting and contemptuous tone, and the scene would certainly have terminated unfortunately if Lady Jane had not informed the Baronet at dinner that there was a young gentleman in her suite who had been with Prince Charles Edward and whom she wished to invite into her cabin to eat something. The Baronet told her that he was in a similar predicament, as the person who acted as his valet was a Mr Carnie, an officer in the Irish brigade in the service of France. We were both invited into the cabin to dinner and, on receiving the necessary explanations, we were very much surprised and made a thousand excuses to each other for our incivility.

I was in a deep sleep when the packet-boat arrived in the quay of Helvoetsluys and all the other passengers were on shore before I was waked. I immediately rushed out of the packet-boat, with my eyes half shut, and began to run as fast as I possibly could from it, as if the captain and his crew had it in their power to arrest me. I could scarcely persuade myself that I was beyond the reach of the English. Lady Jane laughed heartily at seeing me run, and called out that it was entirely useless as I was now out of all danger. I became then thoroughly awake. It is impossible to express the pleasure and satisfaction I felt on seeing myself at last safe, after being six months between life and death! No-one, without having been in a similar situation, can have any idea of the delight I felt at that moment. Ever since the battle of Culloden, the idea that I should end my days miserably upon the scaffold had never ceased to haunt my mind. I now felt myself as if raised from the dead.

After remaining eight days at Rotterdam, I departed with Lady Jane Douglas to the Hague, where she took up her residence. As I had long determined to return to Russia, I immediately wrote to my uncle, acquainting him with the distressing situation in which I was then placed, requesting him to inform his friends, Prince Curakin and Count Gollovin, that I should be in Petersburg in a few days, and to endeavour to induce them to honour me again with their protection, that I might find some employment on my arrival. Had I followed this resolution, I should have been a general officer many years ago. I was on the point of setting out for Russia when Lady Jane persuaded me to defer my departure till we had some positive account of the fate of Prince Charles.

Mr Trevor, the English resident in Holland, presented a memorial to the states-general, demanding that all the Scots who had taken refuge in Holland should be arrested and delivered up to the English government. To the eternal disgrace of this infamous republic, the Dutch were cowardly enough to comply with the requisition, and to violate the feelings of humanity and the law of nations. There were then about twenty

Scotsmen of our party in Holland. Mr Ogilvie was arrested and sent to London; the rest left this worthless country as fast as they could and, as it was necessary that I should remain till I could find an opportunity of going to Petersburg, I repaired in haste to Leyden to enter myself there as a student of medicine— the privileges of this university being so extensive that the states-general cannot arrest any of its students except for the crime of assassination. Having succeeded in obtaining the insertion of my name in the register by means of a few ducats which I gave to Professor Gaubeus, I returned immediately to the Hague, where we learned, a few days afterwards, that Prince Charles had escaped to France. The desire of seeing him again and the hope of another attempt in his favour, determined me to abandon my resolution of going to Russia, and my fate was decided for the rest of my days by my arrival in Paris towards the end of the year 1746.

INDEX

◇

A

Abachie, castle of, 154
Abelard, 154
Aberdeen, 32, 100, 108, 109, 113
Admirable, Mr, 85
Airly, Earl of, formerly Lord Ogilvie, 163n
Alloa, 28, 80
America, 204, 206
Anderson, Mr, 35
Annan, 76, 77
Annandale, 215
Anne, Queen, 7, 45
Anson, Admiral, 205
Argyll, Duke of, 9, 29
Ashbourne, 57, 65
Athol, clan of, 106
Athol, Duke of, 23, 30, 106, 107

B

Badenoch, 100, 140
Bailly, Mrs, 102
Balfour, 176
Balmerino, Lord, 52, 143, 229
Banff, 113, 144, 145-7, 196
Banffshire, 144, 145
Bannockburn, 80, 81, 83, 84, 85, 96, 99
Battereau's regiment, 84
Beaton, Cardinal, 171 & n
Beaton, Mr, of Balfour, 176, 178-9
Beaufort, Duke of, 60n
Belle Isle, 23
Berwick-upon-Tweed, 49, 50
Blair Athol, 27, 100, 107
Blakeney, General, 80, 83, 84, 98
Bland's dragoon regiment, 98
Blythe, Mr, 196, 197, 200
Blythe, Mrs, 196, 197, 199, 202
Borrowstownness, 84

Bradstreet, Captain, 15, 16
Braemar, 9
Brampton, 51
Broughty, 160, 164-7, 170, 175
Brown, Colonel, 89
Brown, Mr, 66, 77, 78, 154
Burn, Jenny, 169
Burn, Mally, 169-70
Burn, Mrs, 168-9
Burrel's regiment, 84
'Butcher, the', 134

C

Cadiz, 10
Cairngorm, mountain, 144
Cameron, Mr, of Lochiel, 25, 69, 75, 111, 117
Cameron, Finlay, 136-7, 141
Camerons, the, 9; clan of, 25, 88; regiment of, 69
Campbell of Lochnell, 25
Campbells, clan of, 29
Canada, 18
Carlisle, 49, 50-52, 60, 70-72, 73, 77-78, 131, 155, 224
Carnie, Mr, 242
Cassini, Monsieur, 48
Charles II, 207
Chebuctoo, 206
Chelsea Hospital, 212
Cholmondeley's regiment, 84
Clifton, Sir —, 242
Clifton-hall, 16, 69, 70, 72, 75, 77
Colville, Mr, 209, 232, 233, 236
Congleton, 15, 56
Cope, General Sir John, 13, 25-28, 29 & n, 32, 34-37, 41, 44, 47, 51, 80, 98
Corstorphin, 32

Rollo, Lord, 30, 144, 145, 149, 164, 175, 196, 199
Rollo, the Misses, 30
Rome, 11, 14, 30, 32
Ross, Lord, 113
Ross, Mr, son of Lord Ross, 113
Ross, Mr, of St Andrews, 173
Rothiemurchus, *see* Grant, Mr, of
Rothiemurchus [village], 137-40, 143-4, 145, 153
Rotterdam, 243
Royal Scots, 25, 58, 81, 113, 122
Russia, 17-18, 170, 235, 243-4
Ruthven, 100, 127, 128, 140-2

S

St Andrews 170, 171, & n, 173-4
St Dennis, 81
St George's regiment, 98
St Ninians, 81, 100
Salmon, a fisherman, 180-6
Samuel, a peasant, 154-63, 164-5, 188, 202
Saxe, Marshal, 48
Scothouse, 40, 116, 123, 124, 135. *See also* Macdonald of Scothouse.
Scots fusiliers, 98
Scott, Mr, a banker in Edinburgh, 211
Seine, river, 49
Sempell's regiment, 98
Seton, Mr, of Dubbieside, 188-90, 191, 195, 205; son of, 188-9; younger brother of, 190, 192-3, 205
Seton, Miss, 189
Shap, 52, 66
Sheerness, the, 105
Sheridan, an Irishman, 23, 127
Sinclair, Master of, 9
Sinclair's regiment, 84
Smith, Mr Peter, 96, 112
Solway Firth, 48n
Spence, Mrs, 171, 173-4, 175
Spey, river, 104, 113, 114 & n, 138

Speymouth, 109
Stamford, 212, 215
Stewart, Mr, husband of Lady Jane Douglas, 200, 203, 204, 208, 209, 211, 216, 232, 242
Stewarts, the, 9
Stirling, 26, 28, 32, 64n, 80, 83-86, 99, 105, 158; bridge, 29; castle, 44, 96-99
Strathallan, Viscountess of, 105
Strathbogie, 108
Strickland, an Irishman, 23
Stuart, house of, 10, 23n, 29, 45-46, 51, 55, 64, 104, 106, 134, 137, 154n, 159, 178, 180, 186, 187, 196, 199, 206-7, 236
Stuart, Mr (Col.) John Roy, 88, 89; regiment of, 122
Stuart, Mr, a Presbyterian minister, 145
Stuart, Prince Charles Edward, the Young Pretender, 8, 10-19, 23 *et passim.*
Stuarts of Appin, clan of the, 25
Sullivan, an Irishman, 23, 24, 33, 94
Sunart, Loch, 25
Sutherland, Countess of, 115
Swiss troops, 48, 63, 74

T

Tain, 110n
Tay, Firth of, 155
Temple-bar, 78
Torbay, 7
Tournai, 74
Tower Hill, 229
Townley, Mr, 56, 72, 78, 224
Tranent, 35
Trevor, Mr, 243
Tullibardine, Marquis of, 10
Turenne, Marshal, 28
Tweed, river, 49
Tweedale, Lord, 29n